Living Color

The publisher gratefully acknowledges the generous support of the Humanities Endowment Fund of the University of California Press Foundation.

Living Color

The Biological and Social
Meaning of Skin Color

Nina G. Jablonski

UNIVERSITY OF CALIFORNIA PRESS

Berkeley · Los Angeles · London

University of California Press, one of the most distinguished university presses in the United States, enriches lives around the world by advancing scholarship in the humanities, social sciences, and natural sciences. Its activities are supported by the UC Press Foundation and by philanthropic contributions from individuals and institutions. For more information, visit www.ucpress.edu.

University of California Press
Berkeley and Los Angeles, California

University of California Press, Ltd.
London, England

Title page. A scene from Brazil's Carnival epitomizes "living color." Mauricio Lima/AFP/Getty Images.

Library of Congress Cataloging-in-Publication Data

Jablonski, Nina G.
    Living color : the biological and social meaning of skin color / Nina G. Jablonski.
        p.   cm.
    Includes bibliographical references and index.
    ISBN 978-0-520-25153-3 (cloth : alk. paper)
    1. Human skin color.   2. Human skin color—Physiological aspects.   3. Human skin color—Social aspects.   4. Human skin color—Cross-cultural studies. I. Title.
    GN197.J34   2012
    573.5—dc23   2012003746

Manufactured in the United States of America

21 20 19 18 17 16 15 14 13 12
10 9 8 7 6 5 4 3 2 1

The paper used in this publication meets the minimum requirements of ANSI/NISO Z39.48–1992 (R 1997) (*Permanence of Paper*).

To George

Contents

Illustrations

MAPS

Preface and Acknowledgments

I had been doing research and lecturing on the evolution of skin color for more than a decade when, in 2002, Alan Zendell, himself an author, approached me about writing a book on the topic. He felt that a discussion of all the aspects of skin color—its evolution and its meaning in our daily lives—was essential because there was such a lack of understanding about it and because it was one of those awkward topics that are always present but rarely discussed.

Several people provided me with vital feedback, encouragement, and support as this book slowly took shape and was written. Regina Brooks, my agent, helped me shape a strong proposal and supported the project even when most publishers didn't want "another book on race." Blake Edgar, my editor at the University of California Press, understood and believed in the project and patiently endured years of excuses about why the manuscript still wasn't finished. His critical reading of the first draft greatly improved the writing, helped me balance the content, and inspired some final flourishes in the illustration program. Without his staunch and sensitive support and critical guidance, I would never have persevered.

George Chaplin, my husband and life partner, best friend, and primary scientific collaborator, helped me keep faith in the importance of this project and loved me when I was in the unlovable state of the obsessed author. We have worked together for many years on the evolutionary biology of skin color, and George's substantive input into the historical chapters was invaluable. The insights we derived together about the history of discrimination and racism based on skin color became the major themes of the latter half of the book. George was my most reliable and critical sounding board and contained his frustration over the slowness of my writing to provide me with daily, loving encouragement.

Theresa (Tess) Wilson, my research technician at The Pennsylvania State University, provided the best possible logistical support during the three years when I was most actively researching and writing. She searched out and screened literally hundreds of books and articles, maintained my bibliographic database, identified potential artwork, and dealt with all of the laborious and complicated communication necessary to assemble the illustration program. She brought to my attention dozens of primary historical sources, especially on the transatlantic slave trade, that proved essential. I thank her for her unstinting hard work, punctilious attention to detail, and generous stores of patience and good humor.

The research that went into this book was conducted mostly at the University Park campus of Penn State, and I am grateful to the several research librarians and interlibrary loan assistants at the Pattee and Paterno libraries for their help in locating scholarly resources. For access to and assistance with resources about the transatlantic slave trade and the African American experience, I am also grateful to India Spartz, senior archivist in the Peabody Museum Archives of Harvard University, and Sheldon Cheek, senior curatorial associate in the Image of the Black in Western Art Research Project and Photo Archive of the W. E. B. Du Bois Institute for African and African American Research of Harvard University.

I am deeply thankful to Fletcher Philanthropy for providing me with an Alphonse Fletcher Sr. Fellowship in 2005. The fellowship made it possible for me to undertake travel connected with research and writing of the book and to purchase the rights to artwork for the illustration program. I feel privileged to have had the support of Alphonse Fletcher Jr. and Henry Louis Gates Jr. for this project since its inception.

I thank Nana Naisbitt for providing great encouragement to me at the beginning of this project and providing insightful feedback on the proposal. I am also very grateful to Marion Tilton, who generously allowed me to stay in her guesthouse at Lake Tahoe for two weeks in the summer of 2009 to begin writing in earnest. I give deep thanks to the many colleagues, friends, and relatives with whom I have discussed ideas that contributed to this book: Lisa Feldman Barrett, Gregory Barsh, Koos Bekker, the late Baruch Blumberg, Carol Boggs, Carol Bower, Elsabe Brits, Keith Cheng, Joel Cohen, Valerie Colangelo, Charles Convis, Lester Davids, Terry Diggs, Jennifer Eberhardt, George Ebers, David Epel, Paul Ehrlich, Susan Evans, Leonard Freedman, Tiny Freedman, Cedric Garland, Barbara Gilchrest, Susan Glassman, William Grant, Elizabeth Hadly, Barry Helft, Brenna Henn, Michael Holick, James Jackson, Wilmot James, Jennie Jin, Rich Kittles, Martha Levinson, Michael Merrill, Suzi Nash, Henry Navas, Bill Nye, Charles Oxnard, Ellen Quillen, Charles Roseman, Charmaine Royal, Sam Richards, Deborah Robbins, Lynn Rothschild, Pat Shipman, Mark Shriver, Fiona Stanley, Thomas Struhsaker, Ania Swiatoniowski, Mark Thomas, Sarah Tishkoff, Desmond Tobin, Elizabeth Vandiver, Jennifer Wagner, Alan Walker, Ward Watt, David Webster, Richard Weller, and Gregory Wray. I apologize to anyone whose name I have accidentally omitted, and I also acknowledge the many people who generously shared their ideas with me in conversation but never identified themselves. I am, of course, responsible for the final distillate.

Finally, I thank the editing, production, and marketing team at the University of California Press for their encouragement and professionalism, and for bringing the book to press in an attractive form: Dore Brown, Erika Búky, Alex Dahne, Nicole Hayward, and Lynn Meinhardt.

Introduction

We are united, and divided, by our skin color. Perhaps no other feature of the human body has more meaning. Our skin is the meeting place of biology and everyday experience, a product of human evolution that is perceived within the context of human culture. An attribute shaped by biological forces, skin color has come to influence our social interactions and societies in profound and complex ways. Its story illustrates the complex interplay of biological and cultural influences that defines and distinguishes our species.

Everyone thinks about the color of their own skin, and usually we can remember when we first gave it serious thought. When I was about twelve, I learned that one of my great-great-grandfathers on my mother's side was a "Moor" from northern Africa. I wanted to know more, but no one seemed to know anything about him, and everyone seemed uncomfortable talking about it. My mother was Italian American, and all I heard growing up was that we had "Mediterranean" skin. In rural upstate New York, where I was raised in the 1950s and '60s, I was one of the most darkly pigmented kids in my school. I didn't understand fully why my relatives avoided talking about our African ancestor or our color, but I realized that it embarrassed them. Some years later, I learned that my mother's brother, a decorated World War II veteran, had been called a "nigger" by a superior officer while serving overseas. I also learned that my mother and her darker siblings had suffered color discrimination while growing up. They had moderately pigmented skin and tanned heavily during the summer, in contrast to the kids of northern European ancestry in nearby neighborhoods who hardly tanned at all. Their dark color was derided by some of their classmates and a few of their teachers, but they made friends among the local "Indians" at the beach because they "all shared the same color and were darker than everyone else." In the minds of my relatives, then, dark skin had many shades of meaning, and some were better than others.

Years later, as a graduate student and then a professor in biological anthropology, I realized just how deeply color anxiety permeated my own academic discipline. Physical, or biological, anthropology is committed to the study of human evolution and human variation, and yet differences in skin color—one of the most obvious and variable of human traits—were mostly only described and not explained. In late-nineteenth- and early-twentieth-century anthropological treatises, explanations of differences in skin color were often given in the context of "definitions" of races. And to some anthropologists of the time, some races were superior to others. The racist tenor of anthropological and scientific writing on human skin color was so repellent to later scholars that after the Second World War, research on the evolution of skin pigmentation or the evolution of races was avoided, as were questions about the origin of skin color variation and its meaning to our biology and health. So, too, scholars skirted around questions of the origin of skin-color discrimination in different parts of the world. Until the past decade, these questions were seen as too divisive and too difficult to explore.

As a graduate teaching assistant, I hobbled through the first classes I taught on human variation and "race" and wished that someone would do research or engage in discussions that would yield deeper insight into these issues. I never imagined that one of those people would be me. Fortunately, today I am not alone in my interests. There are probably hundreds of experts from the fields of anthropology, genetics, sociology, medicine, and many other disciplines who study skin color and its many kinds of meaning. We live in an Enlightenment of color.

My goal in writing this book is to share information on the origin and meanings of skin color and the ways it affects our daily lives. Human evolution and human history are easy to comprehend, but they are rarely discussed in plain language or together. I have tried to write this book in a straightforward manner so that anyone with a basic knowledge of biology and history can understand it, and so that the facts of skin color will become common knowledge.

The first part of the book (chapters 1–6) is devoted to the biology of skin color: how skin gets its color, how skin pigmentation evolved, and what it means for our health. Readers of my previous book, *Skin: A Natural History,* will find familiar material in this section but will also discover a lot of new information derived from recent genetic investigations of skin pigmentation and physiology. Our understanding of the evolution of human skin color is much more extensive than it was even a decade ago. Biology textbooks are filled with examples of evolution acting to bring about changes in the appearance and functioning of insects and viruses, but well-documented examples of evolution in action on humans are rare. Our skin reveals the combined action of the major forces of evolution, from the mutations that provide the basis of variation to natural selection and the other genetic mechanisms that caused changes in skin color as humans migrated around the globe. Every human being represents a walking set of compromise solutions worked out by evolution in the history of our lineage. Skin is our largest interface with the world, and its structure and color beautifully illustrate the concept of conflict resolution through evolution.

The properties of our skin—including color—affect our health. Most of us think that humans have used our collective intelligence to overcome biological limitations in a way that cultureless species cannot do. But at least with respect to our skin, this hubris is unwarranted. Many common health problems, like skin cancer and vitamin D deficiency, are caused by a mismatch between our habits and our heritage. The amount of pigment that our skin contains, which determines how our bodies deal with sunshine, evolved in our ancestors. Today, many of us live under very different conditions from those experienced by our predecessors and pursue dramatically different lifestyles. People living thousands of years ago did not have indoor jobs and go on vacation; they lived outside most of the time and generally didn't travel much or very far. Because of these factors, many of us have an inherited skin tone that is not adapted to our current circumstances, and that mismatch places us at risk for specific health problems. Knowing our own particular risk factors can be a matter of life or death.

The second part of the book (chapters 7–15) is devoted to how we perceive and deal with the social ramifications of skin color. We notice one another's skin because we are visually oriented animals, but we are not genetically programmed to be biased. Over time, however, we have developed beliefs and biases about skin color that have been transmitted over decades and centuries and across vast oceans and continents.

We have no evidence that when people of different skin colors first met in the regions surrounding the Mediterranean Sea, their relationships or business transactions were affected by skin color. As long-distance travel became more common, however, people increasingly encountered others abruptly and were often startled by each other's appearance. The parties involved rarely met on equal terms. European explorers tended to be more exploitative than egalitarian in their attitudes and less than charitable in their descriptions of the peoples they met during their travels. Darkly pigmented or nearly black skin astonished most Europeans, and the tales told and written of encounters with dark-skinned natives often described the color of distant peoples in lurid or unpleasant terms. For centuries, the tales written by European explorers and travelers were the only sources of information available about people living in distant lands, and these accounts had powerful effects on the ways readers and schoolchildren conceived of these others. Demeaning images of blackness, in particular, had an inordinate influence on human history and set in motion some of the most odious behaviors, customs, and laws our species has ever devised. We are still burdened by the biases that were planted in the minds of people centuries ago.

Skin color has been the primary characteristic used to assign people to different "races." These categories, which have always been ill-defined, have varied tremendously from one place to another. Races have been defined as collectives of physical traits, behavioral tendencies, and cultural attributes. They have been considered real and immutable, so that a person having a particular physical characteristic had, by definition, all of the other attributes of the racial category. Roger Sanjek, one of the foremost scholars of race, notes that the global racial order has always included more than just black and white, but these two terms and the social values affixed to them have defined its poles.[1] Systems of racial classification built on skin color and other characteristics have varied from place to place and through time. They are the products of racist ideologies. The aim of these classifications has been not only to physically distinguish one group from another but also to rank these groups in hierarchies of intelligence, attractiveness, temperament, morality, cultural potential, and social worth.

The association of color with character and the ranking of people according to color stands out as humanity's most momentous logical fallacy. While widely recognized as malignant, color-based race hierarchies are still treated as facts of nature by some and are duly upheld and promulgated. A large portion of this book explores the origin and ramifications of this powerful social deception and the many ways in which it has played out in human history. Much is said today about a "color-blind" society and movement toward a " postracial" era, but we are not there yet. In most of the world, darker-skinned people experience prejudice. Despite laws prohibiting color- and race-based discrimination in many countries, many people aspire to lighter skin in order to have a chance at a better life. Understanding all of the different meanings of skin color in our lives may help us as a species eventually to move beyond skin color as a label of human worth and to see it instead as a product of evolution that once caused great misery.

If you are interested in why color matters to humanity, then this book is for you.

PART ONE

Biology

1

Skin's Natural Palette

Skin does so much in so little space. It protects the body against most physical, chemical, and microbial threats and yet maintains an exquisite sensitivity to touch, temperature, and pain. It achieves this and much more in less than one millimeter (about $1/25$ of an inch) of average thickness, with a layer of nearly impervious dead cells covering the living cells.[1] Skin's highly economical construction consists of two layers, the epidermis and the dermis. The epidermis (outer layer) is very thin, waterproof, and abrasion-resistant and contains important pigment-producing and immune cells. The thicker, denser dermis is tougher than the epidermis and contains most of the skin's plumbing and wiring, including blood vessels, sweat glands, sensory receptors, and hair follicles.

Skin color comes from several substances, which are visible to varying degrees in different people. For most of human history, people did not know exactly how skin got its color, so they spun creative tales and theories to explain it. Many of these explanations were ingenious products of astute observations, like that of the Greek philosopher Hippocrates, who ventured that skin became darker when it was parched by the sun over time.

In lightly pigmented people, the skin gets most of its color from blood and from the bluish-white connective tissues of the dermis. The red color produced by circulating hemoglobin becomes more obvious, especially on the face, when the small arteries in the skin expand and become engorged with blood. This is the classic blush. After long bouts of vigorous exercise, the face becomes flushed and sweaty as blood is pumped to the surface of the skin to supply the sweat glands with needed coolant. The most uncomfortable reddening occurs when people flush red with embarrassment or anger.[2] When people "drain of color" as the result of fear or anxiety, the blood vessels narrow and reduce blood flow to the skin.

MELANIN

Although hemoglobin contributes to skin color, the most important substance imparting color to skin is melanin, which is a pigment produced in specialized skin cells. In moderately or darkly pigmented people, melanin provides most of the remarkable range of brown hues. *Melanin* is the collective term for a large family of molecules that can absorb broadly in the visible light spectrum and are dark in color. The unique chemical configuration of melanin also makes it protective against a variety of noxious environmental elements. It is found in a tremendous array of organisms, including fungi (figure 1; box 1), and its ubiquity in the natural world testifies to its long history and versatility. Melanin is one of many compounds that are repeatedly recruited during the course of evolution because they do their job well and usually only require minor tweaking through natural selection to be modified for new functional roles.

Eumelanin is the dominant pigment found in human skin, and I generally refer to it simply as *melanin*. The most important pigment in the animal kingdom, eumelanin both protects the body and gives it color. Its basic building blocks are chemically simple, but these chemical constituents are bound strongly to proteins in the body to make large, linked molecules, or polymers. Eumelanin polymers take on different physical configurations and are remarkably stable.[3] This stability is essential to their function and makes them hard to study: even when bombarded by high-energy radiation or free radicals, eumelanin molecules don't fall apart. There are many kinds of eumelanin, each with a slightly different structure and resulting color.

Eumelanin is remarkable for its ability to absorb a wide range of the wavelengths of radiation generated by the sun, and in particular the higher-energy and potentially damaging wavelengths of solar radiation beyond the visible spectrum, collectively known as ultraviolet radiation, or UVR. Ultraviolet radiation can damage biological systems by breaking the chemical bonds that hold together important mol-

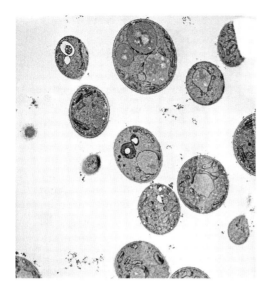

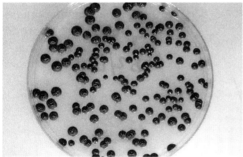

FIGURE 1. Black fungi of the species *Wangiella dermatitidis*, shown in two micrographs at different magnifications, are rich in melanin and thrive in the presence of radiation that would kill many other organisms. Photos courtesy of Ruth Bryan, taken at the Analytical Imaging Facility, Albert Einstein College of Medicine. Photo of melanized *W. dermatitidis* by Christine Polumbo.

ecules, including DNA. This causes a toxic cascade of events in cells that involves the production of "free radicals"—highly chemically reactive atoms or molecules with free electrons that can bind to other molecules—which disrupt normal chemical reactions in cells.[4] When UVR strikes eumelanin, the eumelanin absorbs the radiation without breaking down. This makes eumelanin a powerful sunscreen. Besides blocking damage through physical absorption of UVR, eumelanin prevents free-radical formation and neutralizes free radicals that do form. This is why it is also classified as an antioxidant.

Eumelanin's superior antioxidant properties are put to the test not only in the skin but also in less obvious places like the eye. There, eumelanin is one of the main components of the membrane just under-

BOX 1 **Melanin in Black Fungi**

Many fungi are dark or black because they contain melanin. In these fungi, melanin confers a survival benefit by countering the effects of harmful environmental agents such as heavy metals and UVR. After the Chernobyl nuclear disaster in 1986, black fungi (*Wangiella dermatitidis* and *Cryptococcus neoformans*) colonized the cooling pools and outer walls of the damaged reactor and the adjacent soil. Intrigued, scientists studied the fungi and found that they thrived in the presence of very high levels of ionizing (highly energetic) radiation. The chemical properties and physical structure of melanin protected them from the effects of the radiation. The researchers speculate that these organisms could be used in the future to protect against damage from ionizing radiation.[1]

The fungi may even use the radiation as a source of metabolic energy. If this is the case, the melanin in black fungi serves the same function as chlorophyll in plants: transforming electromagnetic energy into chemical energy capable of sustaining life. Fungi evolved early in Earth's history, before our planet developed the ozone layer that blocks ionizing radiation from space. When the surface of the planet received much higher doses of radiation than it does today, organisms had to evolve ways to use the radiation while protecting themselves from the cell damage it caused.

1. Dadachova et al. 2007, 2008.

---

neath the retina, which is the light-sensitive layer at the back of the eyeball. The retina is constantly bombarded with radiation in the forms of visible light and UVR. The delicate cells of the retina are largely spared damage, however, because the eumelanin in the layer below works to prevent free-radical damage.[5] It is thought that other forms of melanin, tucked away in hidden parts of the inner ear and brain and thus not exposed to any light, may perform similar functions.[6]

All melanins are produced in specialized cells called melanocytes. In the skin, melanocytes are found at the lowest level of the epidermis, at the junction with the dermis (figure 2). Melanocytes come to this position early in the development of the embryo, after their precursor cells migrate into the skin. At this point they establish connections with their neighboring skin cells, called keratinocytes. All babies are born quite pale: although melanocytes start producing melanin early in fetal development, they don't work at full capacity until puberty.

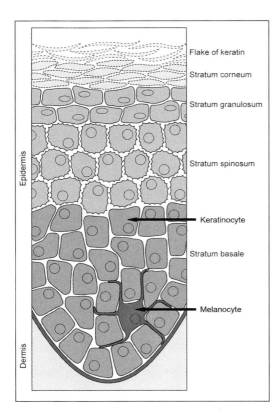

Flake of keratin
Stratum corneum
Stratum granulosum
Stratum spinosum
Keratinocyte
Stratum basale
Melanocyte
Epidermis
Dermis

FIGURE 2. Melanin is produced in melanocytes and then delivered into adjacent keratinocytes within melanosomes. All people have the same number of melanocytes, but they vary in the amount of melanin they can produce and the way it is packaged and distributed in the skin. © 2005 Jennifer Kane. All rights reserved.

Melanin is made within small, membrane-bound packages called melanosomes. As these packages become full of melanin, they move into the slender projecting arms of the melanocyte and from there are transferred into adjacent keratinocytes. Under normal conditions, melanosomes aggregate on top of the nucleus of the keratinocyte and form a protective cap over the genetic material contained in it. One melanocyte supplies melanin to about thirty-six keratinocytes in an intricately choreographed process that is directed by signals from the keratinocytes. These cells also regulate melanin production and melanocyte replication.[7] This is important because disruption of the relationship between melanocytes and keratinocytes wreaks havoc on the body. When melanocytes lose contact with their controlling keratinocytes, they start dividing rapidly and can break free from the confines of the skin altogether and initiate one of the most dangerous of skin cancers, metastatic melanoma. These processes are controlled by genetic and hormonal factors, but in most people they can be accelerated greatly by exposure to UVR.

People have different skin colors mainly because their melanocytes produce different amounts and kinds of melanin. The genetic mechanisms of melanin production involve the regulation of a series of chemical pathways largely governed by the enzyme tyrosinase.[8] Differences in skin color are also caused by differences in the size and distribution of melanosomes in the skin. People with naturally darkly pigmented skin have melanosomes that are large and filled with eumelanin. Those with naturally pale skin have smaller melanosomes that contain varying amounts and kinds of eumelanin as well as of its lighter-colored cousin, pheomelanin.

Like eumelanin, pheomelanin varies in its structure, and its color ranges from yellow to red. It is most obvious in the hair of people from northern Europe (and the British Isles) and in the luxuriant coats of animals like golden lion tamarins and Irish Setter dogs. Pheomelanin not only looks different from eumelanin but acts differently too. Whereas eumelanin is an antioxidant that quenches harmful free radicals produced by UVR, pheomelanin actually produces free radicals when hit by UVR and so can further damage DNA and other components of living skin cells.

Subtle variations in skin color—the reddish, yellowish, bluish, and other hues that are often remarked on in artistic representations of human skin—are due to different proportions of the different forms of eumelanin and pheomelanin in the skin, and most people have both types of melanin in their skin in varying ratios.[9]

Pigment can be unevenly distributed over the surface of the body, and an obvious example of this is freckles. Freckles are small, flat spots of melanin that develop in a random pattern on the skin in response to repeated sun exposure. Occurring mostly in people with very lightly pigmented skin, they vary in color from yellow to dark brown. Ephelides are the type of freckles that most commonly appear on the faces of children. They can occur elsewhere on the body if the skin is exposed to sunlight for longer periods. These freckles can fade if the skin is protected from the sun for a while, and they often disappear entirely by the mid-teens. Sometimes, though, they persist in fair-skinned people who are routinely exposed to strong sun. Another type of freckle is "liver spots" or "age spots" (solar lentigines) that appear on the hands and faces of older people. These tend to be darker than childhood freckles and occur in people with a wide range of skin colors as the result of sun damage. They do not fade, and their persistence is vexatious to many people as they age. Skin bleaching preparations are marketed to eliminate these marks, but this treatment is often not effective.

Large anomalies in the production of melanins in human skin usually leave conspicuous traces. Because the absence of normal skin color on part or all of the body can affect a person's health and self-image, extensive research has been conducted on these afflictions. Absence of pigmentation can arise for many reasons. Various types of albinism are due to genetic mutations affecting different parts of the pigment production pathway or melanocytes in different parts of the body. Melanocytes can be entirely absent or fail to produce melanin, or melanosomes can fail to mature and be transferred into keratinocytes.[10] The end result is the same: no pigment. When the ability to produce pigment in the skin is lost in patches on the body, the result is a condition known as vitiligo.

Albinism is better known and is the collective term for many conditions that reduce pigmentation. Africa is home to people with many hues of brown, melanin-rich skin, but it is also home to many people with albinism, who have greatly reduced levels of melanin. They tend to stand out more in Africa because their pale skin, hair, and eyes contrast strikingly with the features of most of the people around them. Some types of albinism affect just the skin and hair; others affect the skin, hair, and eyes, or just the eyes. All are caused by different genetic mutations involving pigmentation. One of the most common types is oculocutaneous albinism, or OCA, which has many subtypes of varying severity that are caused by different genetic mutations (box 2).

Albinism, especially the OCA2 type, is a serious health problem in Africa because people with albinism are more susceptible to the harmful effects of UVR exposure, including extreme sun sensitivity, skin cancer, and eye damage (figure 3). They also face serious social discrimination because of their appearance. In recent years, this discrimination has taken a dramatic and grisly turn, with dozens of people being killed in ritual murders in Tanzania and neighboring Burundi. Local witch doctors aver that the limbs, hair, and blood of people with albinism are potent ingredients for magic charms, which are said to bring success in business and in gold prospecting. Prices for magic concoctions mixed with ground-up organs taken from people with albinism reportedly start at US$2,000, and witch doctors involved in the sale of products made from albino body parts are said to belong to powerful networks across East Africa. Despite well-publicized trials and govern-

BOX 2   **The Complexities of Albinism**

Different kinds of albinism are caused by genetic mutations on different chromosomes and are diagnosed genetically. In humans, at least four genes (*TYR, OCA2, TYRP1,* and *MATP*) are responsible for different types of the condition and can exert their effects at various points in the biochemical pathways that produce pigmentation, affecting the production of eumelanin and pheomelanin.[1] Albinism is an autosomal recessive condition, meaning that two copies of an albinism gene—one inherited from each parent—must be present in order for someone to be born with albinism. Albinism is more common in some parts of the world than in others, but it is estimated that about 1 in 70 people carry a gene for oculocutaneous albinism (OCA). The most severe type of OCA is OCA1A, which is characterized by a complete, lifelong lack of melanin production. The milder forms—OCA1B, OCA2, OCA3, and OCA4—show some pigment accumulation over time, with different patterns of reduced pigmentation in the skin and hair.

Some of the most serious medical problems faced by people with albinism affect the eyes. Their irises lack melanin pigment, and they have much less melanin in their retinal pigment epithelium, which protects the light-sensitive retina from damage. These deficiencies lead to lower visual acuity, impaired color vision, and considerably greater sensitivity to light. Because their skin lacks protective eumelanin, people with albinism also have a higher risk of skin cancer, especially if they live in sunny places and do not have ready access to sun protection or medical screening.

1. See Carden et al. 1998; Gronskov, Ek, and Brondum-Nielsen 2007.

ment crackdowns against the perpetrators of these crimes, a climate of fear exists among people with albinism in Africa.[11]

MEASURING SKIN COLOR

In doctors' offices and in scientific studies of skin pigmentation today, objective and reproducible measurement of skin color is important. This was an imperfect art for centuries. The earliest classifiers of humankind, working in early-eighteenth-century Europe, used simple and imprecise color words like *yellow, red, black,* and *white* to describe skin tone. They had not observed non-Europeans in person but had only read explorers' and traders' reports of journeys to distant lands.

FIGURE 3. This girl with albinism from Tanzania wears sunglasses and a protective hat and scarf to protect her skin from strong sun. People with albinism living in equatorial Africa are at risk of great damage to their skin and eyes because these organs lack protective melanin. Nonprofit organizations across Africa provide protective hats and chemical sunscreen for many people with albinism. Photo courtesy of Rick Guidotti, www.positiveexposure.org.

By the late 1800s and early 1900s, it was evident that a more nuanced system was necessary to describe the many hues of human skin, and it was then that European scientists began to develop numerical codes for describing skin tone. These systems made use of numbered strips of painted paper or numbered tiles of colored glass in different shades; the latter system gained wide circulation under the name of its developer, Felix von Luschan.[12]

These methods were an improvement over arbitrary color naming, but they failed. Matching methods arbitrarily divided the continuum of skin tones into discrete shades, and the measurements were hard to reproduce from one observer to another because the tiles looked different under different lighting conditions, and matches with skin tone were often judged differently.[13] Because of the inaccuracy of these methods, and the benighted motivations of some of the people using them, the study of skin pigmentation and skin color inheritance lost direction and intellectual integrity during the early twentieth century. A more objective and reproducible method was skin-color

BOX 3 **Reflecting on Skin Color**

Different colors of skin reflect different amounts of different wavelengths of visible light. This fact is nicely demonstrated by the work of the anthropologist Nigel Barnicot comparing the average skin reflectances from a group of lightly pigmented Europeans (mostly British) and a group of darkly pigmented Nigerians of the Yoruba group, shown in the table and figure below.[1]

		Light reflectance by skin (%)		
	Group	Blue light (425 nm)	Green light (550 nm)	Red light (685 nm)
Males	Yoruba	8.0	10.1	23.6
	European	32.8	37.9	45.4
Females	Yoruba	8.5	11.1	13.9
	European	34.3	40.5	63.1

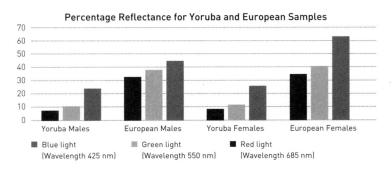

Percentage Reflectance for Yoruba and European Samples

Lower numbers indicate less reflected light and more absorbed light. Melanin pigment absorbs more blue light than red light. Therefore, the reflectance of red light (685 nanometers) is a good measure of pigmentation due to melanin. Reflectance of green light (550 nm) measures in particular the color due to blood in the skin. Note that shorter wavelengths are reflected less (and are absorbed more) than longer wavelengths, and that female skin reflects more light of all wavelengths than male skin. In other words, women tend to have lighter skin than men.

1. See Barnicot 1958. Barnicot's methodology differed from that used in later studies in that he measured the amount of light reflected from the inner surface of the forearm, not the upper arm. The upper-arm site is now favored because it is less frequently exposed to sunlight.

measurement using reflected light of specific wavelengths, often called reflectometry.

The principle of skin reflectometry is simple. The reflectometer measures skin color by shining light through filters of different colors onto the skin and measuring the amount of light that is reflected back. Each colored filter allows light of a specific wavelength of the visible spectrum to pass through. Skin color is measured by the percentages of the different wavelengths of light reflected. Light skin reflects more visible light of all wavelengths than dark skin and gives higher reflectance values, but different skins reflect different amounts of different wavelengths (box 3). Darker-toned skin absorbs more short-wavelength (blue) light than long-wavelength (red) light. Lighter skin absorbs less blue light and more red light. Over the past sixty years various kinds of portable reflectometers have been invented to make it easier to measure skin pigmentation in field situations and in doctors' offices.

SKIN COLOR AND UVR EXPOSURE

Our skin "tans" when exposed to strong, UVR-containing sunlight, but some of us develop a much darker tan than others. (Tanning as a series of physiological responses to UVR exposure is distinct from sun-tanning as a recreational activity, which I refer to as *recreational tanning;* see chapter 14.) Everyone, regardless of skin color, has about the same number of melanocytes, but people with naturally dark skin possess melanocytes that can produce about four times as much melanin as those in people with lighter skin.[14] Higher melanin content offers more protection against damage to DNA and other important molecules. The fourfold difference in melanin content between darkly pigmented and lightly pigmented people translates into a seven- to eightfold difference in protection against damage to DNA, but even the darkest skin does not protect a person completely. Even very low UVR exposures cause measurable DNA damage.

Most people have sufficient melanin in their skin to produce a good natural tan, but some people with lightly pigmented skin make very little melanin to begin with and cannot produce more. They have lost the ability to tan, even if exposed to prolonged or intense UVR.[15] Instead, their skin reacts to the radiation by mounting a strong inflammatory reaction—sunburn. The redness, heat, swelling, and pain caused by sunburn are symptoms of the damage-control reaction, which is the skin's response to excessive UVR. At the cellular level, damage can occur to epidermal keratinocytes; to numerous cells in the dermis, including the resident immune cells; and to the delicate linings of the tiny blood vessels or capillaries in the skin. (Damage to capillaries causes them to leak fluid, which creates blisters on the skin surface.) At the chemical level, the immune response causes molecules that provoke inflammation, pain, and itchiness to be released from skin cells.

From the skin's point of view, a sunburn is a disaster. Even after the redness and pain subside, the damage persists. The connective tissues in the skin and the DNA in skin cells have been seriously harmed, leading to premature skin aging and possibly cancer if the impaired DNA cannot completely repair itself.[16]

Tanning is a complex process that takes place over days and weeks if exposure to the sun persists (figure 4). For some people, the skin's first response to strong sunlight is the rapid development of gray-brown blotches. This reaction, which can cause alarm to the unwary sunbather, is known as immediate pigment darkening (IPD) and is still not well understood. It occurs mostly in people who already have a moderate amount of melanin in their skin. It appears to involve not the production of new pigment but rather the redistribution of existing melanin. The color produced by IPD mostly disappears soon after sun exposure stops.

What we think of as normal tanning is known to dermatologists as delayed tanning to distinguish it from IPD. During delayed tanning, melanocytes are mobilized into vigorous long-term action. Most of the visible darkening that occurs within the first week of sun exposure results from the upward movement of melanin already present in the epidermis, not from newly produced pigment. Increases in melanin production occur later, as chemical reactions gradually increase within melanocytes. Chronic exposure to UVR, like that experienced by many outdoor workers, can result in a near doubling of the skin's melanin content. This is brought about by increases in both melanin production and the number of melanocytes.[17] In people with naturally dark skin, the tanning reaction starts with a dramatic mobilization of melanin upward in the epidermis and continues with increased production of melanin. This reaction accounts for the fact that naturally dark-skinned people get visibly darker after a week or more of sun exposure and then lose the added color over months if they stay out of the sun.

Does tanning really help protect the skin against the harmful effects of sunlight? Some people think it does and attempt to "build up a good tan" early in the summer to protect themselves from a long season of

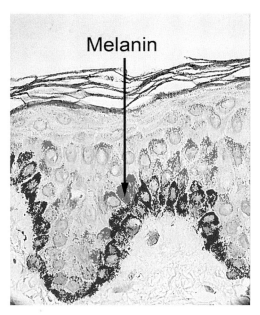

Melanin

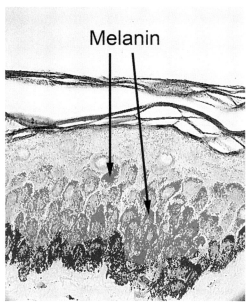

Melanin

FIGURE 4. Sections of dark skin before and seven days after UVR exposure. Before exposure (top), melanin is concentrated at the base of the epidermis, but seven days afterward (bottom), it has moved closer to the surface because melanosomes carrying existing melanin have been transported and transferred into keratinocytes closer to the surface. From Tadokoro et al. 2005. Reprinted with permission from Macmillan Publishers Ltd.

heavy UVR exposure. Unfortunately, a heavy tan affords little more protection than what is provided by naturally dark skin. Tanning does increase melanin content, but this alone does not confer protection from UVR damage. The skin of a naturally darkly pigmented person affords great protection against UVR because of its higher melanin content and the larger and denser caps of melanosomes that protect the DNA within the living skin cells, and because the pigment in dark skin is mobilized faster from deep in the epidermis to a position closer to the surface. In this position, the melanin can more readily absorb UVR that would otherwise damage DNA and other vital molecules. Thus it is not just the abundance of melanin but also its location that determines how much protection it affords.

In prehistory and in early historical times, people tanned in the course of their daily activities. Our ancestors slept in natural shelters or simple huts and spent their days outside acquiring food through gathering, hunting, herding, fishing, and farming. Tanning was part of the skin's adaptation to seasonal changes in the intensity of sunlight. Today, most people in industrialized countries live and work indoors and get only casual exposure to strong sunlight during their normal activities. Seasonal tanning has become a process that people have to seek out and is done mostly in the context of relaxation and recreation (see chapter 14).

SKIN COLOR AND AGING

People fade with age. In people over thirty, the number of active melanin-producing cells decreases on average by about 10 to 20 percent per decade as melanocyte stem cells gradually die. The skin of the face and hands, which is routinely exposed to UVR, has about twice as many pigment cells as unexposed skin, probably because chronic exposure to sunlight continues to stimulate melanocytes. The uneven or blotchy appearance of the hands and faces of older people is due to the loss and uneven distribution of pigment cells and to changes in the interactions between melanocytes and keratinocytes.[18] Darkly pigmented people tend to exhibit fewer signs of aging in their skin than the lightly pigmented because their built-in sunscreen protects them from most photoaging (aging caused by sunlight). Both of the women in figure 5 belong to the Herrero, a group from southwest Africa. The women are the same age, but the woman on the left had a German father. Her lighter skin left her more susceptible to photoaging: the resulting deep

FIGURE 5. Herrero women in southwest Africa. The woman on the left had a German father, and her skin shows more sun damage than that of her friend of a similar age (right), whose parents were both Herrero. Photo courtesy Jeffrey A. Kurland.

lines and wrinkles on her face make her look much older than her companion.

Age-related changes in skin color wouldn't matter much if it weren't for the fact that humans are highly visually oriented animals, like all primates. We critically assess the appearance of other members of our species immediately, unconsciously, and without introspection, and we draw conclusions about their age, attractiveness, and health on the basis of what we see. Recent studies have shown that evenness of facial skin color is one of the main criteria influencing judgments of female attractiveness, age, and—in particular—health.[19] Fewer color irregularities connote better health, general physiological well-being, and greater reproductive potential. These findings drive the continued development and marketing of creams and preparations that can make skin more evenly colored and encourage women and men to protect their faces from sun damage in the first place.

2

Original Skin

Encountering people of different skin colors is now an everyday experience, but it was not so for our ancestors. Before the rise of cities and advances in rapid, long-distance transportation, most people lived and died not far from where their parents and great-great-grandparents had lived. Their skin colors had evolved to suit their environments, and so others they met mostly looked like them.

The sepia rainbow of human skin that exists today evolved over the past 60,000 years, as modern humans dispersed out of equatorial Africa and adapted to new environments. It has only been in the past few thousand years, though, that people have *known* that this diversity existed. During earlier phases of our history, it was rare for people living in distant places to meet or see one another. It took horses, camels, wheels, paddles, sails, and, eventually, engines, trains, and aircraft to bring distant peoples into contact with one another. Our modern ability to travel great distances at high speeds makes it hard to imagine a world of more circumscribed movement. But it is this world that we must revisit to understand how skin colors evolved and what the skin-color map probably looked like before people of all colors spread around the planet.

NAKED SKIN AND HOT SUN

The human lineage originated in equatorial Africa around 6 million years ago, when it split from that of our closest living relatives, chim-

FIGURE 6. An infant chimpanzee is born with lightly pigmented skin all over its body. As its face and hands are exposed to sunlight and UVR, it develops more melanin pigmentation on those areas. Chimps that stay indoors all year (as in some zoos and medical research facilities) retain light-colored skin on their faces and hands. Photo courtesy Leanne Nash.

panzees. Our common ancestor didn't resemble modern chimps but shared many features with modern African apes in its general lifestyle and appearance.[1] We have no confirmed evidence of fossilized skin from human ancestors because skin breaks down quickly after death and is rarely preserved for more than a few thousand years. Because of this, we rely on comparative anatomical and genetic evidence from modern apes and humans to reconstruct the probable appearance and function of our skin millions of years ago.

Compared to our living ape cousins, we stand out as the only naked species. Humans are virtually hairless except for clumps of hair on the head and in the armpits and groin. Underneath the dark hair of our ape relatives is a sheet of pale skin (figure 6). The parts of the body not covered with hair, like the face and the backs of the hands, start out pale in infants and get darker as the animals are exposed to more sun with age. Because this condition is common to all modern primates, we can infer that it was probably shared by early humans.

Fossils tell us that the defining characteristic of our ancestors was habitual bipedalism, the ability to stand and walk on two legs. Evidence of bipedal human ancestors, or hominids, is plentiful in the fossil record. Dozens of sets of fossilized limb bones retrieved from African sites show that we were competent bipeds more than 5 million years ago and energetic striders and runners by 2 million years ago. The major changes in hominid anatomy and behavior that occurred around 2 million years ago heralded the emergence of the genus *Homo*, which includes our species. Well-preserved fossils from east Africa and the Republic of Georgia show that our ancestors living about 1.5 million years ago were tall, active, and able to travel long distances by walking and running.[2] The changes in anatomy and activity that can be detected from fossil bones were also accompanied by less obvious but significant changes in the digestive system, brain, and skin.

Skin is the body's interface with the physical, chemical, and biological environment. It protects our organs and helps to maintain a constant body temperature. When hominids adopted more active lifestyles, staying cool was one of their biggest problems. Active animals, especially those living in sunny places, have to meet the challenge of overheating. A person exercising in the heat will suffer heat exhaustion if the core body and brain temperatures exceed 40°C (104°F); the normal core temperature is 37°C (98.6°F). Hyperthermia, or heat stroke, can occur when the body's core temperature exceeds 41°C (106°F). This is a serious condition that can cause delirium or coma and death, because the nerve cells in the brain succumb to the effects of a toxic cascade of heat-induced chemical reactions and a shutdown of the brain's blood supply.

Different groups of animals have evolved various solutions to the problem of brain cooling, but primates deal with it mostly by sweating.[3] As sweat evaporates, it cools the skin and underlying blood vessels. The cooled blood returns to the heart, is oxygenated in the lungs, and is then pumped to the brain and other organs. This system works well as long as evaporation can continue on the surface of the skin and fluid intake can be maintained to replace the evaporated sweat. Most primates have few sweat glands and easily overheat. Chimpanzees, for instance, produce lots of sweat only in their armpits and suffer heat exhaustion quickly because they can't dissipate their excess heat by other means. They compensate for this by being less active in the hottest period of the day.

The evolution of an efficient whole-body cooling system based on sweating was an important, though largely underappreciated, breakthrough in human evolution. We have sweat glands all over our bodies; those on the forehead, back, and chest are especially quick to respond to heat and exertion. The broad distribution of sweat glands on the body keeps us cool in much the same way an old-fashioned swamp cooler does—by moving air over a wet surface. We still have much to learn about how our sweat glands and cooling system evolved, but insights are coming from genome research and comparisons of key gene sequences between humans and our primate relatives. Some of the important differences between us and chimpanzees are found in genes related to the structure and function of skin.[4] These differences are related mostly to the epidermal proteins that contribute to the barrier functions of the skin, the integrity of sweat glands, and the delicate nature of our body hair. Our skin is tougher, has sturdier sweat glands, and has a coat of finer, more delicate hair.

Another line of genetic evidence also sheds light on the evolution of human nakedness. Naked skin is vulnerable skin. The loss of functional body hair facilitated the cooling function of sweat but left our skin exposed to abrasion, plant irritants, and UVR damage. We coped with the first two problems by toughening up our epidermis and with the third by evolving dark, all-body pigmentation. An important determinant of skin pigmentation in humans is the *MC1R* (melanocortin 1 receptor) gene. In modern Africans this gene exhibits almost no variation, but outside Africa it is highly variable. When geneticists investigated the lack of variation in African forms of the gene, they calculated that the gene probably had undergone strong positive selection—intense, directional natural selection sometimes referred to as a "selective sweep"—around 1.2 million years ago.[5] They reasoned that the African form of *MC1R* was so effective in improving health and reproductive success that people carrying it quickly outnumbered and replaced those who didn't. The African form of the *MC1R* gene makes possible the production of large amounts of eumelanin in the melanocytes of the skin. Thus, at an early point in the history of the *Homo* lineage, we evolved hairless and sweaty skin replete with protective eumelanin. With this array of new adaptations, we could walk, run, and search for food for long periods under a hot sun without overheating and brain damage. We had evolved a covering of skin that buffered us against most environmental challenges.

THE BENEFITS OF DARKLY PIGMENTED SKIN

Darkly pigmented, melanin-rich skin affords considerable protection against UVR damage to DNA and is associated with much lower rates of skin cancer than lightly pigmented skin. The high concentrations of melanin also protect sweat glands from damage. Although some theories about the evolution of dark pigmentation suggest other benefits that might be conferred by dark skin (box 4), none of them has gained much support.

For many years, the most widely held theory about the evolution of dark skin pigmentation invoked the protective effects of melanin against skin cancer and sunburn. This theory was based upon the observation that sun damage to lightly pigmented skin would compromise reproductive success. Visions of sunburned hunters unable to provide for their families were conjured in support of this idea, but with no supporting data. In 1961, these ideas were challenged by the biologist Harold Blum. Blum analyzed data showing that skin cancer and sunburn rarely killed people during their reproductive years. Even if their skin was damaged by UVR, bad sunburns were rarely fatal, and badly repaired DNA took a long time to lead to fatal skin cancer. The harmful effects of UVR damage, Blum reasoned, wouldn't catch up with people until after they had had children. In other words, they had evaded natural selection. Even if they succumbed to one or another form of skin cancer in their post-reproductive years, their DNA had already been transmitted to the next generation. Blum concluded that dark skin was not an adaptive trait and that scientists should not be hasty in assuming that all physical traits confer some kind of benefit in natural selection.

Blum's arguments were flawed and his language pejorative, but his paper had two significant effects on research. First, it put a damper on adaptive explanations for skin color and effectively halted research into the function of human skin pigmentation for more than a decade. A second, more beneficial effect was to encourage scientists to think more critically about the real reproductive advantage conferred by traits assumed to be adaptive.

Blum was correct that skin cancer and sunburn alone did not adequately explain the evolution of darkly pigmented skin. This finding does not trivialize these problems: it simply means that they rarely caused death among our ancestors during their reproductive years.[6] Our research on the distribution of skin color showed that there was a very high correlation between skin pigmentation and UVR intensity, meaning that the vast majority of variation in skin color could be explained by variation in UVR.[7] The distribution of skin colors was, therefore, highly unlikely to have developed by chance.

BOX 4 **Dark Skin—For Camouflage or for Fighting Disease?**

Many hypotheses have been developed to account for variations in skin color. One of the most creative was put forward in 1959 by the zoologist R.B. Cowles, who argued that dark skin evolved because it provided better concealment in dark forest environments.[1] He reasoned that dark pigmentation would have been favored in early phases of human evolution because it afforded greater camouflage and protection than light skin, especially among peoples who hunted or foraged for survival. Cowles's argument sounds daft now but wasn't unreasonable at the time. Only in the 1970s did we learn that humans evolved mainly in open woodland and grassland environments, not forests.

Another hypothesis that has been recycled over the past fifty years suggests that dark pigmentation evolved because it strengthened the immune system against tropical infectious diseases and parasites.[2] Melanin's antioxidant and anti-inflammatory properties were seen as supporting the hypotheses that melanin and melanosomes were important components of the immune system and that organisms (including humans) became darker under evolution when their immune systems were severely challenged by bacteria, fungi, and parasites. According to the antimicrobial hypothesis, the evolution of highly melanized people and animals near the equator had more to do with the importance of melanin's protective effects against microbes than with its protection from UVR.

Two lines of evidence argue against this hypothesis. The first is that equatorial peoples living in humid and cloudy environments are actually lighter in pigmentation than those living in drier and sunnier places. The second is that although there are more disease-causing bacteria, fungi, and other organisms near the equator, their prevalence is greatly affected by precipitation.[3] These organisms are abundant in the wet tropics, which receive year-round rainfall, but far less so in the dry tropics, where most of human evolution occurred and where darkly pigmented skin first evolved. Melanin's antimicrobial properties probably benefit humans living in the wet tropics today, but they were of far less importance in evolution than the protection that melanin provided against the severe and continual damage caused by UVR.

1. Cowles 1959.

2. This idea was first put forward in Wassermann 1965 and later revived without reference in Mackintosh 2001.

3. Many parasitic and disease-causing organisms require a year-round water supply to reproduce successfully. Modern humans have been living at or near the equator for more than 100,000 years, but mostly in dry, forest-margin, or coastal habitats. We did not live in *moist* tropical environments, where the highest diversity of such organisms occurs, until 10,000 years ago. See Guernier, Hochberg, and Guegan 2004.

My own research on the evolution of skin color began in 1991, after I rediscovered a paper written in 1978 that described how strong sunlight reduced the levels of folate in the blood. The authors of the 1978 paper proposed that the light-induced breakdown of this important molecule might be related to the evolution of skin color.[8] Folate is a water-soluble B vitamin that occurs naturally in green leafy vegetables, citrus fruits, and whole grains, and it was known at that time that folate deficiencies caused a serious type of anemia. By the late 1980s folate was recognized as a precursor in the pathway for replication of DNA. This process is necessary for making all new cells in the body, and so all of the chemicals required to make DNA are themselves fundamental to the continuation of life. Epidemiological studies aimed at examining the patterns and causes of diseases had begun to indict folate deficiency as the cause of many health problems, including some birth defects. By the early 1990s the relationship between folate deficiencies in pregnancy and the occurrence of birth defects called neural tube defects, or NTDs (figure 7; box 5), had been established.[9] I recognized that this discovery held a key to understanding the evolution of dark skin pigmentation. If high melanin concentrations in skin protected folate from being broken down by sunlight, and if a high level of circulating folate was needed for normal embryonic and fetal development, then the long-sought connection between skin color and successful reproduction was at hand.

In recent years the importance of folate in early development and throughout life has been reinforced by more laboratory and epidemiological studies. Women need folate to maintain healthy eggs, for proper implantation of the fertilized egg, and for development of a healthy placenta after fertilization. It is also essential for all aspects of fetal growth and organ development, not just that of the neural tube. Folate is also needed for normal sperm production in men: folate status is increasingly being investigated as a reason for male infertility.[10]

Factors that might lower folate levels in the body are being investigated by many research groups. Studies using model systems in which folic acid, the synthetic form of folate, is subjected to UVR have shown that folate breaks down in the presence of UVR and that the longer, more deeply penetrating UVA rays are particularly damaging.[11] Perhaps even more important, the damage and stress caused by UVR simultaneously increase the body's demand for folate and reduce levels of readily available folate. These results support the theory that evolution of dark skin pigmentation is intrinsically related to UVR-mediated

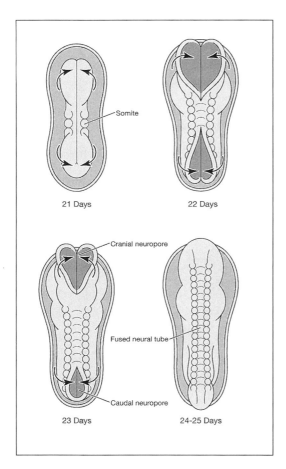

21 Days

22 Days

23 Days

24-25 Days

FIGURE 7. Neural tube defects (NTDs) occur when the neural folds fail to fuse at either end or along the length of the neural tube. Folate deficiency accounts for the majority of NTDs. Spina bifida is the most common. It varies in severity depending on how many layers of the developing nervous system are involved. The prevalence of NTDs has declined greatly in much of the world because of the increasing effectiveness of prenatal screening. Courtesy Jennifer Kane.

changes in folate metabolism and underscore the importance of folate conservation.[12]

Another way to examine this question is to look at epidemiological data and see whether the prevalence of NTDs varies between groups of people of different skin color (other things being equal). This kind of study cannot establish a cause-and-effect relationship between skin color and NTDs, but it can indicate trends that may warrant further investigation. If darkly pigmented skin helps to maintain healthy folate status, we would expect to see fewer NTDs in more darkly pigmented groups—and we do. Many factors probably account for the fact that the most darkly pigmented women suffer the lowest rates of NTDs,

BOX 5 **Folate and NTDs**

Humans obtain folate only from food: our bodies cannot manufacture it. The best sources are green leafy vegetables (the word *folate* comes from the Latin *folium,* for leaf), fruits, and dried beans and peas. Folate is unstable and tends to break down when fresh foods are boiled or stored, or when it is exposed to light or mixed with alcohol. The body converts folate derived from food into various forms that are either used immediately or stored in the liver.

In addition to playing an essential role in the production of DNA, folate regulates gene expression; it is essential for maintaining proper levels of the amino acids that are the building blocks of proteins; it participates in the formation of myelin, the sheath that covers nerves and helps them to conduct electrical impulses quickly through the body; and it is important in the production of many neurotransmitters, including serotonin, which regulates intestinal activity, mood, appetite, and sleep.[1] Folate deficiencies can be caused by insufficient dietary intake, inadequate absorption of it from the gut, or the breakdown of serum folate (the form that circulates in the bloodstream) by alcohol or UVR. In most cases, folate deficiencies can be remedied by eating folate-rich foods or by taking supplements of folic acid, the synthetic form of folate.

Neural-tube defects occur in the developing embryo when the normal processes of cell division in the early nervous system are disrupted. In the fourth week of development, the neural tube closes like a two-ended zipper from the middle simultaneously toward the head and tail ends. At this time, the embryo and its nervous system are particularly sensitive to low folate levels because rates of cell proliferation are high. Failure of the two edges of the tube to fuse securely can cause holes in the tube anywhere along the way (see figure 7). Some of these problems (like anencephaly) are fatal, some lead to a badly compromised lifestyle (the more serious forms of spina bifida), and others are mild and may go undetected (such as spina bifida occulta).

1. There are many good sources of information available on folate and its functions in the body. The Office of Dietary Supplements of the National Institutes of Health provides a good online fact sheet (National Institutes of Health 2009). Good scholarly reviews include Lucock et al. 2003 and Djukic 2007. The latter review emphasizes the roles of folate in infant development and child health.

but studies show that high melanin concentrations in the skin have a protective effect.[13] This finding warrants explicit epidemiological investigation.

The evolution of darkly pigmented skin in high-UVR environments protected DNA and conserved folate, but it raises another interesting question about evolutionary adaptation. High-UVR environments are also generally sunny and hot. Darkly pigmented skin absorbs 30 to 40 percent more sunlight than does lightly pigmented skin. Does this have any effect on a dark-skinned person's well-being? This excess energy appears to be converted to heat. This heat, however, does not raise the body's core temperature significantly: rather, it appears only to warm the surface.[14] This small external heat load is negligible compared to the amount of heat produced when muscles are actively working during exercise. Regardless of skin color, humans have remarkable abilities to dissipate body heat through sweating. Thus the original skin of the genus *Homo* was darkly pigmented to help protect the body from the injurious effects of UVR, and the disadvantage of absorbing heat was mitigated by the sweating mechanism that provided evaporative cooling while hominids searched for food or evaded predators. Under high UVR conditions near the equator, dark pigmentation was a boon and the extra heat load only a negligible disadvantage. As hominids dispersed from these environs to higher latitudes and lower UVR conditions, the natural sunscreening properties of dark pigmentation posed other disadvantages.

3

Out of the Tropics

The origin and early evolution of the human lineage occurred in equatorial Africa. By about 2 million years ago, our hominid ancestors looked much more like modern humans than like apes in their body proportions and in their skin. Our transition to a nearly naked, sweaty, and heavily pigmented skin was complete or nearly so. Ecosystems in Africa underwent many changes beginning about 2 to 1.5 million years ago. As a result of global and regional climatic changes, conditions became more highly seasonal. Rapid and unpredictable changes brought about transitions from forest to woodland and from woodland to grassland. Plants and animals either evolved to cope with these rapidly fluctuating environments or became extinct.

By this point in our history, our ancestors were dependent on herd animals for some of their food requirements.[1] With changes in weather and climatic patterns, herds of hoofed animals ebbed and flowed over the landscapes in search of food. The late archaeologist J. Desmond Clark wrote that in this period of our evolution, human populations followed the seasonal migrations of the herds they depended on, and this behavior drew some populations northward and eastward, out of Africa into Asia. These hominids didn't set out to colonize new realms, nor were they escaping unfavorable conditions: they were simply following game animals.[2] By about 1.8 million years ago, they were living in central and eastern Asia. Tall and strong-bodied compared to their antecedents, they had smaller brains and bigger teeth than modern humans and used simple stone tools. They were not sophisticated by modern standards, but they were more clever, resourceful, and opportunistic than any primate that had lived before.

The first hominid dispersal out of the tropics of Africa required changes in bodies, behaviors, and culture to adapt to new environments and respond to new threats. The intensity and yearly pattern of sunshine in tropical Africa is, and was, very different from that of most of Asia and Europe. The strength of UVR tapers off greatly north of the Tropic of Cancer and south of the Tropic of Capricorn (map 1). Humans living outside the tropics are still exposed to high levels of UVR in the summer months. In the fall and winter, however, levels of UVR are low, and they decrease with proximity to the poles. This trend would at first appear advantageous for protecting human skin from sun damage, but it is not, because UVR serves an important function in the human body: it starts the production of vitamin D in the skin.

THE SUNSHINE VITAMIN

Vitamin D enables the body to absorb and use calcium. Almost every part of the body, from the skeleton to the immune system and brain, requires vitamin D. Our most distant vertebrate ancestors were fish living in the calcium-rich oceans. Fish do not appear to need vitamin D in order to absorb calcium or to stay healthy because they absorb all the calcium they need directly from seawater through their gills.[3] In spite of this, fish consume considerable vitamin D in their diet. The phytoplankton and zooplankton they ingest are rich in various forms of vitamin D, and fish that do not themselves eat plankton eat other fish that do. Fish concentrate vitamin D in their livers, which is why fish liver oil is valued as a vitamin D supplement.

The first land-living vertebrates evolved around 375 million years ago. We refer to them as ancient tetrapods, the four-legged, land-living ancestors of all living amphibians, reptiles, birds, and mammals, including us. Among the challenges facing early tetrapods was how to absorb calcium. They could not absorb it through their gills from seawater, as their ocean-dwelling ancestors had done, so they evolved a way to absorb it from the foods they consumed. This process required vitamin D. Life on land required many new adaptations, and the ability to make vitamin D in the skin from sunshine was one of the most momentous.

Vitamin D production in the skin begins when UVR penetrates the

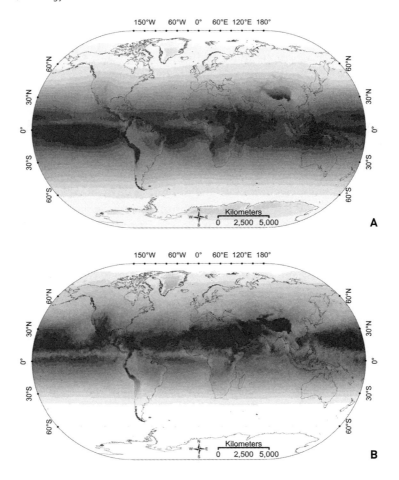

surface of the skin and interacts with a cholesterol-like molecule to form the compound called pre–vitamin D₃. This reaction occurs only in the presence of medium-wavelength UVR, or UVB, not the longer-wavelength UVA. Most of the Earth is bathed in UVA, along with visible light, for most of the year because longer wavelengths of solar radiation pass more easily through the atmosphere than shorter ones. Most UVB and all UVC rays are destroyed or reflected by oxygen, ozone, and dust in the atmosphere. UVB reaches the Earth's surface when it has a relatively straight path from the sun through a thin layer of the atmosphere (figure 8). The farther a place lies from the equator, the less UVB is received, and the less potential it offers for making vitamin D.

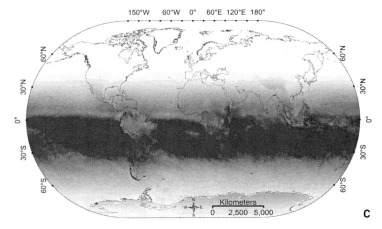

MAP 1. The distribution of medium-wavelength ultraviolet radiation (UVB) at the Earth's surface. The darkest areas are those with the highest UVB. *(a)* Average UVB for the year. The highest average levels of radiation are seen at equatorial latitudes and at high altitudes (in the Himalayas and Andes). Cloud cover and high humidity over equatorial rainforests greatly reduce UVB. The distribution of UVB changes as the Earth revolves around the sun on its axis during the year. *(b)* UVB in June. The areas with the highest levels of UVB are shifted northward. *(c)* UVB in December. The highest levels are shifted southward. In December, most densely populated parts of the Northern Hemisphere receive no UVB. Maps by George Chaplin based on remotely sensed data on UVB (305 nm) from NASA. World Winkel II projection.

By enabling the absorption of calcium from the diet, vitamin D contributes to the building and maintenance of a strong skeleton. Children who do not get enough of the vitamin suffer from the highly visible and disfiguring bone disease called rickets. We now know, however, that vitamin D does a lot more than build bones: it performs essential functions in many parts of the body (box 6).

Now a worldwide health problem, vitamin D deficiency can be particularly dangerous when it persists for many years. Vitamin D deficiencies have become more common in recent decades because more people live in cities, protect themselves from sunlight, or no longer eat vitamin-D rich foods. Vitamin D deficiency doesn't kill its victims quickly and, in fact, it may not kill directly at all. Rather, it weakens bones, compromises the body's ability to prevent the rampant cell division that occurs in cancer, and reduces the immune system's ability to fight infections.

To understand the importance of vitamin D in human evolution and its relevance to skin color, it is helpful to return to the situation

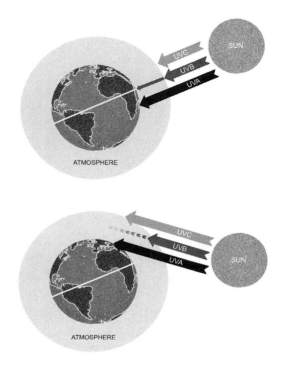

FIGURE 8. The kind and amount of UVR reaching the Earth's surface depends mostly on location and time of year. UVC is almost entirely absorbed by the ozone and oxygen in the atmosphere. At the spring and fall equinoxes at the equator (top), the sun is directly overhead, and some UVB passes through the atmosphere and reaches the Earth's surface. At the height of winter in the Northern Hemisphere (bottom), the sun's rays follow a longer path through the atmosphere, which results in the complete filtering out of UVB. Illustration by Tess Wilson.

experienced by early members of the genus *Homo*. Remains of early *Homo* specimens and the tools they used have been found in equatorial Africa, and in central, eastern, and southeastern Asia in fossil sites dating from 1.8 to 1.5 million years ago. Two of the oldest Eurasian sites, Dmanisi in Georgia and Xiaochangliang in China, date from about 1.7 million years ago and are located just above 40° N latitude. These destinations were a long way from tropical Africa in terms of both distance and latitude.

The dispersal was fast by the standard of mammalian evolution; its swiftness is a testament to the hominids' cleverness and adaptability. We can only speculate how they managed to meet their vitamin D requirements. The African ancestors of these hominids were darkly pigmented, their skin richly endowed with sun-protective melanin. The efficacy of melanin as a sunscreen meant that it would have greatly reduced the production of pre–vitamin D in the skin. Studies have demonstrated that melanin distributed throughout the epidermis readily absorbs the shorter wavelengths of UVB and maximizes its sun-blocking effect.

BOX 6   **Vitamin D, Vitamin Extraordinaire**

Vitamin D (calciferol) is more accurately classified as a hormone because of the way it is produced in the body and controls the functions of various cells and organs. It accomplishes its prime function of maintaining calcium balance in the body by increasing the efficiency of the intestine to absorb calcium from the food. In bones, vitamin D helps mobilize stored calcium so that it can be used for other functions in the body. Pre–vitamin D_3, formed in the skin by exposure to UVB, is converted into vitamin D_3 at body temperature. It is chemically transformed first in the liver and then in the kidney to its active form.

Levels of the active form of vitamin D_3 are closely regulated in the body and do not vary much. A different form of vitamin D_3 is stored by the body in fat and muscle, and this is the type that is most commonly tested to determine vitamin D deficiency. When vitamin D_3 is made in the body after exposure to UVB or after eating vitamin D_3–rich food, it can be stored for about two months in muscle and fat tissue. The stores can be drawn upon and converted to the active form.

Research in the past decade has led to a resurgence of interest in vitamin D and a growing appreciation of the varied and important roles it plays in the body. Vitamin D receptors are found in the cells of the brain, heart, stomach, and pancreas, in many types of cells in the immune system, and in the skin and gonads. In all of these places, vitamin D maintains proper calcium levels and normal cell function. The active form of the vitamin is a potent inhibitor of abnormal cell division in several organs, and this may be why chronic deficiencies in vitamin D appear to be associated with certain cancers. This is one of the most active topics of research in cancer epidemiology, and one that is still being debated.[1]

1. The first study to show a probable causal link between vitamin D deficiency and cancers of the breast, colon, prostate, and ovary was welcomed with considerable media and scientific attention and some skepticism. Since then, cancer epidemiologists have been investigating the question further. The situation is complex because vitamin D status is affected by the amount of vitamin D individuals make in the skin, the amount they eat, and the genes that affect how vitamin D binds to cells. See Garland et al. 2006; McCullough, Bostick, and Mayo 2009.

A darkly pigmented person requires about six times as much UVB in order to make the same amount of pre–vitamin D in the skin as a lightly pigmented person.[4] This is not a problem for dark-skinned people living at or near the equator, because the UVB doses received there are so high year-round that ample amounts of pre–vitamin D can be made from regular sun exposure (figure 8a). The situation is quite different outside the tropics, however, as illustrated in figure 8b. Levels of UVB vary greatly according to location, time of year, time of day, and the amounts of moisture or pollution in the air. Today, heavy air pollution and overcast conditions in many cities reduce the penetration of UVB and the potential to make vitamin D in the skin.

FOSSILS, GENES, AND THE LOSS OF ANCESTRAL PIGMENTATION

Research on the evolution of human skin pigmentation began before information on the DNA sequences of human pigmentation genes was available. Anthropologists deduced that hominids living outside the tropics would have been under evolutionary pressure to lose some of the pigment in their skin as they moved north. This deduction was based on the fact that dark skin and reduced UVB exposure would have made it difficult for people to produce enough vitamin D in their skin to stay healthy and reproduce. Therefore, skin would have had to become lighter. This is the basis for what has long been known as the "vitamin D hypothesis" of human skin pigmentation.[5] Some authorities argued that the body's ability to store vitamin D could get humans through the months of the year when active production in the skin was not possible. But the time limit for vitamin D storage is about two months, not long enough to see our lean and active ancestors at high latitudes through from the last UVB of autumn to the first UVB of spring.[6] Females, with naturally more subcutaneous body fat than males, would have been able to store more vitamin D, but even these stores would not have been sufficient to meet their year-round requirements. For people at high latitudes, loss of pigmentation or depigmentation was not an option; it was essential to survival.

In the past decade, researchers have accumulated extensive information on patterns of variability in human pigmentation genes and what these patterns mean.[7] Many different genes contribute to human pigmentation, including the *MC1R* locus introduced in chapter 2. Most of the variations in the DNA sequence of the *MC1R* gene are associated with variations in skin and hair pigmentation. The results of genetic comparisons of the *MC1R* gene across many living human groups demonstrate that there is little variation in the gene within Africa but a lot outside Africa. The near absence of variation in *MC1R* was established in the early history of the *Homo* lineage by strong natural selection, often called positive selection. Since then, a low level of variation in *MC1R* in native African peoples has been maintained by natural

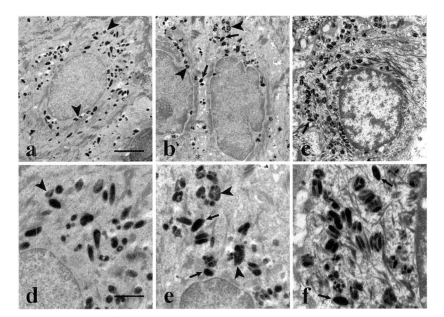

FIGURE 9. The melanosomes of human skin, indicated by arrows, vary in their size, density, melanin composition, and mode of packaging. This figure shows melanosomes from the keratinocytes of the epidermis of three different human populations at low *(a–c)* and high *(d–f)* magnification. Melanosomes in the skin of darkly pigmented African Americans *(a, d)* exist as large, independent units that are packed with UVR-absorbing eumelanin. The skin of East Asians *(b, e)* shows a combination of individual and clustered melanosomes. Those in lightly pigmented Euro-American skin *(c, f)* are small and clustered in membranous compartments; they are filled with pheomelanin, which is much less effective than eumelanin at absorbing UVR. From Thong et al. 2003. Image courtesy of Raymond E. Boissy. Reprinted with permission from John Wiley and Sons/Wiley Blackwell.

selection working to eliminate extreme variations in pigmentation. In contrast, the gene is highly variable outside Africa, especially in northern Europe, where it is associated with red or blond hair and lightly pigmented skin.[8] Insight into the nature and timing of these genetic changes has come from two diverse sources: the zebrafish and Neanderthals.

The skin of native northern Europeans contains relatively little melanin, and most of it is yellow-red pheomelanin, not dark brown eumelanin. The pheomelanin is packaged into small melanosomes that are grouped together in membrane-bound clusters (figure 9). The color of the pheomelanin and the way it is packaged make the skin look pale. When pale human skin is exposed to UVR, it produces more pheomelanin, not the darker and more protective eumelanin. Pheomelanin reacts with UVR to actually *produce* dangerous free radicals in melanocytes, just the opposite of what eumelanin does to neutralize these molecules. The production of free radicals in melanocytes is a deadly chemical reaction because it is the first link in the chain of causality leading to the most serious of skin cancers, melanoma. The facts suggest that lightly pigmented skin evolved in people who lived with generally low levels of UVR.

For many years, scientists were puzzled about the gene or genes that were associated with light skin pigmentation. They knew that variant forms of *MC1R* were associated with red hair and pale skin in northern Europeans, but the curious thing was that different forms of *MC1R* in this group were associated with different hair colors, but not with different skin colors. This led them to suspect that a gene other than *MC1R* was responsible for the slight differences in skin color that are observed in various northern European groups: Scandinavians versus Irish and Scots, for instance. An important clue to this mystery eventually came from a research group studying zebrafish.

Zebrafish are tropical fish named for the pattern of black and white stripes that decorates their bodies. There are other colors of zebrafish, including a golden variety, and this is the one that yielded an important insight about the evolution of human skin pigmentation. Golden zebrafish have fainter and smaller stripes than regular zebrafish. These differences parallel the differences between the melanosomes of lightly pigmented and darkly pigmented human skin. The gene that produces the coloration of the golden zebrafish is the same in structure and function as the gene that produces light pigmentation in human skin (figure 10; box 7).[9]

The zebrafish study had two significant results. First, it led to the identification of the European variant of the *SLC24A5* gene as an important contributor to variability in human skin color. This variant resulted from a single DNA base change (often referred to as SNP, or single nucleotide polymorphism) that then underwent a selective sweep that affected ancient European populations thousands of years ago. (A selective sweep is the process by which variation is greatly reduced or eliminated by strong positive natural selection.) The evolution and spread of the gene accounted for 25 to 38 percent of the difference in skin color between Europeans and Africans. Second, the study found

FIGURE 10. The differences in color between *(a)* normal and *(b)* golden zebrafish shed light on the differences between darkly and lightly pigmented people. Photo courtesy Dr. Keith Cheng. From Lamason et al. 2005. Reprinted with permission from AAAS.

that the European variant of *SLC24A5* was not present in Africans or East Asians. The absence of this loss-of-pigment gene in East Asians was surprising because most eastern Asians have lighter skin than most Africans. This meant that the skin of East Asians must have undergone loss of pigmentation by yet another genetic mechanism, independent of the change seen in Europeans. To date, the gene or genes responsible for depigmentation in East Asians still have not been found, but the search has narrowed down to a few promising leads.

The finding that lightly pigmented skin evolved independently in the ancestors of modern Europeans and East Asians is extremely important. It suggests that at least two distinct genetic mutations occurred and underwent positive selection in two regions of the world that receive relatively low levels of UVR. These genetic findings supported the previous hypothesis that loss of dark skin pigment was an essential adaptation to life in northern regions of the world, where the sun

BOX 7 **Colorful Fish and Human Skin**

The golden zebrafish studied by the research group headed by Keith Cheng at Penn State has a gene named *slc24a5,* or *golden,* that is associated with the production of melanin granules that are smaller, less dense, and more irregularly shaped than those of normal zebrafish. Because the researchers were interested in human skin pigmentation, they decided to study the human equivalent (or orthologue) of the *golden* zebrafish gene, called *SLC24A5.* They reasoned that if the *golden* gene in zebrafish was the same thing as *SLC24A5* in humans, then the human form of the gene should be able to induce pigment production in golden zebrafish embryos whose pigment genes had been inactivated. The researchers injected these "knockdown" golden zebrafish embryos with the messenger form of the human *SLC24A5* gene. They found that the zebrafish embryos started producing golden pigment granules again because the zebrafish pigment gene had been recovered by its human equivalent. This experiment demonstrated that the *golden* gene in zebrafish and the *SLC24A5* gene in humans have not changed throughout the course of evolution, and that the human form of the gene was that associated with the characteristic configuration of small, pale melanosomes seen in the skin of northern Europeans.

shines less brightly. The genetic signature of strong positive natural selection in the European variant of *SLC24A5* indicates that it was strongly favored in evolution until it achieved 100 percent frequency in the population. The most likely reason for this shift was that it was associated with a loss of skin pigment that favored vitamin D production under conditions of low UVB.

Modern humans, *Homo sapiens,* entered into Europe and Asia and underwent loss of pigmentation under natural selection as they dispersed into northerly latitudes beginning about 30,000 years ago. But almost 100,000 years before this, another group of hominids had ventured into Europe and taken up residence there. These were the Neanderthals, belonging to the species *Homo neanderthalensis.* The Neanderthals descended from a branch of early *Homo* that entered Europe about 800,000 years ago. A phenomenally successful line of hunters and foragers, Neanderthals lived in Europe, western Asia, and around the Mediterranean from about 200,000 until 30,000 years ago. We and others before us had concluded from the distribution of Neanderthal fossils that they would have had to be quite lightly pigmented to survive under highly seasonal UVB conditions, especially in central Europe.[10]

Among the many bones of Neanderthals retrieved from fossils, some less than 40,000 years old have yielded DNA that can be analyzed. As studies of the Neanderthal genome have progressed, it has been possible to study the function of some Neanderthal genes.[11] Researchers isolated the *MC1R* sequences from Neanderthal DNA samples, replicated them, and then introduced them into cultures of living skin cells in order to examine the function of the ancient pigment-receptor gene. By "transfecting" cultured cells with the ancient gene, they investigated pigment production in the cells. They found that the specimens had a variant form of the *MC1R* gene not present in any modern humans, including Europeans. The Neanderthal *MC1R* pigmentation gene had a reduced ability to make the receptor protein that alters hair and skin pigmentation, suggesting that at least some Neanderthals had light skin and red hair. This finding meant that inactive forms of *MC1R* had evolved independently in both modern humans and Neanderthals.[12]

The inescapable conclusion from the Neanderthal pigmentation gene study and the zebrafish pigmentation gene experiments is that lightly pigmented skin evolved independently at least three times in human evolution: in Neanderthals, modern Europeans, and modern East Asians. These discoveries argue for the action of natural selection in promoting the evolution of depigmented skin in groups of ancient humans that inhabited northern realms, where sunshine was weaker and where UVB was in shorter supply for most of the year.

Our understanding of human skin-color genetics is still incomplete, but with the tools of modern genetics and comparative genomics, we are making headway. Human geneticists have long known that skin color is controlled by several genes and that these genes interact in complex ways. We now understand that skin, hair, and eye color are all affected by multiple genes and that in some populations some variant forms of the genes account for more of the variation in skin color than in hair color or vice versa. Combinations of different forms of the genes bring about the complex and continuous variation in coloration we see in humans today.

Another important outcome of the genetic studies of the past decade is the finding that pigmentation genes evolve on their own and that pigmentation undergoes evolution independently of other traits: it is not intrinsically linked to other features of appearance, constitution, or behavior. Often when people talk of races, like the "white race" or the "black race," as real biological categories, they assume that skin color and other traits of appearance, or even of temperament, are biologically connected in a heritable package. They are not. Skin color is a biological reality; race is not.

4

Skin Color in the Modern World

Humans have been on the road for a long time. The first dispersers from tropical Africa around 2 million years ago were early members of the genus *Homo* and are generally called *Homo erectus*. Populations of *Homo erectus* spread out to the farthest reaches of Africa and Eurasia. Those who came to inhabit parts of Indonesia, eastern China, and southwestern Europe had tenures of more than 1 million years, but most populations became extinct without trace by about 250,000 years ago.[1] There were some notable exceptions, the most famous being the lineage that gave rise to Neanderthals. The earliest members of *Homo neanderthalensis* evolved nearly 200,000 years ago from one of the regional branches of early *Homo* that colonized Europe. The species reached its peak about 100,000 years ago, when sites of Neanderthal habitation stretched across Europe and western Asia. Neanderthals were superb big-game hunters and lived in close proximity to herds of large mammals. As ice age conditions intensified, the herds thinned for lack of food, and Neanderthal populations waned. The last Neanderthals lived in southwestern Europe until finally becoming extinct around 30,000 years ago.

The first dispersers were not a unitary or cohesive group. They divided and diversified in Asia and Europe for more than 1.5 million years, and then all groups—except those in Africa—eventually became extinct. The Pleistocene (the period from approximately 2.5 million years ago to 10,000 years ago) was a challenging time for most of the world's mammals. The increasingly cold, dry, and seasonal conditions killed off the animals and plants that hominids in Asia and Europe relied on, and few groups survived this crisis. In Africa, descendants of *Homo erectus* continued undergoing evolutionary diversification and adaptation. The first modern humans, *Homo sapiens,* evolved in Africa around 195,000 years ago.

The oldest known *Homo sapiens* fossils were uncovered from a site in a remote river valley in southern Ethiopia. These distant relatives of ours were "anatomically modern": they had large brains, relatively small teeth and jaws, and lithe bodies. They not only looked like us but were also culturally and technologically sophisticated. They made a wide range of sharp-edged stone tools with which they hunted and butchered large animals like hippos. Their own bones bear cut marks and evidence of polishing, suggesting that they cared for the bones of their own dead.[2] We cannot access their thoughts or conversations, but we can judge from their technology and hunting behavior that these people were similar to us.

While descendants of *Homo erectus* in Europe and Asia languished, *Homo sapiens* in Africa thrived and diversified. The period from 80,000 to about 60,000 years ago witnessed dramatic population expansions and changes in human technological, social, and economic patterns in southern and eastern Africa that correlated with rapid climatic changes and increased cognitive capacities. Human remains from this period are associated with body ornaments, sophisticated stone tools, deliberate burials, and other evidence of a rich symbolic life.[3] Humans had become truly modern.

Approximately 65,000 years ago, a small group of people moved from northeastern Africa and probably took an eastward route along the south Asian coastline. This move defined the genetic split between African and non-African people. Current evidence indicates that there was only one such dispersal and that it involved only a few hundred people. The vast majority of modern people stayed in Africa and adapted biologically, socially, and technologically to a wide array of environments.[4]

A HERITAGE OF COLOR IN AFRICA

Modern humans originated in Africa and have been migrating, interacting, and adapting there longer than elsewhere. People living in Africa show high levels of mixed ancestry and more genetic diversity than all the rest of the world's people put together.[5] This diversity is also reflected in skin pigmentation. Africans are not uniform or uniformly dark in their skin color. High levels of skin color diversity exist between different populations and also within most sub-Saharan African groups.[6] This variation illustrates the complex interactions of evolutionary forces that contribute to patterns of variation in skin color at any point in time.

Some of the variation between groups is related to the strength of UVR and is probably the product of natural selection (map 2). Much of the diversity in skin tone within individual groups, however, is related to the long histories of population interchange—due to migrations, climate change, and wars—that have contributed to mixed ancestry for most African groups. Variations in skin color in Africa have very little to do with variations in the *MC1R* skin pigmentation gene, which shows almost no variation in Africa (or in other very high UVR environments like New Guinea), where it works to maintain production of large amounts of protective, sunscreening eumelanin. But other genes have contributed to the subtle differences in skin pigmentation. The shades from light brown through darkest brown, and with overtones of garnet and coal, produced by the play of visible light reflecting off of varying mixtures of eumelanin and pheomelanin in the skin are produced by a symphony of genetic interactions. Variation in skin pigmentation within Africa reflects long histories of natural selection, migration, and the occasional creation of new pigmentation mutations, but the details of the interactions of these forces are still not well understood.

One of the main and earliest areas of human intermingling in Africa was the Nile River. The Nile Valley has a complex population history, and reconstructing this history has been difficult both because the archaeological record is rich and complicated and because many interest groups have stakes in the outcome. The most comprehensive accounts today show that there were episodes of population movement along the Nile Valley from the end of the last ice age through about 3000 BCE.[7] These movements were bidirectional and occurred as the result of language-family dispersals, droughts, and patterns of settlement and military conflict. They resulted in rich exchanges of genetic material and culture and created a changing tapestry of skin color.

Reconstructing the appearance of the ancient Egyptians is difficult because of the complex population history of the Nile Valley. In skin tone, the pharaohs were not monochrome. Some were lighter and some

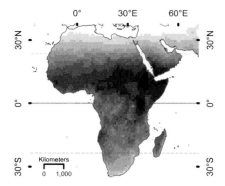

MAP 2. Medium-wavelength ultraviolet radiation (UVB) levels for Africa for March illustrate the wide range of UVR exposure over the continent. The darkest areas are those with the highest UVB. The considerable variation in the intensity of skin pigmentation between African peoples is due in part to this varied sunscape. Levels of UVR are highest over equatorial Africa at the spring and autumn equinoxes in March and September. Note the lower levels of UVR seen in southern Africa, and, at the equator, the contrast between the UVR levels over the eastern deserts and the western rainforests. Map by George Chaplin based on NASA data for UVB at 305 nm. World Winkel II projection.

darker, depending on the time period and their physical location along the Nile Valley. They and their subjects would have had excellent tanning abilities, based upon what we know of the response of "Mediterranean" and African skin to UVR.[8] Enjoying a generally cosseted indoor life without much exposure to sunlight and certainly not tanned from a life of toiling in the fields, Egyptian nobles would have had skin color at the light end of the range of pigmentation for their populations.

The young king Tutankhamun (King Tut) has been an object of particular fascination because of his early death and the gleaming opulence of his tomb and grave goods. Tutankhamun lived from 1341 to 1323 BCE (early in the New Kingdom period) near the mouth of the Nile. Recent reconstructions show him with a lightly built, somewhat feminine-looking skull that resembles those seen among northern Africans today more than those of any other group.[9] The probable hue and tanning ability of Tutankhamun's skin can be reconstructed with reference to the levels of UVR near his home in Lower Egypt. Because these most closely match those found today near the Cape of Good Hope in South Africa, the home of the Khoe-San peoples, we can infer that Tutankhamun's skin tone was similar to theirs. The skin of the southern Khoe-San reflects about 50 percent of the longer wavelengths of visible light and looks moderately pigmented. Along with his literally sheltered existence, Tutankhamun's youth contributed to his relative lightness because melanin production does not peak until after puberty.

THE MOVEMENTS OF PEOPLES AND A HISTORY OF SKIN COLOR

The dispersal of *Homo sapiens* from Africa was driven not by a goal of expansion or escape but by the pursuit of survival. Hominids of this wave moved quickly, initially moving and leapfrogging along coasts, where food resources would have been abundant. First western, then southern, and then southeastern Asia were reached, and no later than 50,000 years ago, *Homo sapiens* made it to Australia. This would have been an amazing experience. We will never know if this remarkable feat was the result of an accident or a plan, but in either case it shows that these people were risk takers and excellent communicators.

Not all of *Homo sapiens* stayed near the coast. Some populations made their way into the hinterland of central Asia, between the Caspian and Black seas. From there, about 45,000 years ago, the species divided again, into a western branch that dispersed into central and northern Europe and an eastern branch that eventually made its way into northeastern Asia. Among the last frontiers of human settlement were the far northern latitudes of Europe and eastern Asia, which were colonized by people beginning about 20,000 years ago. This kind of life would have been unimaginable earlier because the extremes of far northern environments were far beyond human survival capabilities. Technology made these environments accessible to people: clothes, shelters, and new ways of moving across the landscape, making fire, obtaining drinking water, and storing food. The first Americans descended from north-central Asians who worked their way down the American coastline and into the North American hinterland via the Bering land bridge (between modern Siberia and Alaska) beginning about 16,500 to 13,000 years ago. By 10,000 years ago, the Americas had been occupied by a great variety of hunters and foragers. The very last destinations for prehistoric *Homo sapiens* were the distant islands of the Pacific, which were colonized in stages by seafaring people emanating originally from Taiwan and subsequently in waves from islands within Melanesia.[10]

From the sound understanding of the early population movements of our species, we can begin to reconstruct the history of our skin color.

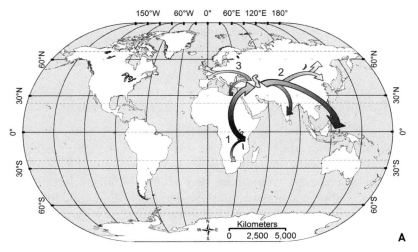

MAP 3. Hominid dispersals and suggested trajectories of skin-color evolution for the early species of the genus *Homo*, above, and *Homo sapiens*, right. Gradations of the grayscale of the arrows correspond roughly to those of human skin color. The *Homo* lineage evolved in Africa close to two million years ago. Our naked skin was permanently darkly pigmented with protective sunscreen. *(a)* The earliest dispersals from tropical latitudes, both southward and northward (1), began around 1.9 million years ago. Adaptation to middle latitudes required loss of pigmentation. Dispersal of *Homo erectus* from central Asia into southeast and northeast Asia (2) over one million years ago involved further changes in pigmentation determined by natural selection in response to local UVR conditions. Dispersal of *Homo erectus* and its descendants (including *H. neanderthalensis*) into Europe was accompanied by depigmentation, and reentry into the Levant, by repigmentation (3).

Between fossils and molecular evidence, we have a good basis for outlining a general evolutionary history of skin pigmentation up to about the time of the origin of agriculture, about 10,000 years ago (map 3).

The reasons for the evolution of varied skin tones in modern humans are much better understood now than they were twenty years ago, but questions remain about the genetic mechanisms underlying differences in pigmentation. We know that several genes contribute to skin, hair, and eye pigmentation in different populations.[11] But exactly how many genes are involved, and what were their roles in different human groups? Natural selection for increased pigmentation evolved as we lost our hair, and that loss of pigmentation occurred as populations moved away from high-UVR environments. The study of ancient population movements in the past also suggests that natural selection might have favored regaining of skin pigmentation as some populations dispersed

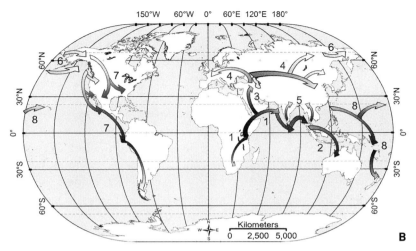

(b) Dispersal of darkly pigmented *H. sapiens* throughout Africa began more than 100,000 years ago. Movement into Eurasia occurred along a coastal route around 65,000 years ago (1). This movement and that into Australasia around 50,000 years ago (2) was probably accompanied by only minor changes in skin color. Overland dispersal of non-Africans into western Asia (3), and from there into western Europe and northeastern Asia was accompanied by independent episodes of depigmentation (4) beginning about 50,000 years ago. Loss of pigmentation also probably occurred in Asian populations dispersing northward from coastal areas (5). Dispersal into the New World, beginning about 15,000 years ago, was by lightly to moderately pigmented people (6), with some tropical reentrants evolving enhanced tanning abilities (7). The last dispersals into Oceania were undertaken by moderately pigmented people less than 10,000 years ago and, for those reentering coastal tropical environments, were accompanied by independent reacquisition of dark pigmentation (8). Maps by Tess Wilson, using base maps by George Chaplin. World Winkel II projection.

back into equatorial realms. One of the most important remaining questions is how long these transitions might have taken. Our research led us to estimate that 10,000 to 20,000 years may have been required for human populations to achieve an optimal level of pigmentation for the regions they ended up in. It could have happened faster, though, if the pressure of natural selection was higher. The length of time would also have been affected by the characteristics of the cultural interface—including the food and the nature of the body coverings and shelters—through which people interacted with the environment. It is thus worthwhile to look in detail at the environmental challenges human populations faced in prehistory as they spread farther away from their equatorial African homeland.

LIFE AT THE EXTREMES

By about 5,000 years ago, humans were living on all of the continents except Antarctica and on most of the habitable islands in the open oceans. The only places where people had not established a year-round presence were at altitudes above 5,000 meters (about 16,400 feet) and on a few extremely remote islands. It didn't take long for most of those islands to be occupied, but extremely high elevations proved a more formidable barrier to human settlement because of the lack of oxygen and the difficulties of finding or growing food. By the end of prehistory there were few uninhabited places on Earth. In the coldest, hottest, highest, and driest places, our bodies were pushed to their biological limits, and in many instances it was only a combination of technology and biology that permitted humans to survive for any length of time. In this context, a few examples of modern humans living at the high and low extremes of environmental UVR warrant a closer look.

The coastal regions of Africa and southeast Asia and the Pacific islands near the equator experience some of the highest UVR levels on Earth. The UVR is invariant except at the spring and autumn equinoxes, when it increases. Two of these regions—the coasts of equatorial Africa and the western Pacific islands of Melanesia—are particularly interesting because they have been inhabited for a very long time. The population history of equatorial Africa is complex because people have been moving across the continent and up and down the coast within the past 5,000 years. Thus, most human movements have occurred in environments with very high UVR. Parts of Melanesia have also been occupied for many thousands of years. The western end of Melanesia, from New Guinea through the western Solomon Islands, was first colonized by modern humans between 40,000 and 29,000 years ago.[12] These islands have been occupied ever since and have long and exciting histories of interchange and invasion.

Natives of Buka and Bougainville at the northern end of the Solomon Island chain in Melanesia and the Chopi people of Mozambique on the southeast coast of Africa have darker skin than their neighbors (figure 11). Although widely separated, these people share similar physical environments and lifestyles. In both regions, they experience extremely high UVR exposures directly from the usually cloudless skies near the equator and reflected from water and sand. Seawater reflects about 10 percent of the UVR that falls on it, and sand reflects between 10 percent and 30 percent, depending on its color.[13] In both regions, many

FIGURE 11. The native people of Bougainville, Papua New Guinea, have some of the darkest skin pigmentation in the world. Photo courtesy Michael Field.

people rely on fishing for a livelihood. Men spend long hours in the water, in boats, or on the beach. Because of the impracticalities of wearing clothing while fishing in such places, culture and technology do little to buffer them from extreme UVR exposure. The skin takes the full brunt of solar radiation. These people are probably near or at the maximum darkness that human skin can attain.

In stark contrast to the UVR-saturated coasts of Melanesia and Mozambique are the UVR-starved reaches of the far Northern Hemisphere. The northernmost parts of Scandinavia, Asia, and northern Canada and Alaska presented some of the greatest challenges to humans in prehistory. A high percentage (24 percent) of the world's land mass is concentrated in polar regions of the Northern Hemisphere that receive little UVR and even less vitamin-D-producing UVB during most of the year. These places were also extremely cold, covered in tundra, dotted with glaciers, and lacking in easily obtainable food. When we plot the distribution of sites of ancient human habitation on maps, we find that this region was uninhabited by modern people until about 12,000 years ago. Archaeologists have attributed this lack of settlement to cultural shortcomings that prevented people from adapting to boreal forests.[14] But it is also likely to have been due to inherent limitations on the production of vitamin D in their skin because of the lack of UVB for most of the year. The pattern of sunlight in the far north is highly seasonal, with complete or near-complete darkness around the clock in the depth of the winter. Even during the bright months of the year, the sunlight contains little UVB. These conditions were not compatible with year-round human habitation because people could not satisfy their vitamin D requirements from exposure of their skin to sunlight alone.[15] In order to live there throughout the year and sustain their health and capacity for successful reproduction, they had to supplement their bodies' own solar production of vitamin D with dietary sources of the vitamin, such as fish, marine mammals, or large land mammals.

Evidence of humans using barbed points and weirs to collect fish dates from 90,000 to 80,000 years ago, and it is likely that humans have been supplementing their diets with fish for considerably longer still, but the first archaeological evidence for true barbed harpoons capable of being used on marine mammals dates from only about 13,000 years ago. Away from the coasts, life in the north was possible only where people could find other good sources of vitamin D on the hoof. Hinterland populations across northernmost Eurasia survive by eating reindeer, which they follow and herd.[16] Reindeer meat, organs, and fat contain high levels of vitamin D, which the reindeer get from eating lots of low- and slow-growing lichen.

Fishing and hunting technologies allowed people of the extreme north to live healthily in places that otherwise would have been off limits.[17] For humans, life in the far north required a combination of biological and cultural adaptations: a depigmented skin and a culture and body of technology structured around the exploitation of vitamin-D-rich foods.

This conclusion raises the question of whether all dwellers of far northern latitudes are lightly pigmented. The Inuit of northern Canada and Alaska live at latitudes mostly within the Arctic Circle, where their exposure to sunlight is highly seasonal. On the basis of their location alone, we would predict that their skin would be maximally depigmented. It is not: it is moderately pigmented and capable of developing a heavy tan. These people's pigmentation can be understood by looking in detail at the nature of their sun exposure and their diet. Over the course of a year, Inuit receive low to moderate amounts of direct UVR, mostly in the form of UVA. The amounts of UVB they receive are negligible, even at the peak of UVB radiation near the summer solstice. The Inuit live in snow- and ice-covered environments and subsist on diets traditionally composed of marine mammals like seals. For much

FIGURE 12. Inuit people develop dark tans on the exposed parts of their bodies because of high levels of UVR (especially UVA) reflected from the surfaces of snow, ice, and open water. Photo courtesy Per Michelsen.

of the year their Arctic habitats are dim and dark, but during the summer the people are active for much of the time, bathed in solar radiation that is reflected by snow, ice, and water. Fresh white snow reflects 94 percent of the UVA and 88 percent of the UVB that falls on its surface, as skiers learn from painful experience with winter sunburns.[18] Inuit skin color is an excellent example of a compromise between biology and culture (figure 12). Their tanning abilities help to protect them from high doses of UVR reflected from the snow, and their naturally vitamin-D-rich diet allows them to remain healthy without maximally depigmented skin.

The Inuit evolved from peoples in northeastern Asia that were mostly depigmented, but still retained tanning potential. The Saami of northern Europe, by contrast, evolved from mostly depigmented European progenitors who had nearly completely lost the genetic ability to tan. Natural selection for enhanced tanning appears to have been tuned up in the Inuit case, leading to darkening of the skin relative to their ancestors, but no similar process appears to have occurred with the Saami.

Traditional cultures of the Inuit and the Saami center on harvesting and eating vitamin-D-rich foods. The dietary focus of both groups has compensated for the vitamin D they cannot produce in their skin. Both peoples remain healthy when they stick to their traditional diets but suffer badly from vitamin D deficiencies when they switch to Western diets that are lower in vitamin D.[19]

IN THE MIDDLE

People living close to the equator are as darkly pigmented as possible, and those living near the poles are generally lightly pigmented. The rest of humanity spans every conceivable shade of brown between these extremes. People living in intermediate latitudes tend to be moderately pigmented and to tan easily. Tanning involves not only the development of more melanin pigmentation in the skin in response to UVR but also the thickening of the top layer of the epidermis, the stratum corneum. Tanning takes place in all darkly pigmented native peoples living near the equator, but it tends to be more noticeable in light-colored people. It affords a small measure of increased protection against UVR rays by increasing the skin's protection factor, but the potential benefit of tanning is highly dependent on a person's starting skin color and the type of sun exposure.

When considering the evolution of skin pigmentation, we should bear in mind that people in antiquity experienced different patterns of sun exposure than we do today because until about 10,000 years ago, most people spent most of their time out of doors. Under these conditions, a person's exposure to UVR would vary seasonally, and the skin would darken or lighten accordingly. For people with lightly to moderately pigmented skin who experienced this natural annual cycle of sun exposure, it is likely that the sun protection afforded by a tan would have reduced their effective lifetime UVR dose by 50 percent.[20] This pattern is in stark contrast to the "vacation" model of sun exposure that is typical for many indoor workers today (box 8).

Because of the unequal distribution of land between the two hemispheres, relatively little habitable land in the Northern Hemisphere lies within the tropics, but a large proportion of land in the Southern Hemisphere does. This geographical bias has had consequences for the distribution of skin color between the two hemispheres. More of the native population of the Southern Hemisphere lives in tropical regions and is darkly pigmented, and more of the Northern Hemisphere's population, living north of the tropical region, is lightly pigmented—or, more correctly, depigmented. The bias in the distribution of the world's land mass and population is something very few people know about or appreciate, but it has had many ramifications for human biological and cultural evolution.[21]

BOX 8   **How Much Sun and UVR Exposure Do You Really Get?**

The amount of sunlight and UVR exposure a person receives depends on the person's location, age, and daily activities. On average, outdoor workers receive about 25–40 percent of the UVR that falls on their area, but typical indoor workers in the same place may receive only 10 percent, even when outdoor exposure on weekends is included. The same indoor workers are likely to receive twice their annual dose of UVR during a two-week vacation in a sunny place.[1] This is a far cry from the pattern of sun exposure that our ancestors experienced, and it poses many problems for the skin and overall health.

The time of day and the nature of outdoor activity also make a difference. When the sun is 30 degrees above the horizon, most of the body is exposed, but only about 8 percent of the UVB in summer sunlight reaches the body, because most of it is filtered out by the thickness of the atmosphere through which the sun's rays are passing. The UVB content of sunlight is greatest when the sun is directly overhead and UVR takes a shorter and more direct path through the atmosphere. A person standing up straight exposes only a small surface area of skin, but a person lying down (for instance, on the beach) at midday in the summer will receive the full impact of dangerous radiation.

1. For research on the average UVR doses received by people under various environmental, work, and vacation conditions, see, for example, Urbach 2001; Diffey 2002; Thieden, Agren, and Wulf 2001.

ANCIENT MIGRATIONS AND THE CULTURAL SHIELD

Modern humans have been adept at adapting to their environments through culture. Until about 15,000 years ago, we had only rudimentary means to protect ourselves physically from the environment. We could make fire, use natural shelters like caves, and cover ourselves with animal skins, but we had no sewn clothing or buildings. Our skin was our raincoat and our parasol.

The importance of "stuff" has increased over time. The complexity of our homes, transportation systems, means of food procurement, and the "essentials" we carry with us every day is staggering. Early *Homo sapiens* living 50,000 years ago or so had almost none of these things. At that time all humans were gatherers and hunters. We had great technological wherewithal and could make many useful things out of objects found or animals hunted, but we carried little with us as we moved from place to place.

FIGURE 13. The skin color of this Ecuadorean man is typical of indigenous South Americans— moderately pigmented with a heavy tan. His bold facial markings were probably made using uruku plant pigment. Photo courtesy of Edward S. Ross.

The Late Pleistocene, from about 50,000 to 10,000 years ago, was a difficult time in human history because much of the world experienced dramatic periods of cold and dry conditions. In the high latitudes in the Northern Hemisphere, tremendous oscillations of temperature resulted in abrupt changes in climate and rapid development of unfavorable conditions for many plants and animals.[22] Human groups living outside the tropics suffered privations because the herds of animals they had come to rely on were dying for lack of food. Many groups dwindled in size or became extinct, while others followed the seasonal movements of animal herds. Some of these people were the ancestors of the first Americans, who began making their way into North America via coastal and inland routes. They came from Siberia and were able to survive because they could construct new interfaces between themselves and their environment, such as clothing made from animal skins, simple shelters, and ways to preserve food. The environment required that they wear clothing most of the time.

This dispersal was unique because it happened in the relatively recent past and involved people who were mostly clad, not naked. These factors contributed to the establishment of a less pronounced gradient of skin pigmentation in the New World than in the Old World. Indigenous Americans vary greatly in appearance and skin color, but most

BOX 9   **Skin Pigmentation in the New World**

Before 1500 CE, the indigenous peoples of the New World represented the descendants of the "first Americans," who could trace their
genetic ancestry to northern Asians from Siberia. Since that time, genetic input from Europeans and Africans has added to the heterogeneity of most indigenous populations, so it is hard to know what
the skin colors of the New World peoples looked like in the days
before Columbus. Studies of skin pigmentation among indigenous
American groups carried out in the twentieth century show that more
darkly pigmented peoples are found in regions of high UVR, but the
gradient of pigmentation from the equator toward the poles is less intense than it is in Africa and Eurasia. Most of the native New World
peoples start out with various hues of moderately pigmented skin and
develop darker color through tanning after exposure to UVR. Thus
the dark skin tones seen among the indigenous peoples of the high-
altitude regions of Bolivia and Peru are mostly acquired tans. The
genetic basis of tanning abilities in New World populations is now
the subject of intense research, and preliminary results indicate that
positive selection for genes conferring enhanced tanning abilities occurred in these groups.[1] New World peoples in high-UVR environments did not evolve dark pigmentation as their baseline; rather, they
evolved abilities to tan prodigiously when exposed to the sun.

1. It has long been recognized that the indigenous peoples of the New World
are more lightly pigmented than those of the Old World, but directly comparable data on skin reflectances are rare. Considering the great range of UVR
regimes in which people live, especially in South America, the amount of
skin-color variation between populations is relatively low. Important work
on the evolution of skin pigmentation in the Americas has been done in the
laboratory of Mark Shriver at Penn State, in particular by Ellen Quillen. See
Relethford 2000; Quillen 2010.

are moderately pigmented with excellent tanning abilities (figure 13;
box 9).

People today can cover long distances quickly while transporting
volumes of stuff. This ability developed with the rise of agriculture, the
domestication of riding and traction animals (like horses and oxen),
the invention of wheeled vehicles, and the development of boats with
sails.[23] It meant that we could transport our lifestyle with us to distant
places, including favorite foods and tools and the technology needed to
protect ourselves from the environment. Thus we could use culture to
create a more or less stable and predictable microenvironment around
us as we moved from place to place. The development of this capacity

revolutionized human life and marked an extraordinary first in evolution: the ability to move thousands of miles and re-create "home" in less than a single generation.

One of the best-documented large-scale movements of people in prehistory occurred in Africa and involved farming peoples who spoke languages belonging to the Bantu language group. Ironworking had become central to the economies of several farming groups in western and northern Africa by about 900 BCE. Iron was used first for ceremonial and decorative objects, but it was quickly adopted as a superior material for making tools and weapons. By about 600 BCE, these ironworkers had brought their agricultural civilization to the coasts of western and eastern Africa, and beginning around 300 BCE they began their expansion into southern Africa. A second wave of migration from eastern into southern Africa took place between about 1000 and 1200 CE.

These movements led to a tremendous geographical expansion of Bantu-language-speaking peoples. The rapid spread of these iron-using farmers south of the equator led to the displacement and elimination of many long-term residents of central and southern Africa, groups of gatherers and hunters who relied on stone tools and spoke click languages. (Click languages make use of distinctive percussive consonant sounds and are distinct from those of the large Bantu-language group.) The equatorial farmers were mostly deeply pigmented, whereas the southerly hunter-gatherers were generally moderately pigmented. The Bantu-language speakers have retained the darker pigmentation of their equatorial homelands and thus represent a good example of a mismatch produced by recent migration between real and expected skin pigmentation based on UVR levels (map 4).

Another interesting example of a skin-color mismatch is found on the Arabian Peninsula. Despite the central position of this region on ancient trade routes, its population history is not well understood. Genetic evidence indicates that the peninsula was inhabited by successive waves of people, mostly from western Asia, who colonized the area quite late in human history. The western Asian peoples who settled the Arabian Peninsula in the last 5,000 or so years were moderately pigmented, with excellent tanning abilities.

Their adaptations to living under some of the most intense UVR regimes on Earth were mostly cultural. Loose wraps or robes, protective headgear, and tents are remarkably effective as sun shields and for keeping cool.[24] These people's mostly cultural adaptation to their

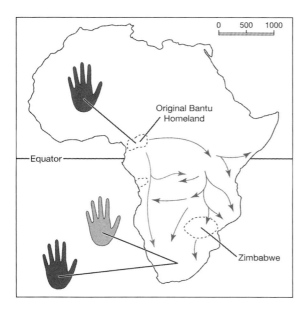

MAP 4. Expansion of Bantu-language-speaking peoples into eastern and southern Africa, with skin tones shown on hands. In southern Africa today, darkly pigmented Bantu-language speakers, who are mostly farmers, live in regions once inhabited by moderately pigmented hunter-gatherers. Courtesy Jennifer Kane.

high-UVR environment contrasts with that of groups living in the desert lands to the west of the Red Sea who have inhabited northeastern Africa for a much longer time. These people, including the Dinka and Nuer, have adapted to their surroundings over many thousands of years by evolving very dark skin pigmentation and a tall, lanky physique that provides a lot of skin surface area for keeping cool in the heat.

Long-distance migrations have become so common in recent centuries that we regard them as commonplace. Our abilities to transport "home" to virtually any place on Earth (or in Earth's orbit) have filled us with self-satisfaction and cultural hubris. Unbeknownst to most of us, these moves have had unforeseen and untoward consequences for our health: these are discussed at length in chapter 6.

5

Shades of Sex

Among the many differences alleged to exist between men and women, skin color is rarely mentioned. Although most people aren't even aware of the difference, artists through the ages have been sensitive to it and generally have depicted men as darker than women (figure 14). The sexes also differ in how skin changes color with age. Men and women are not born different colors: they begin to diverge during puberty, under the influence of sex hormones. Women also gain pigment on parts of their bodies during pregnancy. Although these differences are subtle, they are consistent, and the patterns of sexual difference have warranted investigation and incited controversy.

THE BARE FACTS

In the vast majority of indigenous peoples that have been studied, women have consistently lighter skin than men. This difference is based on measurement of the reflectance of adult skin in an area generally unexposed to the sun, on the inner part of the upper arm. In some groups, this difference is quite noticeable and in others much less so. In all cases, the sexual disparity in skin pigmentation within a group is as great as the color variation we find between groups according to the UVR intensity in their respective locations. Unfortunately, this phenomenon is hard to illustrate because people are generally not photographed showing their armpits.

FIGURE 14. The difference in skin hue between men and women has been formalized in art for centuries. A pair of statues showing painted limestone figures of the royal couple Iai-ib and Khuaut, from Giza in Egypt, date from the Fourth Dynasty (ca. 2575–2465 BCE). Photo by Bruce White. Image © The Metropolitan Museum of Art. Used with permission from the Ägyptisches Museum, Universität Leipzig.

It was thought for some time that men were darker than women only because they spent more time outdoors and tanned more, but this is not the case, because the unexposed skin of men is consistently darker than that of women.[1] When men and women of the same age are exposed to similar amounts of sunshine, women still appear slightly lighter (figure 15). The discrepancy between the sexes in skin color is due to something more than sun-exposure habits: it is indicative of an underlying and genetically based set of causes.

The skin of children becomes darker as they go through puberty because of the action of the sex hormones on the skin. This darkening

FIGURE 15. Differences between men and women in skin hue are evident when both sexes live under similar environmental conditions, as in the case of these individuals, who are probably a Polar Inuit brother and sister from the Cape York or Thule area of Greenland. The woman is said to have lost her nipple to her infant son, who bit it off when they faced starvation. The image, taken by an unknown photographer in the 1880s, was supplied by Per Michelsen.

is especially noticeable in the "sexual" skin of the nipples, the areolae around the nipples, and the labia majora in women and the scrotum in men. In some people the armpits also get slightly darker at puberty. The interaction of genetic, hormonal, and environmental factors in determining adult skin coloration is still not adequately understood, but we know that by the age of thirty or so, men are at their darkest baseline coloration, without considering any effects from tanning. At about the same age, many women begin to experience skin darkening on parts of their body.

Many pregnant women develop the "mask of pregnancy," also called melasma or chloasma, which results in a slight darkening of the cheeks, upper lip, chin, or forehead—any shade from light brown to gray or dark brown, depending on the person. Because melasma is mainly caused by increases in female hormones (progesterone and estrogen), it can also develop in women who take birth control pills or hormone replacement therapy.[2] The mask expresses itself and becomes darker because of sun exposure, and so sun protection is the best defense against melasma.

The melanin-producing cells in the face appear to be "primed" by elevated hormone levels to respond to even minor increases in UVR. In this way, melasma typifies the complex interaction between genetic, hormonal, and environmental factors that occurs in people as they age. Melasma is said to affect between 50 and 70 percent of pregnant women. It fades naturally over time, but the slowness of the reversion to normal pigmentation frustrates many women and causes them to seek quick fixes that are often more disfiguring than the melasma itself.

The areola is particularly sensitive to hormonal, especially estrogen, fluctuations. Slight darkening occurs just before menstruation and more obvious darkening during pregnancy.[3] The skin of the areola darkens with successive pregnancies and generally fades slowly back to the original color, but in some women this skin always remains slightly darker.

ARE MEN DARKER OR WOMEN LIGHTER?

Differences in skin color are always discussed in terms of females being lighter than males. When we look at other species, we see that it is usually the other way around. Darker male coloration is often seen as a departure from a species' baseline condition that is caused by increased testosterone production and other factors (box 10).

Only bare skin stands between us and the outside world. Many other animals have feathers or fur to cover their skin. No matter what colorful differences may have evolved in these animals because of male or female preferences, the basic protective functions of the feathers and fur remain intact. In humans, however, the loss of protective body hair meant the loss of considerable scope for manipulation of built-in coloration. In other words, the evolution of nakedness and the importance of pigmentation as an inherent part of our protective interface with the environment left us with little flexibility for the development of decorative enhancements involving skin color. This is a useful starting place for discussing the theories that have been put forward about whether skin-color differences in humans may result partly or completely from the action of sexual selection, that is, the process by which one sex chooses mates of the other sex.

The observation of systematic differences in skin pigmentation between men and women in most populations has led several scholars to advance the hypothesis that lighter skin in women is the result of sexual selection by men. (No researchers, by the way, have explored the opposite possibility, that women deliberately select darker men!) And

BOX 10   **A Melanodrama of Mallards, Manes, and Mandrills**

Testosterone is a powerful hormone that is produced by both sexes but produced in larger quantities by males. In many birds and mammals, testosterone production is associated with the development of colored skin, plumage, or fur that distinguishes males from females. In a wide range of species, the depth and intensity of coloration of these so-called melanin ornaments is related to testosterone levels and to mating success. In mallard ducks, for instance, the intensity of the iridescent green of the feathers on the head is related to testosterone levels and to male aggressiveness. Males with the showiest heads are not preferred by females, but they tend to win in mating contests against other, less flashy males. In mallards, head coloration is considered an "honest signal" of male competitiveness.[1]

A similar effect is observed in lions, with an added shade of biological meaning. Darker manes in male lions are associated with higher testosterone levels and act as a dominance signal to other lions. Researchers found that males are less likely to engage in competition for food or enter into combat with other males sporting darker manes, and the offspring of the darker-maned lions had preferential access to the carcasses of prey animals. In addition, female lions appear to prefer males with darker manes, so that dark manes act both to discourage lighter-maned males and attract females.[2]

1. The literature on sexual differences in animal coloration due to hormone levels is large and controversial. Debate is intense over which evolutionary mechanisms—female choice or intramale competition—drive the differences between the sexes and regulate the expression of sexually dimorphic ornaments. Melanin ornaments, including the colored plumes of jungle fowl and the green heads of mallards, are termed "honest signals" of male competitiveness because they change the behavior of receivers in ways that benefit the signaler.

2. See West and Packer 2002. The success of darker-maned lions comes at a price, because darker manes cause the animals to suffer greater heat gain, and possibly greater heat stress, than animals with lighter manes.

within this overarching view that males prefer pale, there are many variations.[4] In one hypothesis, female lightness is thought to have been first a byproduct of hormonal differences between the sexes: that is, females did not get as dark as males during puberty because of the different effects of sex hormones on pigmentation. The lighter appearance of females then supposedly became identified subconsciously by men as a measure of hormonal status and childbearing potential and became preferred over darker alternatives.

Another hypothesis views lighter female skin pigmentation as the product of sexual competition between women. In this scenario, women during the last ice age would have competed for the attentions of men, whose numbers were depleted as the result of long and risky trips to hunt large herd animals. Women living at higher latitudes were said to be lighter than their counterparts closer to the equator because their men had to go farther afield to hunt and were more likely to die, forcing the women to compete more strenuously for the remaining males. A related argument suggests that female lightness evolved as part of a complex of childlike traits—including a higher voice, smoother skin, and more childlike facial features—that reduced male aggressiveness and encouraged male provisioning of females. And there's more. One recent paper has suggested that light skin in general, and particularly in females, was the product of parental selection at birth for more lightly pigmented infants.[5]

All of these propositions are untenable. The premise that there was a marked division of labor or separation of roles according to sex in early human gathering and hunting societies is incorrect. Although women have always borne children and have had to deal with the physical and physiological burdens associated with pregnancy, childbirth, and child rearing, these have not stopped them from being active providers. Women in traditional gathering and hunting societies today are active hunters, and—even in high-latitude environments where long-distance hunts are common—they generally do not stay at home waiting to be provisioned.[6] Further, when data on patterns of skin-color difference between women and men were analyzed, no evidence of sexual selection operating at higher latitudes was found. In fact, there is scant empirical evidence that it operates at all. As for parental selection of light-colored infants, especially females, it bears remembering that all babies are born pale, regardless of what their adult color will be. It is highly unlikely that maternal choice of infant birth color would have had any significant effect on overall or female coloration.

Most of the people who have thought about sexual differences in skin color haven't given much consideration to the importance of vitamin D, and some continue to dismiss the role of vitamin D in maintaining health.[7] Our research led us to propose the idea that the slight difference in skin color between the sexes may have evolved originally because of the value of enhancing vitamin D production in women during their reproductive years. Skin pigmentation at any place on the Earth's surface is the product of an evolutionary balancing act between protection against UVR and promotion of vitamin D production. For women of reproductive age, harvesting and distributing sufficient resources to have successful pregnancies and to raise children to a stage of independence pose a major challenge. They must get not only enough energy but also sufficient key nutrients—including vitamin D and calcium—to support the growth of a fetus and nursing infant and to maintain their own health.

Breastfeeding newborns, whose skeletons are growing quickly, make particularly heavy demands on maternal calcium reserves (four times as much as during prenatal development).[8] These needs are met from the calcium reserves in their mothers' own skeletons. The relationship between vitamin D and calcium levels in mothers and neonates is complex and essentially involves maternal sacrifice for infant health: even a mother deficient in vitamin D will dissolve some of the calcium in her own bones to supply her breastfeeding baby. In order to survive her next pregnancy, however, she must restore those calcium deposits. Studies of women after breastfeeding have shown that their skeletons undergo rapid remineralization and that their skeletons regain their pre-breastfeeding bone-mineral content within three to six months.

At this point the trail of medical and experimental evidence goes cold. No studies have examined the relationship between vitamin D levels, calcium absorption, and the recovery of the female skeleton after breastfeeding. Lighter skin in women probably makes a big difference at this stage, enabling them to produce slightly more vitamin D in their skin than men in the same group and to facilitate the recovery of the skeleton after breastfeeding. This phenomenon warrants further research.

Women who are chronically deficient in vitamin D because of successive pregnancies and periods of breastfeeding experience a form of bone degeneration called osteomalacia. This has serious consequences for infants born of later pregnancies and for mothers themselves, who are at greatly elevated risk of breaking bones. It makes sense that protection of female health during the reproductive years would be a top evolutionary priority, so we are now investigating whether, in fact, slightly lighter skin in women might be a fairly simple way of ensuring that women get enough vitamin D after pregnancy and breastfeeding to enable their bodies to recover quickly. The need for maintaining strong female skeletons through multiple pregnancies may have been the ultimate evolutionary reason for the origin of the differences in skin color between men and women.

DRIVING THE WEDGE

The mechanism to facilitate vitamin D production in women's skin and sustain their skeletal health through multiple pregnancies is probably not the only reason for skin-color differences. Sexual selection almost certainly operates to widen the gap between the sexes in skin color, but it is not responsible for the baseline difference between the sexes, which was probably established by regular natural selection. A strong cultural preference for lighter-colored women is found in many societies; in a few, it has been enshrined for so long that it may have worked to systematically increase the discrepancy between women and men. In other words, natural differences in skin tone between men and women have probably been increased by a systematic and culturally stimulated preference of men for lighter women. The best-documented case of culturally enhanced sexual selection is in Japan, where female lightness has been prized, sought, and celebrated in art and theater for centuries. Japanese men prefer whiteness of skin in a woman, evocatively described as "skin like pounded rice": it is associated with femininity, chastity, purity, and motherhood.[9] The degree to which this preference has lightened the female population is not precisely known. Preferences by men for more lightly colored women are also known in India and probably have similarly ancient roots. It is no coincidence that women in these two countries are some of the largest consumers of skin-lightening agents in the world (see chapter 13): if you aren't born with it, you buy it. In some places, though, the preference for visibly lighter skin, especially in females, is a more recent phenomenon that stems from systematic prejudice against darker color in general.

6

Skin Color and Health

Skin color affects health. Whether it works for us or against us depends on where we are and what we're doing. Because skin is the frontline of our body's defenses, nothing about its structure and function has escaped the scrutiny of natural selection. And like skin's other characteristics, skin pigmentation evolved long before we had sophisticated cultural ways of protecting ourselves from the environment. We need only go back about 15,000 years to encounter a time before sewn clothes and constructed shelters when we relied on temporary natural shelters and our skin for protection against the environment.

Because solar radiation has determined the relationship between our skin color, our bodies, and the environment, some of its properties bear reviewing. The sun emits a wide range of radiation, from the most energetic and destructive X-rays and ionizing radiation through UVR, visible light, infrared radiation, and radio waves. Of greatest import to skin pigmentation is UVR. The most energetic and potentially harmful form of UVR is UVC (with wavelengths of 200–290 nanometers), which is absorbed totally by oxygen and ozone in the atmosphere (see figure 8 above).[1] Medium-wave UVR, or UVB (wavelengths of 290–315 nm), constitutes a small percentage of the total UVR hitting the Earth. Depending on the latitude, season, time of day, humidity, and amount of air pollution, only about 1–5 percent of the UVR received at the Earth's surface is UVB. The rest is UVA (wavelengths of 315–400 nm). UVB is fully absorbed by the surface of the skin—the stratum corneum and the top of the epidermis—but up to 50 percent of UVA can penetrate deeply into the dermis in people with light pigmentation and little protective melanin pigment.

People whose ancestors evolved in sunny places with lots of UVR have naturally darker skin and are capable of darkening more deeply through tanning than people from cloudier or more northerly places with less UVR. During their lifetimes, people in prehistory did not move around very much, and the skin of indigenous peoples all over the world adapted by evolution through natural selection to the annual cycles of UVR where they lived. Over time, however, we have become increasingly mobile, thanks to technology, animal domestication, environmental change, a penchant for risk taking, and a strong curiosity about unknown places. In the last few thousand years, this mobility has led people to travel to and settle in places distant from their ancestral homelands. The movements of the last four thousand years, and of the last four hundred years in particular, have been the fastest and farthest in human history and have come at an unexpected price with regard to health.

Some of the most significant translocations of peoples to different environments—such as the transatlantic slave trade and the settlement of convicts in Australia—were involuntary. Whether freely chosen or not, these migrations often had the same result: people moved into solar regimes markedly different from those under which their ancestors had evolved. These shifts resulted in mismatches between skin color and environment. These were most pronounced when the migrations involved dramatic changes of latitude, but other climatic factors also played a role. Some regions that straddle the equator, like western Africa, have high levels of UVR year-round, while regions outside of the tropics have much higher levels in the summer than in the winter. In some parts of Australia, minimum UVR levels in the winter are nearly as high as maximum levels in the British Isles in the summer! High UVR levels in the American Southwest and Australia are caused partly by the prevailing low humidity. People who moved from the British Isles to these locations brought their light skin to places with extremely high levels of UVR, inhabited by indigenous people with dark skin. Conversely, people who moved from western Africa or south Asia to the northeastern United States or the British Isles in the past few hundred years brought with them dark skin well-adapted to high UVR regimes, yet they relocated to places with low to moderate levels of UVR, where the indigenous people have light skin. These were not situations for which evolution prepared us. We are now facing the consequences to health of these global displacements.

Sapiens (wise) may be our species name, but our wisdom is dominated by conceit in matters concerning nature. Most people never consider the fact that they are living under physical conditions different from those of their ancestors. The world we inhabit is largely shaped by human ingenuity and technology, and this cultural cushion has afforded us the luxury of not thinking much about nature or our relationship with it. People—especially the affluent—have become accustomed to moving around and doing things at will and in comfort. In making decisions about where to live or where to go on vacation, it is rare for people to cite "inappropriate solar conditions," even though health statistics suggest that considering them often would be wise. Centuries or even decades ago, people could plead ignorance of the connections between UVR levels, skin pigmentation, and health, but not now.

DARK PIGMENTATION: TOO MUCH OF A GOOD THING?

The human lineage is African in origin, and our ancestors who dispersed from Africa in the past were darkly pigmented. They were leaving intensely sunny equatorial latitudes and making their way into regions with less intense and more seasonal sunshine and UVR. Eumelanin pigment is a natural sunscreen, so effective that it competes with vitamin D precursor molecules in the skin for UVB radiation. Melanin therefore captures most, but not all, of the radiation that could start the process of making pre–vitamin D_3 in the skin. The darker the skin, the longer it takes to make adequate amounts of pre–vitamin D_3. In the course of evolution, hominids evolved depigmented skin to deal with conditions of low UVB, but for people relocating to a new home in the twenty-first century, depigmentation is not an option.

The connection between vitamin D and bone health was first realized when vitamin D deficiency was linked to rickets, a childhood disease that causes bone deformities. The poster children of rickets were the bow-legged waifs of the industrial revolution in the crowded, polluted cities of Britain and northern Europe, where living conditions made it next to impossible for them to receive much UVB exposure even during the summer. Rarely, if ever, do we see or learn about the thousands of descendants of African slaves who suffered from rickets while growing up in the cities of the eastern United States in the years

FIGURE 16. Marion Post Wolcott (1910–1990), *Negro Children and Old Home on Badly Eroded Land near Wadesboro, North Carolina*, 1938. Children and grandchildren of former slaves growing up in the confines of farmhouses and urban apartments in the eastern United States had high rates of rickets due to little exposure to sunshine and diets deficient in vitamin D. Photo courtesy of Library of Congress, Prints & Photographs Division, FSA/OWI Collection [LC-DIG-fsa-8c30011].

after the Civil War. These early industrial cities had famously dark and narrow streets and intensely polluted air. Even when children had opportunities to play outside, the cloudy and polluted atmosphere filtered out most of the vitamin-D-producing solar radiation. Under these conditions, darkly pigmented children would have been at higher risk of vitamin D deficiency. Some children in rural areas suffered from rickets too, especially young girls, who stayed indoors most of the time (figure 16).

Rickets was so common "that doctors in Baltimore, Washington, Memphis and Richmond were convinced that all young Negroes had to suffer from the disease as a kind of rite of passage."[2] In 1894, every child of African ancestry seen by one physician in Washington, DC, suffered from rickets.[3] Physicians noted that rickets appeared to be most common in families who had moved from the rural South to the urban Northeast. Well into the early twentieth century, the causes of rickets in African American children were held to be the unsanitary living conditions of postbellum cities and the poor hygiene and poor diet associated with these conditions. Mothers were encouraged to feed children with rickets diets rich in milk fat. Some of them got better, but most didn't.

After assessing the high incidence of rickets in the Northeast, one observant and resourceful physician, Alfred F. Hess (1875–1933), decided to make a thorough study of the problem in the predominantly African American community of Columbus Hill in New York City. Hess and his colleagues observed many families and noted their living situations and diets and the presence or absence of rickets in the children. They also conducted experimental studies on animals to try to determine what factors induced rickets and what therapies might reverse the disease. After several years of research, Hess demonstrated that rickets was caused not by unsanitary conditions or poor diet but by a lack of sunlight, and that the disease could be reversed through "heliotherapy" (exposure to sunlight) and with dietary supplements of cod-liver oil, which is rich in vitamin D (figure 17). It was as a result of Hess's research that cod-liver oil became a standby in the kitchens and medicine cabinets of twentieth-century American and European cities and that rickets became, mostly, a thing of the past.

Hess's most penetrating insight was to recognize that it was dark skin pigmentation, not race, that predisposed children to rickets:

> The main distinction is . . . that colored infants require a greater degree of the effective light rays than do white infants. That they possess no racial predisposition to rickets is evidenced by their freedom from this disorder in their native homes in the West Indies. The darkness of the skin is, no doubt, a predisposing factor, also, in the susceptibility of the southern Italian, the Syrian and other southern races. These statements do not imply that susceptibility is merely a question of degree of pigmentation of the skin. But rather that light is an important etiologic factor in rickets and that, in turn, pigment is an important factor in determining the efficacy of light.[4]

Hess was thus the first person to establish a connection between skin pigmentation, living conditions, and disease. He reasoned that dark skin pigmentation exerted a filtering effect on sunlight that prevented

FIGURE 17. People with rickets or tuberculosis were often given heliotherapy in order to speed production of vitamin D and their return to health. Photo courtesy of the Beck Archives, Special Collections and Archives, Penrose Library, University of Denver.

bones from developing properly. Rickets thus was not a disease inherently related to African ancestry but one that resulted from an unexpected conspiracy of biological and environmental factors, mainly skin pigmentation and insufficient sunlight. Hess and his colleagues also observed that African American and other darkly pigmented children also experienced muscle weakness and problems with development of their teeth—other conditions that we now consider classic symptoms of vitamin D deficiency.

Problems caused by vitamin D deficiencies are not restricted to children. Those occurring in adults, in fact, are more sinister because they are often invisible and involve the gradual deterioration of bones and a reduction in the efficiency of the immune system. Among African American urban communities of the early twentieth century, such diseases contributed to high rates of death and disability, which in turn were interpreted by some as evidence of the physical and psychological dissipation resulting from emancipation from slavery (box 11). Today

BOX 11 **"The Negro Health Problem"**

In 1915, the *American Journal of Public Health* published a paper titled "The Negro Health Problem" by the physician L. C. Allen, which presented statistics about the incidence of tuberculosis among urban African Americans and European Americans and noted the high rates of this disease in former slaves and their offspring. The following passages from Allen's paper are worth quoting because they illustrate a degree of paternalism and racism almost unfathomable today and ascribe the high incidence of disease among the families of former slaves to a lack of discipline. Allen was among many in the scientific community in the years between the Civil War and the Second World War who enthusiastically subscribed to the ideas that races were real biological entities and that skin color was necessarily conjoined with a series of physical characteristics, psychological attributes, and behavioral predilections. His writing typifies the contorted logic of much "scientific" writing about minority populations:

> Communicable diseases find their favorite propagating grounds in the dirty negro sections of our cities, and in unsanitary negro homes in the country. From dirty homes, in these disease-infested sections, negro people come into intimate contact with white people every day that passes. We meet them in our homes, offices, stores, in street cars, and almost everywhere we go. The fact is not pleasant to contemplate, but is nevertheless true, that there are colored persons afflicted with gonorrhea, syphilis, and tuberculosis employed as servants in many of the best homes in the South today.
>
> It is undoubtedly true that the negro race has deteriorated physically and morally since slavery times. In some ways he is perhaps more intelligent, but freedom has not benefited his health, nor improved his morals. There is more sickness and inefficiency and crime among them now than before the war. All old physicians tell us that in slavery time consumption [tuberculosis] was practically unknown among the negro race. This fact, I believe, is thoroughly established.
>
> Because of the excessive death-rate among the negroes from tuberculosis the impression has gone forth, and has been widely accepted as true, that the negro race has a peculiar susceptibility to this disease. When all the facts are considered it seems to me that such a conclusion is not justified. Why was the negro free from tuberculosis during slavery time? The answer is obvious. Then he was disciplined; then he was made to bathe, and to keep clean; he was furnished a comfortable cabin in which to live, which he was required to keep scrupulously clean; he was given plain, but wholesome food, in generous quantities. . . .

The health of the children was carefully looked after. It was to the slave owner's interest to do these things. The more efficient the slave the more valuable he was. A sickly negro was of very little value—a dead negro none. There was no more healthy race of people to be found anywhere in the world than the slaves of the South before the Civil War.[1]

1. Allen 1915.

we find it hard to comprehend that such attitudes were common less than a century ago, but such was the strength of the mental shackles placed on the minds of even well-educated and seemingly well-intentioned Americans by the institution of slavery. For most people at that time, skin color was inextricably linked to a set of physical, psychological, and behavioral attributes that together constituted "race." And race, in their minds, was a proven scientific fact.

Many decades passed before it was recognized that vitamin D plays an important role in regulating the human immune system and that chronic vitamin D deficiencies render people more susceptible to specific cancers and many kinds of infectious diseases.[5] Vitamin D deficiency increases the risk of developing tuberculosis fivefold and also contributes to higher rates of breast, prostate, and colorectal cancer.[6] This partly explains why darkly pigmented people, especially African Americans, who live in low-UVB environments or who spend a lot of time indoors experience higher rates of some cancers than lightly pigmented people under the same conditions.

LIVING WITHIN FOUR WALLS

Throughout most of our history, we have lived outside. No buildings, in the broadest sense, existed until about 40,000 to 50,000 years ago, and the earliest examples of these were small and poorly ventilated enclosures where people did not spend a lot of time. Cities containing large groups of buildings and large numbers of people have existed only since about 3500 BCE; as recently as 200 years ago, only about 3 percent of people lived in cities. By 1950, that percentage had gone up to about 30 percent; today it is above 50 percent, and it is predicted to be 70 percent by 2050.[7] Not only are more people living in cities, but they are also spending much of their time inside buildings or in vehicles, both of which, in evolutionary terms, are new circumstances. This change of lifestyle has come at a price. City life has been maligned for many reasons, but only recently has the potential for vitamin D deficiency been among them. We have recognized that vitamin D plays a bigger role in human health than was previously thought, just at the time when most people no longer pursue an outdoor lifestyle that permits their bodies to make vitamin D as the result of routine sun exposure.

Modern life means time spent indoors. Some UVA but no UVB is transmitted through windows, so there is no chance of making vitamin D inside a building.[8] People who spend all of their time indoors because of illness or infirmity are at great risk of complete UVR deprivation and a resulting lack of vitamin D. An estimated 50 percent of elderly people worldwide in nursing homes and long-term care facilities suffer from vitamin D deficiency. This finding has prompted programs to mitigate the problem through sun exposure and vitamin supplementation.[9] Typical city office workers expose only their faces if they go outside for lunch. Because tall buildings block much of the open sky, they may only receive 5 to 25 percent of the UVR that would have fallen on a flat, open surface during the same period.[10]

Programs for prevention and treatment of vitamin D deficiencies are being mounted, and government recommendations for vitamin D consumption are being changed, but most of these processes move slowly. Dietary supplements can prevent and reverse vitamin D deficiency without any harmful side effects or the risk of skin damage or cancer from UVB exposure (box 12). This is important for modern people, who generally live to an advanced age and want to avoid skin damage and the risk of skin cancer from UVR exposure. Recently, a British government working group departed from the medical mainstream by suggesting that exposure of the skin to full sunlight for a short period in the middle of the day in summer (when UVB is at its peak) leads to minimal skin damage and maximizes vitamin D production in lightly pigmented people.[11] Controversy continues over which poses the greater risk: vitamin D deficiency or skin cancer.

Much of the cancer-causing damage of UVR can be prevented by wearing protective clothing or chemical sunscreens. The cost of this behavior is the reduction or elimination of the potential to make vitamin D in the skin, but these effects depend on the specific properties of clothing and the way chemical sunscreens are used. Wearing a hat with a full brim protects the face entirely from sun and prevents UVR damage to the skin of the face and the eyes unless glare is reflected

BOX 12 **How Much Vitamin D Is Enough?**

Few common natural foods are rich in vitamin D except for fish oils and oily fish like mackerel and sardines (see chapter 3), so it is difficult to prevent or treat a vitamin D deficiency through dietary means, except with vitamin D supplements. Not all types of vitamin D supplements are equally effective in raising the level of vitamin D circulating in the blood. Vitamin D_2, the form of the vitamin most commonly found in plants, is only about one-third as effective as vitamin D_3 in maintaining vitamin D levels in the blood.[1] Therefore it is important to take a supplement that contains vitamin D and to consult a health professional about the dose that is most appropriate.

The U.S. government recently revised its dietary reference intakes (DRIs) for vitamins The new recommendations on vitamin D_3, published in a November 2010 report by the Institute of Medicine, are that most adults should get 600 IU (international units) per day of vitamin D_3; adults over seventy should get 800 IU per day. Daily intakes should not exceed 4,000 IU.[2] The new DRIs have been criticized by many as being not high enough and not reflecting current understanding of the importance of vitamin D.

A typical vitamin D_3 supplement contains about 400 IU. Taken once per day, this will lead to unchanged or even slowly declining levels of vitamin D in the blood of an average adult. Doses of 1,000–10,000 IU per day resulted in incrementally higher blood levels of vitamin D, which leveled off after about ninety days. No adverse side effects were noted, leading the researchers to suggest that the DRI for vitamin D be reset to a minimum of 1,500–2,000 IU/day in the absence of UVB exposure. The widespread availability and low cost of vitamin D_3 supplements today argue in favor of long-term vitamin D supplementation as the safest method to achieve healthy levels of circulating vitamin D for most people.

The potential for making vitamin D in the skin is enormous. When exposed to UVB over the entire surface of the body for ten to fifteen minutes, a lightly pigmented person can produce and release into the bloodstream 10,000–20,000 IU of vitamin D. A darkly pigmented person of African or subcontinental Indian heritage will produce about one-third of this amount for the same exposure.

1. See Armas, Hollis, and Heaney 2004; Hollis 2005. The 2005 paper summons considerable evidence in favor of an increased dietary reference intake for vitamin D_3 and levels of supplementation averaging 2,000 IU per day.

2. See Institute of Medicine 2010.

BOX 13 **The Veiled Threat of Vitamin D Deficiency**

The wearing of full-coverage clothing for modesty or religious purposes is routine in some cultures, especially among women. It is also becoming more common among both sexes for sun protection in places like Australia and the southern United States. A recent summary of several studies has shown that these customs can lead to vitamin D deficiencies and resulting diseases.[1] A study of vitamin D status in Orthodox versus non-Orthodox Jewish women found significantly lower levels of vitamin D in Orthodox women who routinely wore modest clothing. Lower levels of vitamin D also occurred in Australians of European origin living in Queensland who consistently wore long-sleeved shirts and long trousers to protect their skin from sun damage.

Muslim women who routinely wear the veil are more likely to suffer from weakening of the bones (osteoporosis and osteomalacia), and children who routinely wear concealing clothing are more likely to develop rickets. These findings indicate that old and new cultural practices of concealment from the sun can have unexpected health consequences, and that these customs must be compensated for by new habits like taking vitamin D supplements.

1. Springbett, Buglass, and Young 2010.

from below. It also entirely prevents vitamin D formation in the skin of the face. Most clothing reduces the amount of UVB reaching the skin, but white cotton blocks only about 48 percent, compared to black wool, which blocks nearly 99 percent.[12] One of the presumably unintended consequences of the routine wearing of black wool garments for modesty or religious purposes, then, is complete elimination of the possibility of producing vitamin D precursor in the skin. This behavior strongly predisposes wearers to chronic vitamin D deficiencies and osteoporosis (box 13).

Chemical sunscreens can also reduce or completely prevent vitamin D production in the skin. The specific type of sunscreen and the SPF (sun protection factor) of the product make a difference, but the greatest predictor of reduction of vitamin D–making ability in the skin is how much sunscreen is applied. Most people fail to comply with the manufacturers' directions to apply sunscreen liberally before sun exposure and then reapply it after sweating or swimming.[13] As a result, sunscreen use usually does not completely inhibit vitamin D production.

PLATE 1. The thirty-six Von Luschan color tiles for assessing the color of unexposed skin. The tiles provided the standards for recording skin color until the introduction of reflectometry in the mid-twentieth century. © 2011 President and Fellows of Harvard, Peabody Museum No. 2005.1.168.

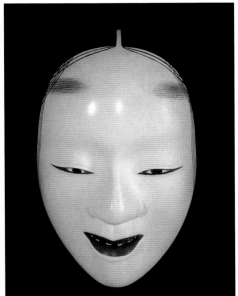

PLATE 2. (OPPOSITE TOP)
Alexa Wright, *Skin: Maxine*. Vitiligo is caused by cessation of melanin production in patches of skin. People affected by vitiligo sometimes suffer psychological discomfort because of their appearance, and support networks help affected people to cope. Reproduced courtesy of the artist.

PLATE 3. (OPPOSITE BOTTOM)
This Khoe-San woman and her baby from South Africa have moderately pigmented skin capable of tanning. Their skin is typical of people who have evolved in the middle latitudes under seasonally strong UVR. Photo courtesy of Edward S. Ross.

PLATE 4. (ABOVE) The contrast in skin hue between men and women is emphasized in these highly stylized masks used in Japanese Noh theater. Photos courtesy of T. Inoue, Inoue Corporation, www.nohmask21.com.

PLATE 5. (ABOVE) Muslim women in Afghanistan wearing traditional burqas cannot produce vitamin D in their skin even under the sunniest conditions. Black wool prevents nearly 99 percent of UVB from reaching the skin. Photo courtesy of Edward S. Ross.

PLATE 6. (RIGHT) Wall of the tomb of Sebekhotep in Thebes (Eighteenth Dynasty, ca. 1400 BCE). Several men, probably Nubians, were depicted with black skin by Egyptian artists. Photo © The Trustees of the British Museum. All rights reserved.

PLATE 7. Jan Mostaert, *Portrait of an African Man* (ca. 1520–30). Many of the Africans who arrived in Europe in late medieval and early Renaissance times became scholars and advisers. Photo courtesy of the Rijksmuseum Amsterdam.

PLATE 8. Skin tones vary according to levels of UVR and are darker near the equator and lighter toward the poles. The gradient is more obvious in the Old World and less so in the New World, where people have lived for only about 10,000 to 15,000 years. Illustration © Mauricio Antón 2011.

PLATE 9. Mattel's Malibu Barbie was marketed to girls in the early 1970s, before the dangers of sun-tanning were fully appreciated. The glamor, sex appeal, and studied leisure associated with a tan and with tanned celebrities contribute to the continued popularity of the tanned look today.

THE PERILS OF PALENESS

Consider now the plight of a lightly pigmented person in a very sunny place. The lightest-skinned populations in the world evolved in far northwestern Europe, specifically northern Scotland and northern Scandinavia. These people evolved maximally depigmented skin so that they could harvest the measly amount of UVB radiation available in the summer months. Because there is not sufficient UVB in the sunlight most of the year to start the process of making vitamin D in the skin at far northern latitudes, evolution favored people carrying mutant pigmentation genes (including variants of *MC1R*) that produced less and less protective melanin pigmentation. Thus depigmentation was positively selected for under extreme low-UVB conditions.

Until about five hundred years ago, people born under these conditions lived outdoor lives as farmers, herders, or fisher folk and experienced seasonal fluctuations in UVR intensity. These patterns had two important implications for their health. The first was that they did not receive enough UVB from sunshine alone to supply their bodies' needs for vitamin D, and so they relied on a diet that supplied vitamin D, including fresh and preserved oily fish and reindeer. The second was that they experienced few serious sunburns because their skin adapted to gradually increasing UVR during the spring months by thickening the most exposed areas, on the face, neck, and hands.[14] When people moved from these conditions to places with consistently higher levels of UVR, as in the case of English colonists moving to India, Africa, or Australia, their concerns were focused on serious damage from the sun, not insufficient vitamin D (figure 18; box 14).

In the past twenty years, most people have become aware of the risks of skin cancer and premature aging of the skin caused by UVR, and they take preventive action at least some of the time. People of European or northern Asian descent living in sunny places like Australia, Florida, and the American Southwest tend to adhere more closely to sun-protection guidelines because of public health campaigns that emphasize the risks of UVR exposure. People who live in regions with strongly seasonal patterns of sunshine are less likely to be "sun smart." Many people reading this book may recognize this behavior. After a long winter with little sunshine, people tend to splurge on sun exposure in the spring and summer because it feels good and because others tell them that they look good with a tan. On summer weekends, the normally sun-deprived spend longer periods outdoors than they would otherwise,

FIGURE 18. The tropical explorer's suit and similar sun-protective outfits were considered essential to the preservation of the health of light-skinned European men working under the intense sun of African and Asian colonies in the late nineteenth century. This particularly well-tailored example was worn by Sir Henry Morton Stanley. Photo courtesy of the Smithsonian Institution Libraries, Washington, DC.

often without adequate sun protection. The "vacation effect"—the tendency for people to ignore sun-exposure guidelines while on vacation in the summer or in a sunny place—has a big effect on the amount of UVR a person receives and the likelihood of developing a sun-related disease.

The vacation effect is a new problem in human history, and it is not trivial. When it takes hold, the city clothes come off, the skimpy vacation attire goes on, and the cookout begins. Sunscreen is rarely

BOX 14 **Keeping Covered in the Colonies**

Northern Europeans who emigrated to Africa, Asia, and Australia from the 1600s onward faced solar conditions remarkably different from those they knew at home. The intense sun was blamed for numerous ills and difficulties, among them a condition that came to be called tropical neurasthenia. This disorder, said to be caused by overstimulation of the nerves by the "actinic" rays of the sun, was characterized by a bewildering array of symptoms, including fatigue, irritability, loss of concentration, loss of memory, hypochondria, loss of appetite, diarrhea and digestive disorders, insomnia, headaches, depression, palpitations, ulcers, alcoholism, anemia, sexual profligacy, sexual debility, premature and prolonged menstruation, insanity, and suicide.[1] One well-regarded authority wrote in 1898: "It is the almost universal opinion that the European cannot colonize the tropics, but must inevitably fall, sooner or later, a victim to the influence of their deadly climate. I will endeavour to prove that this statement is wrong, and that there is no reason why the European should not conquer the tropical world."[2] Protection from the sun was thus considered important both to individual survival and to the success of colonial enterprises.

The major deficiency in the European constitution for conquering the tropics was recognized as pigment: "The skin of the white man is unprovided with the protective pigment which adapts the coloured man to his environment."[3] The development of sun-protective fabrics and outfits became a challenge to which several enterprising companies and entrepreneurs rose. In the late 1800s and early 1900s, field experiments were conducted to test the properties of different colors and fabrics under conditions of extreme sun, heat, and humidity. The fabric called Solaro, developed by the physician L. Westenra Sambon, became popular because it "imitated nature" in being sun-protective yet was "pleasing to the eye, and in texture comfortable to the body." Solaro, a fine and densely woven wool, is still manufactured today by Smith & Co. Ltd. in London and used for some "tropical-weight" tailored suits.

1. This exhaustive list of symptoms is quoted directly from Kennedy 1990, 123.
2. Sambon 1898, 589.
3. Johnson 2009, 531.

applied thickly or often enough to afford sun protection, and the result is often a sunburn. Intense doses of UVR delivered to inadequately protected or totally unprotected skin lead to repeated sunburns and soreness and eventually to visibly aged skin. This problem is compounded because people typically expose much larger areas of skin while lying on a lounge chair or a beach towel than on a typical day at home. The cancer-causing damage to the DNA of the skin is invisible immediately after exposure, and for this reason many people intent on getting a tan do not change their behavior.[15]

Skin cancers account for one-third of all cancers diagnosed worldwide, and rates continue to rise dramatically. Ultraviolet radiation causes 80 to 90 percent of these cancers, but most people don't think that skin cancer is serious and thus do not take adequate precautions. This attitude has perplexed public health experts, who have conducted vigorous risk-awareness campaigns in print, broadcast, and digital media for forty years. People seem reluctant to believe that skin cancer will adversely affect their lives, much less result in death.

Melanoma accounts for 75 percent of the deaths from skin cancer in the United States, some 8,650 per year. According to the American Cancer Society, 68,720 new melanomas were diagnosed in the United States in 2009. This is a small percentage of the more than one million new cases of all skin cancers reported annually in the United States each year, but the lifetime risk that an American will develop melanoma is now 1 in 58, compared to about 1 in 500 in 1950.[16] A melanoma diagnosis means a lifetime of follow-up examinations and major modifications of lifestyle, including vigilant sun avoidance and protection against UVR.

A worrying trend is that melanoma is now becoming more common in people with moderately or darkly pigmented skin who were considered at lower risk for the disease. Rates of new cases of melanoma are rising in Florida among Hispanics and "non-Hispanic blacks," and some of this increase appears to be due to the very high UVR on the Gulf Coast. Many moderately or darkly pigmented people don't consider themselves to be at risk for skin cancer and therefore don't protect themselves from UVR.[17] Because the surrounding skin is darker, many melanomas are not detected before the tumor invades underlying tissues.[18] For lightly pigmented people, repeated sunburns are a risk factor for developing melanoma, and according to the most recent statistics, 46 percent of men and 36 percent of non-Hispanic light-skinned women in the United States are sunburned at least once each year.

Incautious sun exposure also significantly increases the risks of contracting nonmelanoma skin cancers, such as basal- and squamous-cell carcinomas. These cancers are not considered dangerous because they can usually be removed in doctors' offices and require no follow-up care, but they are not always innocent afflictions. Individuals with a history of nonmelanoma skin cancers are at a higher risk of developing other cancers (including melanoma) than people with no such history.

The problem with getting people, especially lightly pigmented people, to take seriously the dangers of UVR relates to perceptions of risk. Young adults engage in the riskiest UVR behaviors: young men are more likely to get sunburned while outdoors, and young women are more likely to frequent tanning salons. Testimonials from youthful skin-cancer survivors are common features of women's magazines, lifestyle blogs, and documentaries, but their deterrent effect on UVR exposure is unproven. For young adults, appeals to vanity may strike a more resonant chord than portents of death. Accordingly, public health authorities are now emphasizing the risks of premature skin aging as an unavoidable consequence of insufficient protection from UVR. Skin cancer may not kill you, but the sun will spoil your looks. In a world that prizes youth and beauty, the prospect of saggy, wrinkled, and mottled skin carried into a long old age may be a more effective deterrent than death.

RECREATIONAL TANNING

Despite the wealth of information disseminated by public health officials on the dangers of UVR exposure, the attractions of a deep suntan die hard (see chapter 14). Ironically, for most of our history, getting a tan was a byproduct of outdoor activity and not a goal in itself; only within the past few decades has tanning been considered desirable. In the early days of human history, people didn't undertake rapid, long-distance migrations, didn't experience the vacation effect, and didn't indulge in full-body recreational tanning. Instead, they gradually gained and lost tans by being outside and experiencing the slow increases and decreases in solar UVR that are part of the seasonal cycle. Tans gained this way were sufficient to protect people from the worst damage (the sunburns and intensified competition for available folate) caused by the maximum UVR they could experience in their location (see chapter 2). Long before the days of farmers, many people had farmers' tans.

The ability to tan varies greatly among people. Generally, those who start out with the darkest skin and the most melanin have the greatest ability to tan. People with the lightest skin and those with albinism have no ability to tan.[19] The biggest differences resulting from sun exposure are seen in people who start out with moderately pigmented skin: the change is dramatically visible where "tan lines" delineate areas of exposed skin, in which melanin production has occurred, and unexposed skin.

The enduring popularity of recreational tanning in the United States, Latin America, and much of northern Europe continues to frustrate dermatologists and public health experts and has them looking to countries like Australia, where campaigns promoting vigorous protection against UVR have been more successful. Australia has the highest skin-cancer incidence and mortality rates in the world. To slow the skin cancer epidemic, the Slip! Slop! Slap! campaign was introduced in 1980 to encourage Australians to protect themselves from the sun by slipping on a shirt, slopping on sunscreen, and slapping on a hat. Despite its modest budget, the campaign caught on famously because it was promoted on TV by a silly-looking bird named Sid the Seagull, who sang a catchy jingle that everyone could remember.[20]

Australia's sun-awareness campaign wisely stressed multiple methods of sun protection: in addition to the "Slip! Slop! Slap!" mantra, it advocated seeking shade, avoiding sun exposure, and wearing sunglasses. The campaign has been supported by laws that require employers to protect workers from UVR in sunlight and reduce the hazards associated with working in a hot and sunny environment. Australian schools are legally required to ensure that children are adequately protected from harmful UVR. At most Australian schools, children wear hats, clothing, and sunscreen during outdoor activities. Full-brimmed hats are commonly worn by women and men while out of doors.

Australia's success in convincing its populace to use many forms of sun protection contrasts with the situation in United States, where people have come to rely more heavily on chemical sunscreens. Because sunscreens are rarely applied properly or sufficiently often, their practical effectiveness is limited. Advertised improvements in chemical sunscreen technology have emboldened many people to forsake other means of protection and undertake longer bouts of sunning, sometimes leading to higher doses of UVR than if they had spent a shorter time in the sun without any protection at all.[21] This has led to a high incidence of sunburns and is thought to be contributing to the continued increase in skin cancers in the American population, particularly among young women.

BEING A HEALTHY HOMINID IN A CONFUSING WORLD

Modern lifestyles and mobility have created new health problems, and the mismatch between skin pigmentation and our living environments is one of them. Vitamin D deficiencies and UVR overexposure are now concerns for everyone, not just for people with extremely dark or light skin or risky lifestyles. Two main health goals are clear: achieving and maintaining healthy vitamin D levels, and engaging in behaviors that prevent premature skin aging and skin cancer from UVR. These goals are easily attainable with the help of a few simple guidelines. First, people need to know what their ancestry is, how their skin color compares to that of others, and what the UVR levels are where they live (in many localities, a UV index is available). Second, they need to examine their lifestyle and diet. This means determining how much UVR exposure a person is receiving daily and from season to season, and how much vitamin D is being obtained from the skin and diet. Doctors and other health professionals can provide guidance on these matters. Third, people must make changes as needed. Individual "sun prescriptions" are just that; there is no one-size-fits-all solution.

PART TWO

Society

7

The Discriminating Primate

Humans wouldn't be so interested in skin color if it weren't for the fact that we are highly visual animals. We form our impressions of others and the world around us primarily through what we see. We size up people and places, and decide what to do from one moment to the next, by comparing new visual perceptions to visually based memories. Our reliance on vision permeates every aspect of our lives as social beings. We assess the age, mood, and intention of others mostly from what we see, not what we hear or smell. We observe people around us keenly, and when we don't know what to do, we often decide by watching the actions of someone we know well or respect. "Monkey see, monkey do" expresses this tendency succinctly. Although the mechanisms of imitation are intensely debated among psychologists and neuroscientists, there is no debate about imitation being the most important process of social learning in humans.[1]

As infants, we observe and imitate our mothers and caregivers, and as children we imitate older siblings, relatives, and teachers. We attend closely to the social nuances conveyed by facial expressions, postures, and gestures. Heightened visual awareness and adept imitation help to ensure that that we fit into our social group and learn what we need in order to survive, physically and socially. These activities are also conducive to our being liked and having positive behaviors directed toward us.

We not only look at how authorities are acting, but we also listen to them carefully and pick up on the labels and social categories that they use. As small children, we learn a lot from subtle visual and verbal cues about who is in our group and who is not, who is nice and who is not, and so forth. Young children prefer individuals or groups that the adults around them have emphasized in their behavior or language, even if the adults have never said anything explicitly good or bad about them.[2] The transmission of bias starts slowly and subtly. We learn to put people into categories based on similarities in the way they look or act or the ways in which our authority figures act around them. Our minds appear to be organized in a way that makes it easy to classify people into distinct groups and then to favor our own group, the "in-group." Partiality toward members of a person's own group occurs even when people are randomly assigned to groups—for example, after a coin toss.[3]

The tendency to exhibit bias in favor of one's own group, however arbitrary, is called the "minimal group paradigm" and is universal.[4] It was probably favored in our evolution because it promoted our ability to detect social alliances and cooperate within small and vulnerable social groups. It is reinforced by alterations of neural responses in the brain that develop as we detect fear or anxiety among those around us and begin to feel it ourselves. These reactions are strongest in the amygdala, which is the part of the brain involved in learned emotional responses and the center of fear and anxiety. Its activation in response to members of "out-groups" is an important aspect of our evolutionary legacy.

Although people can identify others according to categories, they may not always activate the stereotypes associated with these categories. Brain reactions to out-groups aren't all or nothing and by themselves don't create stereotypes. But repeated reinforcement of positive or negative associations, especially by verbal labels, does. Stereotypes and biases formed in this way can be durable. Responses to out-groups, however, are not fixed: they are constantly subject to change because the underlying neural responses can be modulated by situations and by motivations. Conscious effort can compensate for the automatic activation of a negative response toward a member of an out-group. We are hard-wired to be receptive to visual differences between people and responsive to the reactions of authority figures. The tendency to develop stereotypes is universal, but our reactions to them are culturally determined and contingent. Just how tenacious or moldable beliefs about others are over the lifespan is a major focus of research.[5]

This abstract discussion about the importance of vision and visual assessments and the development of biases relates directly to social discrimination based on skin color or other physical attributes. A dramatic experiment to examine this issue was conducted in 1968 by Jane Elliott, a teacher at the Community Elementary School of Riceville, Iowa. Deeply disturbed by the assassination of Martin Luther King Jr., Elliott wanted to teach her class of eight-year-olds about discrimination in a way they could understand. She believed that social discrimination had to be felt personally to be understood, and that the only way to achieve this in her classroom was to divide the class into two groups. With the consent of the class, Elliott divided the children according to eye color: blue eyes and brown eyes. The two groups were accorded different attributes, rights, and privileges.

Within hours, the children in the eye-color group labeled "superior" were acting dominant and outperforming the other group, who had been labeled "inferior." It was a lesson that neither Elliott nor her class would ever forget (box 15). By the time the two-day experiment was completed, the children had thoroughly grasped the mechanics and meaning of discrimination and the arbitrary nature of bias based on differences in appearance. They also understood the purport of Elliott's lesson. "Martin Luther King," wrote one child, "wanted Negroes to have what they wanted just as white people do. And he was killed for doing this. He was killed by discrimination." With her classroom exercise, Elliott showed that in-groups and out-groups, and behavioral stereotypes, could be established quickly and on the basis of a barely noticeable physical trait like eye color. This has happened often in human history, most famously and pervasively on the basis of skin color, but also on the basis of other traits.[6]

Humans are suggestible. If a physical trait is associated with something bad, a negative stereotype can develop quickly. An excellent example is the negative personality traits associated with red hair. This bias dates from biblical times and is derived from the suspicion that Satan and Judas Iscariot—the apostle who betrayed Jesus—were redheaded. The association of treachery and perfidy with redheads pervaded much of European literature from Chaucer onward and encouraged their persecution during the Spanish Inquisition.[7]

What this example and Elliott's class experiment demonstrate is that specific traits can quickly become salient in defining group distinctions, which can then be readily converted into stereotypes. Salient traits are often physical characteristics like skin color, eye color, and hair color, but they also can be entirely socially constructed characteristics, such

BOX 15 **Jane Elliott's Daring Experiment**

On the first day of her experiment in social discrimination, Elliott told her class, "The blue-eyed people will be on the bottom, and the brown-eyed people on the top. What I mean is that brown-eyed people are better than blue-eyed people. They are cleaner than blue-eyed people. They are more civilized than blue-eyed people. And they are smarter than blue-eyed people. It's true. It really is." She proceeded to tell the brown-eyed children that they could use the drinking fountain as usual, have extra time at recess, and have second helpings at lunch. The blue-eyed children were denied these privileges and told that they could play with the brown-eyed children only if they were invited. When she asked the class who should sit in the front, the brown-eyed children responded enthusiastically, "The brown eyes!"

The events of that day surprised and shocked Elliott because within a few hours, the brown-eyed children in the class were acting as if they were indeed superior. They treated the blue-eyed children with disdain and actually performed better in class than the blue-eyed children. The blue-eyed children became increasingly disconsolate and anxious, especially when their brown-eyed friends of the day before turned against them. The next day, the tables were turned, and the blue-eyed children were accorded the privileges that had been withheld from them the day before. Elliott expected that the blue-eyed children would be sensitive to the feelings of the brown, but they were not. They gloated and enjoyed their superiority. The only thing they modified was the degree of their viciousness to their brown-eyed classmates. Toward the end of the second day, Elliott ended the experiment and asked the class, "Does the color of your eyes have anything to do with the kind of person you are?" The class answered resoundingly, "No!" On the third day, Elliott asked the class to write a composition defining discrimination and describing how they had felt on the previous two days. "Discrimination," wrote one student, "is being judged by the color of your skin or the color of your eyes or the church you go to." Another wrote, "On Monday I was happy. I felt big and smart. Then we got five extra minutes of recess. We got to do everything first. And we got to take out the playground equipment. I do not like discrimination. It makes me sad. I would not like to be angry all my life."[1]

Elliott led classes through "discrimination days" in subsequent years and in 1969 was filmed with her class by ABC News for a documentary that was watched by millions of people in the United States.

1. Peters 1987, 32, 33.

as religious affiliation. The concept of human "races" developed when skin color became attached to sets of other physical, behavioral, and cultural traits, which were then considered an immutable package; this package subsequently became associated with the idea of inherent social rank. It was propagated widely by respected authorities and transmitted faithfully as a stereotype. "To be sure a stereotype may be so consistently and authoritatively transmitted in each generation from parent to child," wrote the American political commentator Walter Lippmann, "that it seems almost like a biological fact."[8] Eventually, people could no longer see the individual elements of the constructed racial package—skin color, body form, behaviors, or moral qualities— except in the context of the package. Most people accept the realities of racial categories as fundamental truths; but the categories exist only because people and societies believe them to be true. Racial categories have become institutional facts because their very existence requires special human institutions such as language. Specific bodily traits do not define a group so much as stand as imperfect markers for it and as signals that trigger a stereotyped response.[9] In this way, skin color becomes a symbol for the institutional structure of race.[10]

ATTRIBUTING SIGNIFICANCE TO SKIN COLOR

Children begin to attribute significance to skin color at about three years of age. But they don't develop ideas of race based on what they see. They recognize skin color, but this perception alone does not become attached to a group label until they have perceived from verbal information just how that group is different.[11] Verbal information is potent in installing bias against an out-group member, even in the absence of face-to-face experience, especially when the information is imparted by someone who is respected, like a parent, teacher, or elder. Cultural knowledge is acquired from others mostly from their talk, especially when it involves abstract ideas about group identity and value.

By about age six, children appear to have developed detectable, implicit attitudes about social groups. The development of what is called "categorical thinking" in connection with race in children is important because the mental construct of races guides the processing of relevant information about people they will encounter in the future and profoundly influences the nature of their recollections and expectations. When adults see people of other races in photos or historical depictions, they call upon their mental reference library of racial categories to judge the qualities of the people depicted, even if they have no personal knowledge of such individuals. Often, if they know little about an out-group, they find it harder to differentiate individuals within the group. This problem is referred to as the "cross-race recognition defect," sometimes paraphrased as "They all look alike."[12] Similarly, when people create depictions—cartoons, paintings, or sculptures—of individuals of other races, they bring to those depictions connotations of the nature and personality of those individuals based on social knowledge of the racial characteristics of the group.[13] This is one way that historical images packed with prejudices and stereotypes can be passed down from one generation to the next. Such images represent not what others were really like but portrayals of what was in the mind of the images' creators (figure 19).

Unflattering or negative depictions or descriptions of out-groups can become potent determinants of individual fate. Consider the vast and varied set of in-group and out-group images, memories, and stories that a juror brings into the courtroom or the ways in which a witness's description of a crime or crime suspect can influence jurors' perceptions. In such cases, negative depictions or negative adjectives—sometimes irrelevant to the matter under discussion—can influence the emotional reactions and judgment of people making important decisions about an individual's fate. Race labels that are associated with negative depictions and narratives can have powerful effects on members of out-groups and can also have remarkable effects on in-groups by planting in people's minds the idea that their own group is superior, inferior, smarter, stupider, stronger, or weaker than another. The race label itself thus becomes determinative of personality and individual experience.[14] Over the past decade, many studies have been conducted to examine how people's brains react to photos of the faces of people with different skin colors. These studies are based on the fact that our brains are adept at interpreting faces. The cortical face-processing network comprises several areas in the brain and provides us with abilities to instantaneously draw inferences about a person's age, health, relatedness, mood, intention, and attractiveness.[15] We react more strongly to famous faces and to those with whom we have a strong emotional association, but we react to all faces nonetheless. So primed are we to interpret information from faces that the mere suggestion of a face in a sketch activates the face-processing network. Further, a neutral face can acquire a negative social value after one viewing if it is associated with negative gossip.

FIGURE 19. Images can be powerful in reinforcing group stereotypes, especially when they are issued under the imprimatur of a government. The Mexican government's 2005 issue of stamps showing the cartoon character Memin Pinguin sparked outrage because it signified that the government supported the unfavorable portrayal of people of African ancestry. Courtesy Tess Wilson.

Reactions to faces of out-group members have been studied mostly in the United States, where the two categories tested were "black" and "white."[16] Activation of the amygdala occurs in most people when they look at someone whose skin color is different from their own, but there is great variation between individuals' reactions. The strongest responses occurred in people who scored highest on standard tests of racial prejudice, including the implicit association test (box 16). The longest-lasting fear responses—derived from fear conditioning of the amygdala—were elicited in response to out-group faces. When faces were paired with an unpleasant stimulus, "white" individuals exhibited more persistent conditioned fears in response to pictures of "black" faces than to pictures of "white" faces. The opposite was true for "black" participants. Thus, individuals from a group other than a person's own were more readily associated with an unpleasant stimulus than were those of a person's own group.

These findings do not imply that we are neurologically predestined to be biased against particular individuals. Our attitudes are constantly subject to change through experience and, importantly, conscious choice. Biases can be modified and eradicated on the basis of experience and motivation. Stereotypes are handy because they allow people to get by without thinking carefully about others and paying attention, as in a "knee-jerk reaction" to a person or situation. Stereotypes are subject to change, however, when people are motivated to think about someone, even temporarily, as a member of their own group.[17] Even subtle exposure to a positive, counterstereotypic image can reduce implicit prejudice due to negative stereotyping, as demonstrated in

BOX 16 **The Implicit Association Test for Race**

Implicit biases or unconscious attitudes constitute the "cognitions, feelings, and evaluations that are not necessarily available to conscious awareness, conscious control, conscious intention, or self-reflection."[1] In the past decade, many implicit association tests (IATs) have been developed to measure preference for racial, ethnic, or other groups. They are based on the differential association of two target concepts (for instance, *flower* and *insect*) with an attribute (*pleasant* and *unpleasant*). The basis of IATs is that more closely associated pairings, like *flower* and *pleasant,* will elicit faster responses than less closely associated pairings.

The most popular IATs for race and skin tone measure the strength of association between the target concept of race or skin tone (African American or European American; dark-skinned or light-skinned) and an attribute (good: joy, love, peace, wonderful, pleasure, glorious, laughter, happy; bad: agony, terrible, horrible, nasty, evil, awful, failure, hurt). On a popular version of the racial IAT, participants first press a key when they see either an image of an African American face or a word, such as *tragedy* or *rotten,* that has unpleasant connotations. They press another key when they see either an image of a European American face or a word, like *love* or *health,* which has pleasant connotations. Participants then rapidly press the same key in response to either African American faces and pleasant words and another key when shown either European American faces or unpleasant words. The developers of the IAT reasoned that the faster the responses, the stronger the associations. Many American test takers are faster to link African American faces with unpleasant words and European American faces with pleasant words. Although test takers can learn to cheat, the IAT does a good job at tapping into implicit biases. A new generation of implicit association tests explores the neural processes underlying these responses using functional studies of the brain and facial muscles.[2]

1. This quotation is from the website maintained by Project Implicit: http://projectimplicit.net/about.php. Research papers published by participants in the project are listed on the website and may be requested from the authors: http://projectimplicit.net/articles.php.

2. See Ito and Cacioppo 2007.

studies of the "Obama effect" on levels of prejudice.[18] Humans are suggestible, and their assumptions about who is good or bad can be easily changed, especially by contact with real people from out-groups previously perceived as negative. As one researcher put it: "Activation [of categorical classifications of people] is easy when people encounter verbal labels, harder when they encounter photographs, and hardest when they encounter real people."[19]

The past five centuries have witnessed great changes in how we come to learn about others and form opinions about them. We have moved from a situation of knowing hardly anything about the appearance and culture of others to knowing a lot. Most of the information we receive today is from indirect reports and is not value neutral. Consider how we are affected by the many images of "attractive," "famous," "poor," "affluent," "homeless," or other variously described people from around the world that are electronically captured and propagated globally by the media, cell phone, social media, and advertising. The narratives that accompany these images are rarely simple descriptions: they tend to cast the attributes of a person in a positive or negative light. This highly dynamic and ever-growing reservoir of visual imagery affects how people translate perceptions of appearance into judgment. From these processes they develop preferences, aversions, and personal aspirations of appearance, without conscious thought.

THE EFFECTS OF STEREOTYPES

Stereotypes have powerful effects on behavior, including performance. Nearly twenty years ago a team of social psychologists published what is now a classic paper on the phenomenon of "stereotype threat."[20] They theorized that the underperformance of African Americans on standardized tests was due to influence of the prevalent cultural stereotype on their performance. When a difficult test was represented as being diagnostic of ability, it caused African American students to feel under threat of judgment by a racial stereotype and undermined their performance. Since that publication, similar studies have supported and extended the findings. Stereotype threat has been found to be influential in many contexts: Euro-American, "white" men perform more poorly on math tests when they are told that their performance will be compared with that of Asian men. Girls perform worse on math tests when they are told that girls are considered less naturally adept in math than boys. And Euro-American men perform more poorly than African Americans on a motor task when it is described to them as measuring innate athleticism. Human suggestibility thus extends to self-actualization of negative stereotypes about one's own group. Fortunately, the adverse effects of stereotype threat on test scores and implicit bias can be reduced if a strongly positive and overtly successful role model buffers the negative effects of racial stereotypes.

Most people are not aware of the influence of stereotypes on their own thought processes, and this lack of awareness in connection with stereotypes based on skin color has had profound effects on human history. Recognizing our obsession with the visual and our susceptibility to influences from the cultural mélange, we need to examine how skin color and impressions of skin color have affected human social interactions and the course of history.

8

Encounters with Difference

For most of the history of *Homo sapiens,* humans lived in small groups and did not travel much. Our ancestors would have seen their relatives regularly, and probably other people living in neighboring groups, but it would have been uncommon for people to travel far enough to encounter people who looked different from them. *Homo sapiens* has been around for more than 160,000 years, but only in the last 10,000 years or so have routine contacts between distant populations occurred.

The earliest contacts between people with visibly different skin tones took place in the context of routine trade. The exact times and places where this occurred are not certain because the encounters took place before systems of writing were developed.[1] As people became more proficient at hunting and gathering, and then especially at agriculture, their productivity increased and populations grew. Contacts between population centers became more common, and the number of trade routes and traders increased. Most early meetings probably involved small groups of people who would have taken stock of each other's appearance in the course of preliminary social exchanges. They were no doubt initially cautious or suspicious of others whose appearance or dress was different, but the face-to-face meeting of well-intentioned parties would have gone far to allay fears of sinister intentions. At that point the meetings were mostly concerned with trade. The social contacts established may have led to intermarriage and to people settling in trading centers far from their homes. The archaeological record shows us only that materials were traded and ideas exchanged: it is mute on the subject of people's reactions and feelings.

Evidence of the first recorded contacts between peoples of different skin color thus warrants attention. The earliest such evidence comes from ancient Egypt. We also have evidence of interactions between people of different skin color during the early history of southern Asia. However, the interactions and impressions generated in Asia did not significantly influence the development of the philosophical basis of Western attitudes toward skin color.[2] Later, people of different skin colors met and interacted in the ancient Mediterranean worlds. These categories do not include the peoples who contributed to the rise of agriculture and the first cities along the Tigris and Euphrates Rivers in Mesopotamia, who were more similar in skin tone to one another than were the inhabitants of the Nile Valley and the lands around the Mediterranean. The ancient history of Greece and Rome and adjacent lands leads naturally into an examination of the attitudes toward color in the early Jewish, Christian, and Islamic traditions that developed in the last centuries of the Roman Empire.

EARLIEST RECORDED MEETINGS: EGYPT

The Nile Valley was a highway of human interaction. Because of its north-south orientation and great length (6,650 kilometers, or 4,132 miles)—crossing fifteen degrees of latitude and traversing UVR zones from intense to moderate—the river and its valley brought together people of visibly different skin tones who had adapted to markedly different solar regimes.

Ancient Egypt comprised most of the modern country of Egypt and part of northern Sudan. After the end of the last ice age—from about 11,000 years ago (9000 BCE) to about 4,350 years ago—this area received abundant rainfall, which promoted the growth of lush vegetation and a proliferation of wildlife. The annual inundation of the Nile because of heavy seasonal rains made it possible for farmers to plan regular cycles of planting and harvesting. The adjacent areas, which are now deserts, were then well watered and were habitable, and conditions were conducive to flourishing agriculture and population growth. These trends led to increased communication between human groups. Being largely sedentary (rather than nomadic) and agricultural, the population of the Nile Valley was amenable to centralized control.[3]

The Nile River was punctuated by six cataracts of shallow and less navigable water that created natural boundaries between population centers. These centers were inhabited by peoples of moderate skin pigmentation with excellent tanning abilities. The lands south of the First Cataract belonged to Lower Nubia and Upper Nubia and were separated by the Nubian Desert. Today, Lower Nubia is part of Egypt, and Upper Nubia is part of Sudan. Upper Nubia—at the confluence of the White and Blue Niles—was inhabited by people with dark skin pigmentation. This area is often referred to as Kush (Cush) in Egyptian and Old Testament sources. Contact and exchange between farmers and herders in Egypt and Nubia began in Egypt more than five thousand years ago and intensified under moist conditions during the Early Dynastic (3100–2686 BCE) and Old Kingdom (2686–2134 BCE) periods.[4] Contact between people in Egypt and southwest Asia (Mesopotamia) also began in the Early Dynastic period but never involved large numbers of people.

By Early Dynastic times, the societies of Egypt and Nubia were structured, and people could be identified by class. Pharaohs and their queens were worshipped as divine beings and surrounded by nobles, who were in turn served by scribes. Peasants and serfs made up most of the rest of the population. They worked the lands owned by the pharaoh or the nobility on a sharecropping system. Because they could not be bought or sold, serfs were not slaves, but they were nonetheless bound to the land.[5] Between seasons in the fields, they were drafted to build the massive pyramids and other monumental architecture throughout the Nile Valley. Slaves constituted a separate class of Egyptian and Nubian societies that included the captives of war. When fortresses fell after successful sieges, people were captured, along with livestock, and enslaved by the victors. Siege warfare resulting in the taking of slaves within and between Egypt and Nubia was common from the late Predynastic period onward. Slaves were considered the property of the gods and the pharaoh: they could not be bought or sold privately. They were put to work as cooks, weavers, and field hands. Some joined the peasants as laborers on monumental constructions. Because most of them worked with serfs, they ended up marrying them and becoming sharecropping serfs themselves.

Slaves and peasants alike worked outside most of the time and would have been exposed to moderate to high levels of UVR on a seasonal basis, depending on whether they were closer to the mouth of the Nile Delta in Lower Egypt or the confluence of the White and Blue Niles in Upper Nubia. Those with moderate levels of genetically determined pigmentation (primarily from Lower and Upper Egypt) would have tanned heavily and looked considerably darker than the pharaohs and nobility. More darkly pigmented peasants and serfs (mostly from Upper Nubia) would have become darker than those who were exposed to less UVR, but the difference between the outdoor workers and the privileged upper classes would have been less noticeable. The visual diversity of population centers increased as contacts became more common between Egypt and Nubia and then between Greater Egypt, Palestine, and Libya.

The long history of contact between peoples along the Nile before the rise of cities and organized conflict meant that parties involved in warfare were familiar with each other's appearance.[6] In ancient Egypt as a whole, people were not designated by color terms, and slavery was not associated with darker skin. Egyptian inscriptions and literature only rarely, for instance, mention the dark skin color of the Kushites of Upper Nubia. We know the Egyptians were not oblivious to skin color, however, because artists paid attention to it in their works of art, to the extent that the pigments at the time permitted. Egyptian men were consistently depicted with reddish complexions and women with skin of a yellowish cast. Nubian (Kushite) nobility were rendered by Egyptian painters in black or dark brown and had themselves painted dark brown in reliefs.

INDIA

A vast region that covers significant expanses of latitude with varying solar regimes, India contains peoples of highly varied skin tones. It experienced a significant influx—what many have called an invasion—of people from central Asia beginning about 3,500 years ago. India is here discussed as a region, not as the modern country that bears the name.

Agriculture first developed in India between 6,000 and 5,000 years ago and was concentrated in the valleys of the Indus River that are part of Baluchistan and Sindh in modern Pakistan. It was here that cotton was first domesticated. The cities that arose in the well-watered Indus Basin gave rise to the Harappan civilization (2500–2000 BCE), which was distinctive for its absence of palaces and imposing burials, its apparent lack of a commitment to warfare, and the presence of intensive trade routes covering great distances.[7] Our knowledge of the Harappans is limited because they had neither a written script nor a tradition of visual art that recorded the details of their lives or interactions. Rather, the earliest extensive written records of life in India come from the invading waves of people who entered from the northwest and who called themselves *ārya* (literally meaning "noble" or "honorable," whence the word *Aryan*).

The Aryans were a pastoral but militarily powerful people, equipped with horses and chariots, who worked their way into the upper Indus Valley and eventually extirpated the Harappans. The process took more than a millennium, probably because the Aryans were greatly outnumbered by the sedentary farmers they sought to displace. The Aryans had a paltry material culture compared to the Harappans, but they left behind a vast body of literature called the Vedas, including hymns that provide a rich record of their lives and complex belief systems.[8] Early Vedic writings show that when they first contacted the Harappans, the Aryans had a simple, two-tiered class structure consisting of a nobility and ordinary tribespeople or commoners. The Aryan nobility soon subdivided into separate classes of priests and warriors, thus creating a total of three classes, which were ranked hierarchically as to holiness and affinity to the truth. These social divisions were associated with the concept of *varna,* which means radiance and color.[9] *Varna* has come to refer to both social class and skin color, but it is debatable whether at this time the term referred specifically to skin color. In the oldest work of India's ancient Vedic literature, the Rig Veda, the term usually is taken to mean *luster. Varna* in this sense was considered an attribute of the gods: the word could be applied to everything from humans to pearls. In its original usage, *varna* did not refer to a specific color or a specific group.

With increasing contact and mixing between the populations, pressure mounted within the upper classes of the Aryans to distinguish themselves from the remaining indigenous people and from the Aryans who had intermarried with them. In the late Vedic period, about 2,500 years ago, society had become divided into four classes that were religiously sanctioned and considered fundamental: the three Aryan classes of priests, warriors, and peasants and a fourth class of serfs, which included Harappans and the offspring of mixed unions. At this time the term *varna* came to be used to describe the cultural development of each class. The highest class of priests was associated with white (and purity), warriors with red, peasants with yellow, and serfs with black. The classification also came to have some association with skin color (especially of the face) because many serfs were descended from the darkly pigmented Harappans. Skin color did not affect perceptions of attractiveness, however, for a beautiful woman could be "dark or brown or golden-skinned."[10]

By the end of the Vedic period, about 500 BCE, classification of people according to *varna* had become codified in law and regarded as the essential feature of society. Skin color did not denote a person's class. *Varna* was associated with the role an individual played in connection with communal sacrifice and was determined by concepts of taboo, pollution, and purification. It thus reflected a person's access to the spiritual realms. When the social roles in these rituals were assigned distinct colors (white, red, yellow, and black), the use of *varna* in relation to color was confirmed.

The line dividing the three upper, Aryan classes from the fourth, non-Aryan class was strictly enforced.[11] The evolving connection between *varna* and skin color appears to have incorporated ideas about the relationship between tanned skin and outdoor activities, because both warriors and peasants who labored outside were generally darker-skinned than priests. Skin color was not strictly equated with class, however, because a person with darkly pigmented or very tanned skin could belong to one of the three upper social orders. Over time, *varna* became part of a more comprehensive system of social classification based on spiritual purity, in which the purest were considered white and the most impure were considered black. Purity was associated with occupation, among other traits: people such as brewers and distillers, slaughterers and executioners, hunters and fishers, and basket makers were thought to be impure and were described as having the quality of blackness, regardless of their skin color. Outsiders who were descended from non-Aryans and who did not speak the Indo-European tongues of Sanskrit or Pakrit were similarly considered black and were excluded and despised. Serfs had the quality of blackness by virtue of their descent from non-Aryans.

Although *varna* has been interpreted as evidence of a universal human tendency to classify people by skin color, this view is not correct. Only much later in Indian history, in the fifteenth and sixteenth centuries, with the hardening of the Hindu caste system and the installation of more commercial ties with Europe, did the *varna* line become a color line. This attitude prevailed most strongly in territories where Aryans were dominant; it was reinforced by the fact that most serfs were considered to be the descendants of darkly pigmented non-Aryans.

THE MEDITERRANEAN WORLD

The Mediterranean Sea is surrounded by lands with varied landscapes and irregular climates. The low to moderate fertility of these lands meant that early agriculture was a precarious enterprise. The early population centers on the Greek mainland and Crete that existed around 3000 BCE (when Predynastic Egyptian civilization was thriving along the Nile) were physically isolated from one another. The first evidence of contacts between previously independent cultures, especially in the eastern Mediterranean, dates to about 2500 BCE.[12]

The city-state of Athens—the heart of ancient Greece—was one of several to emerge in the Mediterranean region during the first millennium BCE. Its people were unified by economic, religious, and political ties. These city-states had a central urban core and a rural hinterland and were initially fairly small. They buffered themselves from the unpredictability of agriculture by the enslavement of war captives and failed debtors and, later, by invasions of adjacent lands. During the Homeric period (roughly 1200–800 BCE), slaves were worked hard in the fields, kitchens, and weaving workshops but were treated with dignity. Their living standard was only slightly below that of free workers. However, slaves were not citizens and had no rights. Because slaves could be acquired through war between separate Greek city-states (for instance, Athens and Sparta), many were ethnically the same as their owners. There was no single slave class or group.

The number and relative importance of slaves increased in Greece and other city-states of the eastern Mediterranean in the fifth century BCE, driven largely by the economic pressures of war. Some of the shortfall was met by the capture of women whose men had fallen in battle, but the need for strong male laborers necessitated the capture or purchase of slaves from ever more extensive areas, including most of modern Turkey. Towns were occasionally captured by the Greek army and navy for the express purpose of enslaving and selling the entire population, netting both human capital and profit.[13] The random aspect of slave recruitment in ancient Greece in some respects made it more equitable, because it was not based on class or appearance. In the words of the historian William Westermann, "Granting that slave status in general was an unenviable condition, there are many indications that deeper racial and class antipathies, such as those based upon differences in skin coloring, were totally lacking in the Greek world."[14] Slaves lacked many of what we recognize as human rights, but they could not be abused by free Greeks because they were not regarded as less than human. They could be freed by manumission—released by their owner—and when this occurred, the person's history as a slave was officially forgotten.

The intellectual tension over the status of slaves and nonslaves was first explored by Aristotle (384–322 BCE). He deemed that some people were physically and spiritually adapted for slavery or strenuous labor, while others were innately equipped for the freedoms of the citizen. The belief that slaves and low-class laborers were inherently unfitted for the responsibilities of citizenship in Greece reflected his broader philosophy that non-Greeks were, by definition, ill-suited for political development and governance.

Skin color did not figure in the Greek attitude toward slavery, although Greeks' moderate level of skin pigmentation, capable of tanning in response to strong sunlight, was seen as superior to both darker and lighter skin tones. To Aristotle, Greece's privileged intermediate geographical and climatic conditions favored the development of humans with superior physiques, mental faculties, and social equipoise. In this he followed Hippocrates (approximately 460–370 BCE), who established Greek ideas about the relationship between humans and their physical environment in his treatise *Of Airs, Waters, and Places*. Hippocrates was the first to make generalizations about temperament, the practice we now call stereotyping.[15] People who could not speak Greek fluently were further diminished by the epithet *bárbaros*, barbarian (box 17).

The full formulation of the climatic theory of human nature led to the establishment of the concept of the physiological norm, or mean, by which the skin color, physique, and mental qualities of a person were judged against the standard of a free Greek male citizen.[16] We now look upon Aristotle's pronouncements as inventive after-the-fact justifications for claims of Greek superiority. They are exceptional only for the strenuous mental effort and elaborate gathering of evidence that Aristotle summoned to achieve his formulation of ethnic and national preeminence. Others have achieved the same end with less inventiveness.

Aristotle's views on the superiority of Greek skin color did not presage the establishment of a skin-color hierarchy. To him, and to the Greeks and Romans that followed him, all skin tones that fell outside the intermediate range of colors he observed in the Greek citizenry were inferior. His philosophy led to entrenchment of the belief that a

Barbarians

The word *barbarian* was first applied in ancient Greece (from the fifth through the third century BCE) to describe non-Greeks or people who did not speak Greek fluently. The Greeks used the term freely to refer to people of all ethnicities and persuasions, no matter how "civilized." *Barbarian* provided a succinct description of otherness, with connotations of fascination and fear. Over time, it came to imply inferiority.[1] The Greek concept of *barbarian* flourished in ancient Rome, and a similar concept was developed by Aryans to describe non-Aryans in India.

The most elaborate notion of *barbarian* was developed in imperial China more than two thousand years ago: the kingdom was seen as the center of the world, surrounded by alien peoples. Each alien tribe was assigned a symbolic color associated with one of the points of the compass. Although skin color did not determine the symbolic color of the tribe, it "branded the barbarian with the indelible stigma of animalism. A mythical country in the west was inhabited by white people whose long hair covered their shoulders. Barbarians from another tribe had a human face, 'but their eyes, hands and feet are entirely black.'"[2]

1. See Thebert 1980.
2. Dikotter 1992, 6.

people's skin color reflected the qualities of their ancestral environment and their innate value relative to the Greek ideal.

The enslavement of masses of people did not become common in the Mediterranean world until the late third century BCE, when large numbers of slaves were captured in the conflicts between the armies of Greece, Carthage, and Rome. It was accepted and expected that the conquered would be enslaved. Over time, wars between Mediterranean powers became more geographically extensive because highly trained armies and navies could travel farther and faster. These conflicts, along with trade missions and diplomatic contacts, brought together people who looked different from one another in physical appearance and in dress.

Greeks and Romans referred to people with very darkly pigmented skin as Æthiopians. This designation included all people with darkly pigmented skin from the south of Egypt, both sides of the Red Sea, the southern fringes of northwest Africa, and India. They were "burnt-faced people," whose color was their most characteristic and unusual feature, and whose overall appearance and temperament were considered products of their physical environment (box 18).[17] The Romans, especially, developed many ways to express degrees of Æthiopian blackness, including terms for the gradations of color seen in children born of one darkly and one lightly pigmented parent. These children were described by the Latin words *decolor* or *discolor,* the same words that were applied to some Indians and Mauritanians. The climatic theory that related human features, dispositions, and cultures to the environment had a long tenure and broad influence, especially in medicine. These beliefs were incorporated into the medical treatises of the Persian philosopher and physician Avicenna and were influential in Europe until as late as the early eighteenth century.

Greek philosophy had a pervasive influence on the development of Roman government and the Roman belief that non-Romans were culturally inferior. Other peoples who were conquered by the Romans— Greeks, Gauls, Carthaginians, Egyptians, Æthiopian peoples, Germans, and Britons—were considered equally and inherently inferior: skin color and physical appearance did not enter into the Roman judgment of the worth of others.

Where the Romans differed from the Greeks was in the development of slavery on an industrial scale, involving hundreds of thousands of people. Beginning around 300 BCE, the combined effects of tremendous losses of Roman lives in military campaigns and the prodigious needs of the larger Roman cities and army for food and raw materials drove the capture of large numbers of war prisoners and their sale into slavery. Slaves were taken as spoils of war from newly conquered lands, and many thousands more were enslaved when they revolted against central Roman authority and were captured and then sold to private slaveholders.

The last decades of the Roman Republic, from about 206–27 BCE, witnessed a great increase in slave numbers and many instances of extreme exploitation of slaves. Many of these people came from the modern Balkan countries and Turkey. During the years of the Roman Empire (27 BCE–476 CE), many slaves came from Egypt, from the lands bordering the Red Sea, from Gaul, and from lands beyond the Rhine and the Danube. Romans became more fearful, suspicious, and contemptuous of slaves, and attitudes toward them—especially those exploited in mines and mills—became rigid. Even so, many slaves were treated decently or even kindly by more compassionate owners. There

BOX 18　**The Climatic Theory**

Aristotle developed the idea, first introduced by Hippocrates and Herodotus, that climate and topography determined a person's physical and mental characteristics. Aristotle asserted that these traits could be transmitted over generations, thus formalizing one of the earliest theories of the inheritance of acquired characteristics. As one modern historian summarized it, "Climate, geography and institutions all go together in producing peoples of uniformly good or bad character." Skin color was among the traits determined by climate. Light skin tones were produced by excessive cold and dark ones by excessive heat. According to the Roman naturalist Pliny the Elder, Æthiopians were "scorched by the heat of the sun which is nearby and are born with a singed appearance." The Greek historian Strabo agreed and noted that the skin of Indians, with whom people in the Mediterranean world by then had contact, was "not so mercilessly burnt."[1]

To Aristotle, the fact that Greece enjoyed an intermediate geographical position and an equable climate—neither too cold nor too hot, neither too wet nor too dry—meant that the environment imbued its inhabitants with the highest qualities of spirit and intelligence and enabled them to attain the highest level of political development, the capacity for governing other people. People who inhabited less commodious climates had physical characteristics and mental aptitudes that precluded such attainments and rendered them inherently inferior.

1. Isaac 2004, 65, 80.

are many accounts of highly erudite slaves who were the constant companions of their masters and some tales of slaves who became wealthy and powerful because they regulated access to a master or a household. For slaves in Rome, as in Greece, manumission was possible and common, especially for those working in private homes.

From late Neolithic times to the end of the Roman Empire, then, human populations of the Mediterranean region grew, intermingled, and waged war against one another. The major cultural centers of Egypt, Greece, and Rome were mostly tolerant of diversity in physical appearance, and differences did not affect social status, marriage prospects, status of offspring, judgments of beauty, or assessments of physical strength, courage, and fitness for battle. Differences in skin color were noticed and commented upon, but skin color itself did not determine a person's value. The greatest tolerance of physical diversity existed in Egypt, where the long history of population intermingling along the Nile had made contacts between people of different skin colors routine. In ancient Greece and Rome, a person's worth was measured by the yardstick of citizenry, not color. Noncitizens were fully human but were not considered naturally disposed to political development and governance over others because their ancestors had not benefited from the superior physical and climatic conditions of those polities. This discrimination was based on class and social status, not on skin color or other physical characteristics.[18]

EARLY JUDAISM AND CHRISTIANITY

At the same time that the classic civilizations of Greece and Rome were thriving, Judaism and Christianity were emerging among peoples living on the eastern shores of the Mediterranean Sea and the shores of the Red Sea about 3,000 and 2,000 years ago, respectively. The early adherents of these faiths did not invade the Mediterranean world from distant lands. They were indigenous people who shared distinct beliefs and common cultural values and who had been socially marginalized or enslaved. The earliest Jewish people lived in Egypt and Mesopotamia and distinguished themselves by their belief in a single god and by their unique culture. As Judaic beliefs became more popular and widespread in ancient Rome, Jewish populations became more heterogeneous in appearance and language. Because Jewish lands were frequently crossed or occupied by the dominant powers of the day and the people were often captured and enslaved, their belief structure, Hebrew language, and shared culture became their unifying distinctions and common defense. Skin color and other aspects of appearance had no influence on a person's suitability for faith.

Early Christianity developed from one of the three main branches of early Judaism, and its followers adopted similar attitudes toward skin color and physical differences. Christians living in parts of Asia belonging to ancient Greece and Rome adopted the attitude that differences in skin color due to climate were inconsequential and that all humankind was one. In Christian efforts to proselytize among surrounding peoples, neither skin color nor ethnicity was used to exclude new adherents. The dark skin color of Æthiopian people living in Kush, for instance, was noted in early versions of the Old Testament, but no value judgment was implied. Because of a long history of prior contact, the early Christian attitude toward Æthiopians was one of exaggerated solicitude compared to that displayed toward more distant groups like Scythians, with whom they had little prior experience. The conversion of such diverse peoples was seen as proof of the unity of humanity under one God. More salient than color was the fact that Kushites hailed from the "ends of the Earth," as the region was known at that time. This provenance came to be interpreted by later Christian scholars as a misfortune visited upon them by God.[19]

EARLY ISLAM

Islam first arose in the sixth century, near the eastern shore of the Red Sea in Mecca (in modern Saudi Arabia). The holy book of Islam, the Koran, laid out five basic obligations of the faith and provided a code of religious, social, and political laws, which included rules for the treatment of the poor and oppressed and of slaves and orphans. It recognized differences of color and culture between peoples but without a suggestion of superiority. Islam was the first religious movement in human history to combine military conquest with the propagation of a faith, and this enterprise is what accounted for the rapid spread of Islam to millions of people.[20] Non-Muslims, who were referred to as infidels or unbelievers, had little choice but to accept the Islamic faith. Large numbers of slaves were taken by Islamic generals as they conquered major cities in Egypt, Syria, and Persia in fairly quick succession toward the end of the first millennium. The Koran stipulated, however, that slaves could be taken only in just wars and that they had to be treated benevolently and given an opportunity for emancipation.

The early Muslims in Arabia, like most others of the ancient world, attached no stigma to skin color that was different from their own. That attitude changed, however, as Muslim armies penetrated farther into Africa and Europe and captured large numbers of dark- and light-skinned slaves. The Muslim attitude toward African slaves became more negative over time because they were perceived as having less "developed" characteristics than the conquered peoples of southwest Asia and southern Europe. This attitude hardened when African slaves belonging to a group called the Zanj rebelled in the late seventh century. Large numbers of Zanj, who hailed from populations along the East African coast, had been enslaved and put to work in what is today southern Iraq. Under the leadership of a man who had proclaimed himself a new Prophet, the Zanj rebelled against their Arabian owners, galvanizing the poor and disaffected as they went. The central power of the Muslim state eventually triumphed over the Zanj, who were again enslaved. Despite the Islamic injunction against prejudice, the Zanj rebellion intensified the negative attitude toward darkly pigmented Africans. It is also likely that Muslim discrimination against dark-skinned people was influenced by the beliefs of the Persian-based Zoroastrian religion, which conceived of a fundamental cosmic conflict between good, represented by light, and evil, represented by darkness.

Perhaps the most profound influence on early Islamic attitudes toward skin color came from the philosopher Avicenna (or Ibn Sina, ca. 980–1037), who revised Aristotle's climatic theory. Avicenna believed that climate crucially affected human temperament and that exposure to extremes of heat and cold developed peoples suitable for slavery. In his view, the European peoples like the Slavs and Bulgars lived at an "excessive distance" from the sun and were frigid in temperament. "Thus, they lack keenness of understanding and clarity of intelligence, and are overcome by ignorance and dullness, lack of discernment, and stupidity." At the other extreme were those who experienced the "long presence of the sun at the zenith," leading to their "temperaments [becoming] hot and their humors fiery, their color black and their hair woolly." As a result, they "lack self-control and steadiness of mind and are overcome by fickleness, foolishness, and ignorance. Such are the blacks, who live at the extremity of the land of Ethiopia, the Nubians, the Zanj and the like."[21] This philosophical reasoning justified the enslavement of people of light and dark skin colors on the grounds that their natures were inherently suited to slavery. The numbers of slaves who were involved in the Islamic slave trade in the years from 650 to 1600—particularly the routes across the Sahara, from the coast of the Red Sea, and from East Africa—were prodigious: estimates range from nearly 5 million to more than 7 million.

As commerce in Europe and the lands around the Mediterranean intensified toward the end of the Middle Ages, improvements in sailing technology made possible ever-longer voyages to distant lands. From ports throughout the Old World, explorers and traders prepared to embark on voyages that would fundamentally change the world of commerce and human affairs.

9

Skin Color in the Age of Exploration

By the end of the fourth century CE, Europe, eastern Africa, and Asia were dominated by powerful empires, which maintained highly mobile armies and controlled large bodies of slave labor. More trade routes, over both land and water, allowed empires to extend into new territories and obtain commodities and people from ever more distant lands.

Whereas the empires of the ancient Mediterranean world had been fairly tolerant and embraced cosmologies that included many gods, the empires of the medieval period were dominated by the monotheistic, proselytizing faiths of Christianity and Islam. New lands were conquered in order to acquire new resources and new converts. As one historian puts it, "Distinctions between 'Us' and 'Them' became more explicitly religious: Christians and heathens; Muslims and infidels."[1] Although the role of skin color and other physical attributes in establishing these distinctions is debated, differences in skin color often coincided with differences in religious or other social attributes and so provided a convenient means of distinguishing people with different belief systems.

Few documents directly attest to attitudes toward skin color during the Middle Ages and early Renaissance. Most of the information we have comes from descriptions written by European Christian explorers and traders and a smaller number written by northern African Muslim traders and scholars. These convey impressions of peoples encountered in sub-Saharan Africa, South Asia, and the Americas. Hardly any written accounts exist of the reactions of sub-Saharan Africa, south Asia, and the Americas to visitors, traders, and explorers. Those extant were written by missionaries and explorers. This fundamental asymmetry means that most of the descriptions were created by Europeans who were describing peoples they considered distinct from themselves. The establishment of the European white male as the standard against which all other humanity was judged would form the basis of the skin-color and racial hierarchies to come.

The ways in which "others" were described in the Middle Ages and early Renaissance provide important insight into the prevailing attitudes of the time and the later development of entrenched cultural biases. One concerns Muslim attitudes toward African slaves. According to the Koran, it was the duty of the believer to free any slave as soon as feasible, and the enslavement of other Muslims was forbidden. Nonetheless, the legitimate trade in slaves was important to the economy of the Muslim empire from its inception through medieval times. There were always both lightly and darkly pigmented slaves, but from the seventh century onward, most of the slaves held within the Muslim empire were Africans with dark skin color.

After the Zanj rebellion of 868–883, darkly pigmented slaves began to suffer social discrimination even after they were freed. This bias was probably due to many factors, including their potential to rebel, the perceived danger of violence, and their former slave status. But it is significant that, at this time, the Arabic word for a darkly pigmented slave, *abd,* came to mean any darkly pigmented person, slave or non-slave.[2] Muslim scholars and clerics continued to emphasize that skin color had nothing to do with legitimizing slavery, but associations of light with good and black with bad became more common in Muslim poetry and in literature after the Zanj rebellion.

In practice, many Muslims of medieval and early modern times fell short of strict adherence to the precepts of the Koran and those developed by Muslim moralists. Muslim slave trading in sub-Saharan Africa laid the foundation for the later European colonial slave trade. Darkly pigmented Africans were not the only people reduced to slavery in the Muslim world, but they epitomized the trade because they generally did not enjoy the opportunities for upward mobility available to lightly pigmented groups.[3]

Slaves from sub-Saharan Africa were mostly confined to northern Africa before the Muslim Moors conquered Spain in 711; after that, people from northern and sub-Saharan Africa began making

FIGURE 20. Albrecht Dürer's *Portrait of Katharina* (1521) depicts a young woman who had presumably been brought to Europe from Africa as a slave early in the Renaissance. Photo courtesy of Scala/Ministero per i Beni e le Attività Culturali/Art Resource NY.

their way steadily into Spain, France, and Italy. Before the Moors were driven from Spain in the late fifteenth century, large numbers of slaves from West Africa had been brought to Lisbon and Seville, and later to Marseille, London, and Amsterdam (figure 20). The supply of slaves from the southern Slavic regions had been interrupted by Ottoman conquests of these areas. Demand for slaves for agricultural work in southern Europe was high, and slaves from western and central Africa were widely available. By the late fifteenth century, sub-Saharan African people constituted the vast majority of slaves entering southern Europe.[4] Despite European prejudices against dark skin, many African slaves achieved freedom and obtained an education in Europe during the Renaissance, and several rose to prominence as scholars.[5]

In general, however, darker skin was stigmatized. In the mid-1400s, Christian forces wrested control of Spain from the Moors. The issuance in 1449 of the first Statute of the Purity of Blood by the municipal authorities in Toledo, Spain, was an attempt to distinguish between original Christians and recent converts from Judaism or Islam. By the time of the Christian reconquest of Spain in 1492, royal and aristocratic families were much concerned with the concept of purity of blood, *limpieza de sangre,* and accorded higher status to families of lighter complexions who had not intermarried with Moors and Jews. Family genealogies were carefully scrutinized for evidence of mixture with unwanted groups and for evidence that such admixture had been concealed. Military orders and trade guilds began to demand proof of cleanliness of blood. The use of the term *blue blood* is said to have arisen at this time, possibly from the practice of requiring a nobleman to display his blue veins, visible under the light-colored skin of his arm, as evidence that he had not been contaminated by dark, Moorish blood.[6] As the Spanish began to colonize the New World in the fifteenth century, the precise accounting of ancestry became essential for establishing personal classification and social standing.

SKIN COLOR AND DIFFERENCE IN THE AGE OF EXPLORATION

The Age of Exploration, or Age of Discovery, is recognized in European history as the period from the fifteenth through the nineteenth centuries during which "new" lands were "discovered" and described by explorers. These enterprises were fueled by the transfer and development of technology and built on trade routes and networks established over previous millennia. The monikers dignify what was, in reality, the beginning of the Age of Plunder and Commercialism and the rise of the first territorial nation-states or countries, with clearly mapped and defended boundaries.

Until about 1400, most long-distance commercial trade involved luxury goods such as gold, spices, and silk and was conducted overland, along the ramifying byways of the Silk Routes. By the early fifteenth century, trade in luxury goods was also conducted by sea routes connecting Europe and Asia, the Middle East and Africa, and China and Africa. These new routes added to the already vigorous trading network that had been established between Christian-held ports in Europe and Muslim-held ports along the Atlantic and Mediterranean coasts of North Africa early in the Middle Ages.

The creation of overseas trade routes benefited from firsthand reports. Scholars were enlisted to compile the accounts of travelers and informers into usable form. One such individual was the Muslim geographer and cartographer Al-Idrisi (1100–1166), who advised the court of Roger II of Sicily and wrote a book whose title translates as "The Book of the Travels of One Who Cannot Travel Himself."[7] The bulk of these accounts were taken up with descriptions of the distinctive topography, animals, and desirable trade goods encountered. Descriptions of indigenous people emphasized differences in their skin color, physique, dress, and customs compared to those of Europeans. Some of these accounts were quite matter-of-fact, such as Al-Idrisi's description of the Zanj of the East African coast, probably written around 1154: "Opposite the Zanj coasts are the Djawaga islands; they are numerous and vast; their inhabitants are very dark in color, and everything that is cultivated there, fruit, sorghum, sugar-cane and camphor trees, is black in color."[8]

The chronicles that generated the most attention and were reproduced most extravagantly, however, were those that described inhabitants of foreign lands in sensational and judgmental terms. Marco Polo (ca. 1254–1324) never visited East Africa, but he included an account of "Zanzibar"—by which he meant the whole East African coast—when he dictated his *Travels* around 1295. His information, which probably came from Chinese or Indian sources, contrasts dramatically in content and tone with the descriptions of Al-Idrisi:

> Zanzibar is a large and splendid island some 2,000 miles in circumference. The people are all idolaters. . . . They are a big-built race, and though their height is not proportionate to their girth they are so stout and so large-limbed that they have the appearance of giants. I can assure you that they are also abnormally strong, for one of them can carry a load big enough for four normal men. And no wonder, when I tell you that they eat enough food for five. They are quite black and go entirely naked except that they cover their private parts. Their hair is so curly that it can scarcely be straightened out with the aid of water. They have big mouths and their noses are so flattened and their lips and eyes so big that they are horrible to look at. Anyone who saw them in another country would say that they were devils.[9]

The *Travels of Marco Polo* was one the most widely read books of its time, and the impressions of foreign lands and people contained in it were influential for centuries after the author's death. His notions, vivid images, and misinformation instilled biases in European readers that remained for generations.

Another medieval travel writer who had great influence on European views of the lands and life of Asia and Africa was Sir John Mandeville, whose accounts were written originally in French and compiled about 1360. These sensational accounts of life outside continental Europe have been extensively scrutinized and criticized by scholars (box 19). Although the accounts may have been mostly or completely fabricated, Mandeville's *Travels* were translated into eleven languages and sustained the imaginations of people in Europe and then the Americas for five centuries with tales of "fantastic otherness."[10] His writings and those of Marco Polo are said to have inspired Christopher Columbus and numerous other explorers of the fifteenth and sixteenth centuries. Over decades and centuries, the misleading impressions of foreigners propagated by Marco Polo, Mandeville, and many others contributed to a cascade of prejudice against people who did not look European.

European travel literature was obsessed with skin-color differences. Associations of light with good and darkness with evil were common in classical and early Christian culture and tended to dominate perceptions of other peoples with different skin pigmentation.[11] In the absence of personal experience to counter these associations, they were passed from one generation to the next and became endemic stereotypes.

Information gained from travelers' accounts enabled Europeans to venture directly to Africa and circumvent the Muslim ports and Jewish intermediaries who had controlled African trade for centuries. Prince Henry of Portugal (1394–1460, known as Henry the Navigator) is said to have committed himself to a life of exploration from an early age, when he first heard of the ancient caravan traffic that brought gold, slaves, and other riches from Guinea in the African interior across the Sahara to the Atlantic coast of Africa. Starting in the 1440s, Henry initiated voyages to locate the sources of African gold and take control of the gold trade. Fortifications were established near the African coast, including on the Cape Verde Islands, by 1460. Successive journeys brought the Portuguese into the Gambia, where negotiations were conducted directly with local chiefs. By the end of the fifteenth century, the Portuguese controlled much of the gold traffic from the African interior that had previously been handled by Muslim intermediaries. In return they sent cloth, silk, and horses, which were much in demand.

The yield of gold proved to be disappointing in some places, but the yield of slaves was not. The increased demand for African slaves by the end of the fifteenth century saw Portuguese vessels carrying African slaves to Europe. The trade was brokered by Portuguese middlemen, not North African Muslims.[12] Spanish traders joined the business, too, and raided the interior for gold and slaves, often using Spanish-speaking Africans to engage with local people. Many other expeditions were launched to convert people to Christianity rather than capture

Mandeville on the Chaldeans

The Travels of Sir John Mandeville was written by Jehan (Jean) de
Bourgogne and appears to have been compiled from many sources,
including the works of the Roman historian Pliny the Elder.[1] The
author passed himself off as an Englishman and a knight, though
he was neither, and claimed to "have seen and gone through many
diverse lands, and many provinces and kingdoms and isles . . . where
dwell many diverse folks, and of diverse manners and laws, and of
diverse shapes of men." His accounts glorified European maleness
and vilified almost all other forms of humanity, as is evident in the
following passages from his *Travels*, chapter 17: "Of the Land of Job;
and of His Age. Of the Array of Men of Chaldea. Of the Land Where
Women Dwell Without Company Of Men. Of The Knowledge and
Virtues of the Very Diamond." The "description" of Ethiopians who
had one large foot with which they shaded themselves while lying
down is particularly outrageous and ludicrous.

> This land of Chaldea is full great. And the language of that
> country is more great in sounding than it is in other parts of the
> sea. Men pass to go beyond by the Tower of Babylon the Great,
> of the which I have told you before, where that all the languages
> were first changed. And that is a four journeys from Chaldea.
> In that realm be fair men, and they go full nobly arrayed in
> clothes of gold, or frayed and apparelled with great pearls and
> precious stone's full nobly. And the women be right foul and
> evil arrayed. And they go all bare-foot and clothed in evil gar-
> ments large and wide, but they be short to the knees, and long
> sleeves down to the feet like a monk's frock, and their sleeves be
> hanging about their shoulders. And they be black women foul
> and hideous, and truly as foul as they be, as evil they be.
>   In Ethiopia all the rivers and all the waters be trouble, and
> they be somedeal salt for the great heat that is there. And the
> folk of that country be lightly drunken and have but little appe-
> tite to meat. And they have commonly the flux of the womb.
> And they live not long. In Ethiopia be many diverse folk; and
> Ethiope is clept Cusis. In that country be folk that have but one
> foot, and they go so blyve that it is marvel. And the foot is so
> large, that it shadoweth all the body against the sun, when they
> will lie and rest them. In Ethiopia, when the children be young
> and little, they be all yellow; and, when that they wax of age,
> that yellowness turneth to be all black. In Ethiopia is the city
> of Saba, and the land of the which one of the three kings that
> presented our Lord in Bethlehem, was king of.

1. For details, see the brief but erudite review by Malcolm Letts (1946). The
quotations are from Mandeville et al. 1964, 102–103.

FIGURE 21. Detail from a Bini-Portuguese salt cellar, ca. 1525–1600, made in the kingdom of Benin, which is part of present-day Nigeria. The ivory from which the piece is carved conveniently depicts the surprisingly pale color of the skin of the Portuguese sailors, which, along with their prominent noses, was a source of wonderment. Courtesy of the National Museums Scotland.

and enslave them, with the avowed goal of spreading Christianity and reversing the spread of Islam or adherence to "heathen" practices. By the commencement of the direct transatlantic slave trade in 1525, large numbers of African slaves had already been Christianized.

In the late fifteenth and early sixteenth centuries, nothing we would recognize as an objective scientific account of Africa or Africans existed. The continent had been mapped, but little had been written about the peoples or environment of its interior. The fascination with darkly pigmented skin persisted, and sensationalized and derogatory descriptions of Africans that circulated in print were increasingly used to support the slave trade. This practice was aptly summarized by one historian who wrote that "culturally arrogant and ethnocentric observations of non-European peoples were given immortality in western culture by the printed page."[13]

The few extant descriptions of Africans' reactions to Europeans indicate that they found the light-skinned appearance of European explorers arresting and disturbing. In 1455, when the explorer Cadamosto encountered natives on the Senegal River, he commented that "they marveled no less at my clothing than at my white skin," and "some touched my hands and limbs and rubbed me with spittle to discover whether my whiteness was dye or flesh."[14] Similar experiences were recorded by the Kongolese of the Congo River, who encountered Portuguese explorers in 1483. They regarded their visitors as voyagers who had arrived by sea from the world of the dead. The Europeans looked like inhabitants of the underworld whose skin had been painted with white pigment, and their prominent noses were unlike anything that had been observed before (figure 21). The sense of benign otherworldliness about Europeans was reinforced by the vessels in which they sailed, the varied gear they carried, and the opulent-looking goods they often offered in trade. When the intent of the visitors became clear, depictions of Europeans became less charitable.

PEOPLE AND CATEGORIES

The exploration of Africa and Asia and the establishment of overseas trade networks between the seats of Christian power in Europe and other parts of the Old World in the fifteenth century brought goods of unexpected abundance and diversity to Europe. Similar ventures to the Americas in the early sixteenth century yielded even more and different wondrous things. New plants, foods, animals of every description, and people flooded the royal houses and salons, and collections of "curiosities" became fashionable. The realization that the living things of these new places were massively different from those of Europe was at once exciting and disconcerting. Attempting to classify them systematically gave rise to the practice of natural description.

Natural description was not natural philosophy but rather what we would think of today as natural history. A guide to birds is a good example of a collection of natural descriptions that we use today. New discoveries were brought to public attention via printed catalogs in which things were grouped according to their external appearance. Among these curiosities, of course, were people. Most naturalists of the time, however, suffered from the disadvantage that they, sitting in their libraries in Europe, had not seen these people themselves. They had to rely on the accounts of others, for better or (usually) worse.

The only exception was François Bernier, who traveled widely, observed people himself, and then wrote descriptions of them. Bernier was the first to use the term *race* in relation to people in his *New Division of the Earth* of 1684: "For although men are almost all distinct from one another as far as the external form of their bodies is concerned, especially their faces, according to the different areas of the world they live in, and while they differ so clearly that people who have travelled widely can thus often distinguish unerringly one nation from another, nevertheless I have observed that there are in all four or five Types of Race among men whose distinctive traits are so obvious that they can justifiably serve as the basis of a new division of the Earth."[15]

Bernier's classification of humans appears not to have been widely read or circulated. Much more widely known was work of the Swedish naturalist Carl von Linné, or Linnaeus (1707–78), who in 1735 composed the first edition of *Systema Naturae,* a systematic catalog of nature (figure 22). Linnaeus divided the natural world into three kingdoms: mineral, vegetable, and animal. His system had the advantages of being consistent and practical. Each kingdom was divided into subgroups and each of those subgroups into smaller divisions, creating a hierarchical classification. Animals were divided into six main groups. The group Quadrupedia contained the subgroup Anthropomorpha, which held the group *Homo,* humans. This category was further subdivided into four geographically based subgroups: *H. Europaeus, H. Americanus, H. Asiaticus,* and *H. Afer.*[16] These further corresponded to the four humors, or basic substances (blood, yellow bile, black bile, and phlegm), recognized since the time of classical Greece.

Humans were only listed, not described, in Linnaeus's original catalog: the intestinal worms found in the human gut were given more attention than humans themselves. In the tenth edition of *Systema Naturae,* published in 1758, Linnaeus changed the name Anthropomorpha to the more familiar name of our order, Primates. He also fully described humans, using descriptions of both appearance and temperament (box 20). The character attributes assigned to Europeans had uniformly positive associations; those for other groups were, at best, mixed.

In the decades after Linnaeus's death, classifications of humans expanded to include descriptions of the native peoples of South Asia and Polynesia. These treatises tended not to be systematic, objective, or anthropological because they were written on the basis of second- or thirdhand information. They were filled with value judgments and exaggerations. Accounts of the lands and peoples of the Americas and Oceania were abundant, but the greatest fascination was generated by Africa and its peoples. This attraction can be traced to the cultural obsession with darkly pigmented skin.[17] By the seventeenth century, Europeans had fetishized blackness. The paintings of European artists emphasized the contrast in skin color and social position between Euro-

FIGURE 22. Linnaeus (Carl von Linné) introduced a formal system of naming organisms and was the first to describe and classify humans of different appearance. Photo courtesy of the Smithsonian Institute Libraries, Washington, DC.

peans and Africans (figure 23), and European naturalists struggled to determine how skin was made dark.

One of the natural scientists most fascinated by dark skin was George-Louis Leclerc, comte de Buffon (1707–88). Buffon was a keen observer of nature and a student of what we would now call adaptation. He believed that the Africans' dark coloration would be lost if they were transported to northern climes and lived there for several generations. He stated this opinion enthusiastically throughout his career, but by his later years it had become clear, at least to his colleagues, that no loss of color was occurring among the Africans who had lived for generations in Europe.

The discovery of the seeming immutability of skin color had serious consequences for the understanding of human diversity. Buffon was convinced of the theory of monogenesis, which held that humans were a single species comprising several varieties. The fixity of skin color posed a problem for monogenists: how could a single original population of human beings of one color have given rise to human beings of different colors? Several authorities at this time proposed an alternative theory, called polygenesis, asserting that the different colors and forms of humans must have had separate origins. The debate

BOX 20 **Linnaeus on Humankind**

The first edition of Linnaeus's *Systema Naturae* (1738) gave short shrift to humans, simply listing *Homo* within the group Anthropomorpha, along with *Simia* (apes, including the "Satyrus"), and *Bradypus* (sloths). By the tenth edition, published in 1758, Linnaeus had warmed to the task of describing humanity. He placed *Homo* within the group he called Primates, along with lemurs, apes, and bats, and devoted five pages to a complete description of *Homo sapiens*.[1] His description of *Homo* begins with a listing of the occurrences of *Homo ferus,* the wild people, under the heading of *H. diurnus*. Linnaeus gave six examples of wild people in this edition, including the "bear boy" and the "wolf boy." All were four-footed, mute, and hairy, and—to people of Linnaeus's time—subjects of extreme curiosity. (By the twelfth edition of 1766, this group had grown to nine and included a "wild girl.")

He then described five varieties or forms of humans that were synonymous with *Homo sapiens*. Linnaeus's diagnoses included cultural and sociological observations along with observations of anatomy. Four of the five varieties he described were regular human beings.

> *Homo americanus:* red, choleric, erect; hair black, straight, thick; nostrils wide; face harsh; beard scanty; obstinate, content, free; paints himself with fine red lines; regulated by customs

> *Homo europaeus:* white, sanguine, muscular; hair yellow, long; eyes blue; gentle, acute, inventive; covered with close vestments; governed by laws

> *Homo asiaticus:* pale yellow, melancholy, inflexible; hair black; eyes dark; serious, proud, avaricious; covered with loose garments; governed by opinions

> *Homo afer:* black, phlegmatic, relaxed; hair black, tangled; skin silky, nose flat, lips tumid; crafty, indolent, negligent; anoints himself with grease; governed by caprice

The fifth variety was *Homo monstrosus,* a category containing dwarves, giants, people with large or deliberately deformed heads, and various others.

Linnaeus's descriptions of humans and humanlike creatures were distilled from various written accounts and were concerned more with problems of nomenclature than with comparative anatomy or direct observation. His system of classification was revolutionary in that it included humans with other parts of the natural world, but it was old-fashioned in its mixing of old myths with new science, ancient traditions, and contemporary evidence.[2]

1. For a taxonomist's perspective on Linnaeus's description of humans in the tenth edition of *Systema Naturae,* see Spamer 1999.

2. For an insightful examination of Linnaeus's classification of normal and feral humans from the perspective of social science rather than taxonomy, see Douthwaite 1997.

FIGURE 23. Circle of Gilbert Jackson, *Portrait of Florence Smythe*, ca. 1650. Many seventeenth-century European portraits show young European children or families with African pageboys or musicians. This example is typical in that it shows a young girl posed in front of the pageboy, leaving no doubt as to the social position of the two individuals. The comparison with Jan Mostaert's *Portrait of an African Man* (plate 7) is striking. Courtesy Bristol Museum and Art Gallery (Museum No. K622S).

between monogenists and polygenists was to have perfidious social consequences.

Toward the end of the eighteenth century, the challenge of understanding and developing classification systems was taken up not only by naturalists, botanists, and zoologists but also by natural philosophers. Among them was Immanuel Kant (1724–1804). Kant was an important figure in the history of taxonomy because he considered carefully the problem of human variation and how it should be catalogued. He was the first to define race as a fixed natural entity. His races were defined by characteristics that were handed down faithfully from one generation to the next.[18] From catalogs of stable distinguishing characteristics, identification keys could be developed, and groups could be separated.

Kant firmly believed that all humans sprang from a single origin and that the appearance of individuals depended on the conditions of air, sun, and diet where their "pre-existing seeds" were raised.[19] Skin tone was the most important characteristic in his classifications. The "lineal root genus" was of "white or brownish color": within this category, the "first race" was "noble blond (from northern Europe), born of humid cold"; the "second race" was "copper red (from America) from dry cold"; the "third race" was "black (Senegambia) from humid heat"; and the "fourth race" was "olive-yellow (Asian-Indians) from dry heat."[20] To Kant and like-minded taxonomists, color was the kind of unique and nonoverlapping characteristic that allowed the creation of identification keys.

During his career, however, Kant faced a rising tide of evidence against divisions of humanity based on sharp boundaries of skin color. Among the most articulate of Kant's critics was Johann Gottfried von Herder (1744–1803), whose passionate denial of the existence of races and insistence on the unity of humankind presaged modern thoughts on the subject: "In short, there are neither four nor five races, nor are there exclusive varieties on earth. The colors run into one another; the cultures serve the genetic character; and overall and in the end everything is only a shade of one and the same great portrait that extends across all the spaces and times of the earth. It belongs less to the systematic history of nature than to the physical-geographic history of humanity."[21] Despite evidence and entreaties, Kant remained committed to his race definitions, and by virtue of his established reputation, he eclipsed von Herder and others who remonstrated against him. Kant's opinions became the authoritative basis for powerful stereotypes that characterized the physical and mental constitutions of all humanity and swayed the opinions of intellectuals and political leaders for a century (see chapter 10).

Within months of Kant's first essay on this topic, "Of the Different Human Races," an important dissertation was published by the young scholar Johann Friedrich Blumenbach (1752–1840). Blumenbach's thesis, *De Generis Humani Varietate Nativa,* presented a taxonomic system for humans more complex than Kant's because it was based on more than just skin color. In fact, he made clear that skin color was not a reliable characteristic for differentiating people and that "on account of the multifarious diversity of the characters, according to their degrees, one or two alone are not sufficient." He also made clear that the different varieties of humans overlapped to the extent that definite limits between them could not be drawn. Blumenbach published three editions of his thesis, and it is the last of these, from 1795, that is generally cited because it is the first that introduces the name *Caucasian* for one of the five human varieties. The others he defined were *Mongolian, Ethiopian, American,* and *Malay.* After lengthy comparison of the varieties based on the anatomical evidence at hand and study of the treatises published by others, Blumenbach intoned his most famous conclusion: "No doubt can any longer remain but that we are with great probability right in referring all and singular as many varieties of man as are at present known to one and the same species."[22]

EMERGENCE OF A SCIENCE OF SKIN COLOR

Naturalists of the eighteenth century were not only interested in classifying the natural world; they also sought reasons for why it existed as it did. Skin color, the most noticeable and salient of the human characteristics, begged an explanation. The first scientific effort to compare and understand the origins of different human skin colors was "Essay upon the Causes of Different Colours of People in Different Climates," published in 1744 by the Virginia physician John Mitchell (1711–58). Mitchell had a sophisticated understanding of the structure of the skin and of physics of light. He recognized that light skin reflected more light than did dark skin and that dark skin contained a substance that rendered it more opaque. He observed that the sun caused skin to darken, and he was the first person to use the verb *tan* to describe the process. His theory for why different colors had developed ran counter to prevailing explanations and invoked observable phenomena of heat and light: "The Power of the Suns Heat in hot Countries . . . is the remote cause of the Blackness, and the different Degrees of Blackness of the Inhabitants of the Torrid Zone: Whereas the luxurious Customs, and the effeminate Lives of the several Nations of white People, in the northern Climes, are the remote Causes of their respective fair Complexions." He concluded: "For the different Colours of People have been demonstrated to be only the necessary Effect, and natural Consequences, of their respective Climes, and Ways of Life; . . . So that the black Color of the Negroes of Africa, instead of being a

Curse denounced on them on account of their forefather Ham as some have idly imagined, it is a rather a Blessing, rendering their lives, in that intemperate region, more tolerable, and less painful."[23]

Mitchell was the first of two American scientists of the late eighteenth century to make significant observations about the probable causes of variation in skin pigmentation. Samuel Stanhope Smith's essay on skin color was even more modern in its approach, findings, and style of writing. Smith (1751–1819) observed that seasonal changes in skin color were due to changes in the intensity of the sun and that sunburn could be expected on the first exposure to the sun of previously covered skin. Skin habitually exposed to the sun would thicken, like that of the faces and hands of laborers and seafarers. He did not attribute darkly pigmented skin solely to the action of the sun, however. He opined instead that extreme heat caused excess production of bile, and this in turn contributed to dark skin tones. "Encircle the earth in every zone," he wrote, "and . . . each zone is seen to be marked by its own distinctive and characteristic complexion."[24]

The acuteness of Smith's observations on the geographic distribution of skin color was astounding for its time: "In these extensive countries in which the surface of the earth is more uniform than in Europe, and not so much broken and intersected by mountains, seas, and bays running up into the land, the gradation of colour holds a more regular progression according to its latitude from the equator."[25] He also recognized that in "extensive countries" such as China, there had been less recent migration, and the historical gradient of skin color that had developed from "ancient times" was still observable. He was the first to note that the peoples of the New World were lighter in color than those of the Old World at the same latitude. Smith also expounded less convincingly on the probable effects of climate on hair texture, facial features, and disposition, but his observations of climatic conditions, skin pigmentation, and the pattern of human dispersals and migrations were not to be improved upon for several decades.

By the end of the eighteenth century, much was known about how human skin color varied around the globe. Careful observations of how environmental conditions varied relative to pigmentation were beginning to shed light on why variations existed. All naturalists made use of skin color as a characteristic for classifying humans into groups, but some lent more importance than others to the trait as a defining feature. Although taxonomists like Linnaeus and Blumenbach were not necessarily charitable in their classification of non-European peoples, they were reserved and contained in their descriptions of the dispositions and characters of others. Natural philosophers like Kant did not share this reserve, and the value judgments they installed in their taxonomies were to influence the history of the world.

10

Skin Color and the Establishment of Races

The philosopher Immanuel Kant (introduced in chapter 9) was one of the most influential racists of all time. Kant was convinced that skin color denoted qualities of personality and morality. It was the primary criterion he used for sorting people into the categories he called races. To Kant and his followers, the equation of skin color with character signified that lighter-colored races were superior and darker-colored ones inferior, and that members of darker-skinned, inferior races were destined to serve members of lighter-skinned, superior races. Contemporaries who challenged his views were mostly eclipsed and forgotten. Kant established the modern agenda of racial polarity on the basis of his personal opinions alone. His ideas about color and character achieved wide acceptance because of a confluence of three important factors: his writings were widely circulated; he commanded respect as a highly regarded philosopher and scholar; and for the most part, his audience was naive and generally had no personal experience with the darkly colored—mostly African—people whom he disparaged in his writings. Through his writings and lectures, Kant successfully instilled some of the most trenchant and potent classifications of humanity into the minds of inexperienced and unsophisticated readers and students.

Kant's interest in physical and moral differences among people arose early in his career and permeated his writings. His views on the inferiority of non-Europeans predated his definition of races and were based on his conviction of the superiority of European "spirit." In his unpublished notes, he wrote that Europeans contained "all talents, all predispositions to culture and civilization," while "Blacks can become disciplined and cultivated but never truly civilized." He concluded that "[Native] Americans and Blacks cannot govern themselves. They thus serve only as slaves."[1] Kant first determined that nonwhite races were inferior in their intellectual and moral capacities. He then defined races on the basis of visible traits, primarily skin color. He spent decades pondering and writing on the origin and meaning of human variation and the division of humanity into races.

Although Kant's views on the subject are not easily summarized, it is clear that he saw races as fixed and immutable, their distinctive characteristics having developed through a purposeful natural process. The dark skin color of sub-Saharan Africans reflected, for instance, "the perfect purposefulness of the development of the Negro to his motherland."[2] Humans contained the "seeds" of traits that would develop as they interacted with particular environments. People moving into Africa became black when their "seeds" interacted with the hot and damp environmental conditions that prevailed there. Races developed as a consequence of movement away from a geographical core in central Europe and western Asia toward peripheral and less desirable environments in Africa, the Americas, south Asia, and northern Europe.

Once the "seeds" of the diverse races had germinated, the changes effected in bodies and intellects were irreversible. The changes that Kant lamented most were the loss of motivation and drive. When people lost their ability and desire to improve the future of humanity, then, in his opinion, they were fit only for servitude. In an infamous passage, Kant correlated an African man's stupidity with his blackness: "In short, this fellow was quite black from head to foot, a clear proof that he was stupid."[3] The linking of blackness with otherness, sin, and danger was an enduring theme of medieval Western and Christian thought, but Kant transformed this loose network of suspicion and hearsay into a lattice of environmental detail and supposed historical truths. In the history of humanity, few intellectual constructs have carried so much weight and produced such a river of human suffering.[4]

Kant's views were readily embraced by the intelligentsia of western Europe and eventually by the general populace because they supported existing stereotypes and long- and widely held Judeo-Christian religious beliefs. Many who subscribed to the climatic theory, which held that originally light people turned black because of exposure to extreme heat, considered that the transformation from light to dark was a form of degeneration, a departure from the norm. Great meaning was attached to human blackness because black had consistently negative connotations in Indo-European languages, and darkness—such as the darkness of night—had a long-standing association with evil.[5] Some Jewish and early Christian biblical scholars then attempted to connect the blackness of sin with the blackness of skin. The most influential of these was the Christian scholar Origen (about 185–254 CE) who applied the metaphor of blackness as sin to Æthiopians mentioned in scripture, condemning them as not having known God and having been born and lived in sin. At the time, these references did not reflect a negative evaluation of darkly pigmented peoples, but over time, negative connotations of blackness were cultivated and came to have great longevity and power, especially when illustrated in works of art in later centuries.

The meanings of skin color that could be traced to the Bible became significant in later history because they provided divinely ordained justifications for slavery. Interpretations of the Bible from the first and second centuries CE cited allusions and curses that were believed to account for the fate and appearance of people. These provided more cogent and authoritative explanations of differences between people than climatic theories alone and came to be viewed by some Christians (and Muslims) as literal fact. They explained the foreign and the poorly known, clarified the causes of skin color, and cemented the foundations of slavery.

THE MARK OF CAIN AND THE CURSE OF HAM

As contact between Europeans and Africans increased in the seventeenth and eighteenth centuries, the question of the origin of African blackness loomed large in the minds of many Europeans. No consensus was forthcoming, except that dark skin was more than a simple physical trait. The French author Voltaire (1694–1778) described "prodigious differences" between Africans and non-Africans and declared that they were different "species of man."[6] Like many Europeans, Voltaire was struck by the differences he perceived between Africans and Europeans, but concerns extended also to native Australians, Pacific Islanders, Asians, and American Indians. These people were so different that there had not been enough time for all of them to have descended from Adam and evolved under the influence of climatic factors alone. Two alternatives presented themselves. Either God had created them from the offspring of Adam instantly, or they were not descended from Adam at all.

Voltaire was one of the most influential believers in the idea that humans sprang from multiple origins (polygenism). Voltaire embraced what came to be known as pre-Adamism, a philosophy centered on the idea that various human races arose before Adam from separate acts of creation. Pre-Adamism became most closely associated with the French scholar Isaac de la Peyrère, who wrote the work *Prae-Adamitae* in 1655. In the book of Genesis, Cain was banished to the land of Nod, east of Eden, after killing his brother, Abel. Bearing the mark given to him by God, Cain settled in Nod, where he took a wife and had a family.[7] According to de la Peyrère's reasoning, Cain's wife must have existed separately from Adam and Eve, and so Cain had married into a pre-Adamite stock.

Many pre-Adamites took de la Peyrère's interpretation as the starting point for avowedly anti-African and antiblack theologies and racist ideologies. By the nineteenth and early twentieth centuries in Europe and America, many pre-Adamite theorists averred that the biblical "mark of Cain" was blackness or that he had married a black-skinned wife. Thus the punishment for Cain's evildoing was the blackening of his body or his union with dark, inferior beings.[8]

Although pre-Adamism gained some popularity in Europe and the Americas, the idea that humanity sprang from multiple origins was not satisfactory to most biblical scholars and philosophers. They mostly accepted the suggestion that Africans had become dark as a result of intense tropical heat, but they saw the transformation as a degenerative process from an original white or light condition. All humans, according to these beliefs, had a common origin, and the various races arose from accidental and external circumstances. In the eighteenth century, most believers in a single origin of humanity accepted that all humans descended from a single father, the biblical Adam. The question then became how they had become differentiated.

The curse of Ham was the most plausible explanation offered in the book of Genesis (see box 21). Noah, angry with his youngest son, Ham, condemned Ham's son, Canaan, to be a "servant of servants." Theological arguments, counterarguments, and commentaries about the meaning of the curse of Ham are lengthy and tortuous, but the interpretation of the curse by proslavery interests can be simply summarized. Noah's three sons—Shem, Japheth, and Ham—were considered the founders of the major divisions of people in the world. While

BOX 21 **The Curse of Ham**

The text of the curse of Ham comes from Genesis 9:18–26. The wording varies slightly among different versions of the Bible. The text below comes from the 1769 King James Version. The interpretation of this passage has been controversial for centuries because it says nothing about the skin color of Canaan, his descendants, or any of Noah's other grandsons.

> And the sons of Noah, that went forth of the ark, were Shem, and Ham, and Japheth: and Ham is the father of Canaan. These are the three sons of Noah: and of them was the whole earth overspread. And Noah began to be an husbandman, and he planted a vineyard: And he drank of the wine, and was drunken; and he was uncovered within his tent. And Ham, the father of Canaan, saw the nakedness of his father, and told his two brethren without. And Shem and Japheth took a garment, and laid it upon both their shoulders, and went backward, and covered the nakedness of their father; and their faces were backward, and they saw not their father's nakedness. And Noah awoke from his wine, and knew what his younger son had done unto him. And he said, Cursed be Canaan; a servant of servants shall he be unto his brethren. And he said, Blessed be the LORD God of Shem; and Canaan shall be his servant.

not described explicitly in the Bible, the descendants of Shem were held to be Asians, those of Japheth Europeans, and those of Ham Africans (figure 24).[9] The Africans referred to were dark-skinned Æthiopians and Kushites, and the phrase "servant of servants" was taken to mean that Africans were destined to serve the descendants of Shem and Japheth. It was also believed that *Ham* derived from the Hebrew root meaning "dark," "brown," or "black," so the identity of the descendants of Ham appeared to be reinforced by the origin of his name.

The association between servitude and darkness was powerful. Descriptions by the English chronicler Samuel Purchas in 1625–26 crystallized the interpretation of Ham's offspring as being dark-skinned Africans: "These are descended of Chus [Kush], the Sonne of cursed Cham [Ham]; as are all of that complexion, Not so by reason of their Seed, nor heat of the Climate; nor of the Soyle [soil], as some have supposed; for neither haply will other Races in that Soyle proove black, nor that Race in other Soyles grow to better complexion; but rather from the Curse of Noe [Noah] upon Cham in the Posterities of Chus."[10]

FIGURE 24. Ivan Stepanovich Ksenofontov, *Noah Damning Ham.* There is no extant illustration of the curse of Ham that shows Ham as darkly pigmented. This nineteenth-century painting shows Noah driving off a dark-haired Ham (right) with a light-haired Japheth (left) looking on. Photo © culture-images/Lebrecht.

Belief in the inferiority of the descendants of Ham became more pronounced with intensification of the slave trade, and the very fact of slavery made the curse of Ham more credible. The rise of chattel slavery was the most potent influence on European perceptions of darkly pigmented Africans. A stereotype that could ultimately be ascribed to God himself was not subject to discussion. The stereotype established

Reverend Clarkson on the Curse of Ham

Objections to the color-coded interpretation of the curse of Ham came from many quarters—scientific, philosophical, and theological. The literate and impassioned passages from the American cleric Thomas Clarkson, first published in 1787, would have caused discomfort to many readers, because he reasoned that the gradient of skin color that existed from tropics to poles would eventually bring all humans, including the slave masters themselves, under the yoke of slavery.

> With respect to the curse of Ham, it appears also that it was limited; that it did not extend to the posterity of all his sons, but only to the descendants of him who was called Canaan: by which it was foretold that the Canaanites, a part of the posterity of Ham, should serve the posterity of Shem and Japhat. Now how does it appear that these wretched Africans are the descendants of Canaan ?—By those marks, it will be said, which distinguish them from the rest of the world. But where are these marks to be found in the divine writings? In what page is it said, that the Canaanites were to be known by their *colour,* their *features,* their *form,* or the very *hair of their heads,* which is brought into the account? . . .
>
> For if you admit the *form* of men as a justification of slavery, you may subjugate your own brother; if *features,* then you must quarrel with all the world; if *colour,* where are you to stop? It is evident, that if you travel from the equator to the northern pole, you will find, a regular gradation from black to white. Now if you can justly take him for your slave, who is of the deepest die, what hinders you from taking him also, who only differs from the former but by a shade. Thus you may proceed, taking each in a regular succession to the poles. But who are you, that thus take into slavery so many people? Where do you live yourself?[1]

1. Clarkson 1804, 114–115, 118. Clarkson demonstrates his detailed knowledge of the anatomy of the skin and the mechanisms of inheritance, as they were understood then, and demolishes arguments made about the biological separateness of people with darkly pigmented skin.

a hierarchy of groups, which were differentiated by power and divinity. Race had become an institutional fact. It also was on its way to becoming a stratifying practice that created identity and hierarchy through social interaction.[11]

After the restoration of the English monarchy in 1660, slaves from sub-Saharan Africa were traded as things, along with other commodities. Proslavery theologians attempted to persuade doubters that enslavement of Africans was sanctioned by the Bible because the black-skinned were the cursed descendants of Ham. Other religious scholars and scientists in Britain and America wrote vigorous and well-reasoned rebuttals. The physicist Robert Boyle (1627–91) wrote that "even a naturalist may without disparagement believe all the miracles attested by the holy scriptures, yet in this case to fly to a supernatural cause, will, I fear, look like shifting out of the difficulty, instead of resolving it; for we enquire not the first and universal, but the proper, immediate and physical cause of the jetty colour of Negroes; And not only we do not find expressed in the scripture that the curse meant by Noah to Cham was the blackness of his posterity but that he should be a servant of servants."[12] One of most articulate critics of proslavery interpretations of the curse of Ham was the American reverend Thomas Clarkson, who railed against the inhumanity and crass commercialism of the slave trade and the alleged divine endorsement of it (box 22).

Nevertheless, the African slave trade thrived with the biblical justification of the curse of Ham. Biases against dark-skinned Africans grew, reinforced by the demeaning conditions of slave capture, transport, and forced labor. The dye of blackness had cast the die of the institution of slavery.

11

Institutional Slavery
and the Politics of Pigmentation

By the late 1700s and early 1800s, dark skin was associated with inferiority and slavery in much of the world. To light-skinned Europeans, people such as American Indians and many Asians were savages and heathens, but Africans were considered a particularly depraved branch of humanity because of their darkly pigmented skin. Backed by interpretations of the Bible that viewed Ham as the father of dark-skinned Africans cursed with eternal slavery, the slave trade had been legitimized. What could have been an obscure theological debate became a debate over human worth as signified by skin color. The word *Negro* itself made darkly pigmented skin into a signifier of the potential to be enslaved.[1] The possession of lightly pigmented or "white" skin became the norm from which others deviated.

The slave trade brought tens of thousands of individuals from sub-Saharan Africa to continental Europe and Britain and to plantations in the West Indies and the Americas. In the early decades of the seventeenth century, most of the American colonies relied on European laborers and servants for agricultural and household labor. The transportation of African slaves to North America started slowly, with the introduction to the Jamestown colony in 1619 of people sold as cargo from a Dutch ship. Over time, dependence on African slaves increased as tobacco cultivation became more important to the colonial economy. At the same time, in the Caribbean islands, the explosive growth of sugarcane plantations brought demands for labor that were met almost

BOX 23   **Historical Dehumanization of Africans through Imagery**

As early as 1688, European maritime explorers described the people of western Africa as being more closely related to apes than to themselves. The Negro-ape metaphor, as it came to be called by sociologists, permeated popular culture and science. As details of human evolution began to be understood in the late nineteenth and early twentieth centuries, depictions of the history of the human lineage invariably showed a linear sequence from hairy apes through dark "ape-men" to lightly pigmented (European-looking) modern humans. Africans and people of African descent were assumed to occupy a place somewhere between the latter two groups and definitely lower than the Europeans.

The association of people of African descent with apes was a persistent theme in early-twentieth-century movies (e.g., *King Kong,* 1933), commercials, and popular art. Despite the ebbing of anti-African discrimination and the dramatic reduction in pejorative imagery, the link persists.[1] It is pernicious because it alters visual perception and attention: among other consequences, it leads to endorsement of violence against crime suspects of African ancestry. A recent study showed that exposure to these representations was more likely to encourage indifference to or justification of racial inequality.[2]

1. Goff et al. 2008.

2. This conclusion comes from the unpublished research of Shantal Marshall and Jennifer Eberhardt.

exclusively by African slaves. During the eighteenth and nineteenth centuries, slave labor made agriculture highly profitable throughout the New World. Casting dark-skinned Africans as less than human made it easier to expand the slave workforce without moral impediments, and it was a cornerstone of business and government policy in England and in its Caribbean and American colonies. This attitude persisted through the early history of the United States of America, until the Civil War.[2] The process was facilitated in no small part by pictorial depictions of Africans as apelike (box 23).

Most of the slaves who came to the Caribbean and American colonies were transported by English slave traders. The English entered the business of trafficking in human slaves later than their Portuguese and Dutch counterparts, but they lost little time in developing the slave trade's ideology and vocabulary. A key figure in the history of proslavery rhetoric was the Jamaican slave owner Edward Long, whose acerbic

BOX 24 **Authorizing Discrimination
with the *Encyclopaedia Britannica***

The *Encyclopaedia Britannica* has been the most authoritative digest of knowledge for most of the English-speaking world for nearly two hundred years. The dramatic change in attitudes toward darkly pigmented Africans that paralleled the expansion of African slavery toward the end of the eighteenth century is vividly illustrated in the two passages below taken from the first (1771) and sixth (1823) editions, respectively.

NEGROES, properly the inhabitants of Nigritia in Africa, also called blacks and moors; but this name now given to all the blacks.

The origin of the negroes, and the cause of their remarkable difference from the rest of the human species, has much perplexed the naturalists. Mr. Boyle has observed, that it cannot be produced by the heat of the climate: for though the heat of the sun may darken the colour of the skin, yet experience does not shew that it is sufficient to produce a new blackness like that of the negroes.[1]

NEGRO, *Homo pelli nigra,* a name given to a variety of the human species, who are entirely black, and are found in the torrid zone, especially in that part of Africa which lies within the tropics. In the complexion of Negroes, we meet with many various shades; but they likewise differ far from other men in all the features of their face. Round cheeks, high cheek-bones, a forehead somewhat elevated, a short, broad, flat nose, thick lips, small ears, ugliness, and irregularity of shape, characterize their external appearance. The negro women have the loins greatly depressed, and very large buttocks, which gives the back the shape of a saddle. Vices the most notorious seem to be the portion of this unhappy race; idleness, treachery, revenge, cruelty, impudence, stealing, lying, profanity, debauchery, nastiness, and intemperance, are said to have extinguished the principles of natural law, and to have silenced the reproofs of conscience. They are strangers to every sentiment of compassion, and are an awful example of the corruption of man when left to himself.[2]

1. Smellie 1771, 395–396.
2. Maclaren 1823, 750–754.

writings against dark-skinned Africans catalyzed extreme reactions in the Caribbean and American colonies that developed into persistent racism. Long's *History of Jamaica* portrayed Africans as closer to animals than to the civilized world of humanity and advocated slavery as the perfect and obvious restraint for people living in such barbarity. In Long's book, every opportunity was seized to contrast the key qualities of the bodies and minds of slaves with those of free persons. Black was not considered a natural color for human beings and, according to some observers, it not only covered the bodies of Africans but also extended into their internal organs, signifying corruption. Blackness distinguished "a brutish sort of people" and was a portent of future misconduct.[3] As one scholar put it, "The harsher the image of black life, the stronger appeared the case for slavery."[4]

In the early decades of American slavery, it was possible for African slaves in the Virginia and Carolina colonies to demand release from bondage if they converted to Christianity. This loophole was eliminated in 1667, when legal status was tied to skin color and the Virginia assembly ruled that "baptisme of slaves doth not exempt them from bondage."[5] After about 1680, the word *white* began to be widely used for self-identification in the American colonies, and by the end of the seventeenth century whiteness was equated with freedom and blackness with slavery.

The tremendous profits involved, especially in the transatlantic slave trade, convinced many European leaders to drop their opposition to slavery. As slave numbers and the profits from slave labor grew, a rising tide of rhetoric promoted the dehumanization of darkly pigmented Africans (box 24). The effectiveness of this indoctrination is manifest in the extreme cruelty and violence against slaves that were later recorded in slave narratives. Physical abuse was a hallmark of slavery, not an occasional aberration. The experiences of the fugitive slave John Brown were harrowing because they involved experiments on his body in addition to the customary beatings and maltreatment. Brown's experiences at the hands of his owner, a doctor, were particularly gruesome because they involved dissections of his skin to determine the origins of its blackness. The atrocities Brown suffered prefigure those perpetrated in East Asia and Europe during World War II:

> Having completed his series of experiments upon me, in the heated pit, and allowed me some days' rest, I was put on a diet, and then, during a period of about three weeks, he bled me every other day. At the end of that time he

FIGURE 25. Descendants of Sally Hemings and Thomas Jefferson, with the playwright Sandra Seaton (unrelated), photographed in 2001. Back, left to right: Julia Jefferson Westerinen, Sandra Seaton, Karen Richardson. Front, left to right: Shay Banks-Young, Kelly Richardson, Connye Richardson, Dorothy Westerinen. Photo by Robert Barclay, University Communications, Central Michigan University.

found I was failing, so he left off, and I got a month's rest, to regain a little strength. At the expiration of that time, he set to work to ascertain how deep my black skin went. This he did by applying blisters to my hands, legs, and feet, which bear the scars to this day. He continued until he drew up the dark skin from between the upper and the under one. He used to blister me at intervals of about two weeks. He also tried other experiments upon me, which I cannot dwell upon.[6]

No less a figure in American history than Thomas Jefferson wrote about the inferiority of darkly pigmented Africans and supported their lifelong enslavement and unsuitability for emancipation, despite his outspoken advocacy of freedom and happiness (box 25). Scholars have noted Jefferson's ambivalence toward the institution of slavery and his unease at owning slaves, but evidence of these attitudes does not alter the fact that he refused to free his slaves. The height of Jefferson's hypocrisy was revealed when it was demonstrated that he had fathered a child with one of his female slaves, Sally Hemings, in May 1808 (figure 25).

BOX 25   **Thomas Jefferson on Blackness and Slavery**

Thomas Jefferson's ambivalence about slavery is reflected in many of his writings, but he clearly regarded dark-skinned Africans as distinct, less attractive, and inferior humans, as evidenced in these passages from his *Notes on the State of Virginia:*

> The first difference which strikes us is that of colour.—Whether the black of the negro resides in the reticular membrane between the skin and scarf-skin, or in the scarf-skin itself; whether it proceeds from the colour of the blood, the colour of the bile, or from that of some other secretion, the difference is fixed in nature, and is as real as if its seat and cause were better known to us. And is this difference of no importance? Is it not the foundation of a greater or less share of beauty in the two races? Are not the fine mixtures of red and white, the expressions of every passion by greater or less suffusions of colour in the one, preferable to that eternal monotony, which reigns in the countenances, that immovable veil of black which covers all the emotions of the other race? . . .
>
> The improvement of the blacks in body and mind, in the first instance of their mixture with the whites, has been observed by every one, and proves that their inferiority is not the effect merely of their condition of life. . . .
>
> This unfortunate difference of colour, and perhaps of faculty, is a powerful obstacle to the emancipation of these people.[1]

Jefferson's views on blackness were shared by the antislavery pioneer Benjamin Rush and others who considered the darkness of Africans to be due to a "disease of the skin."[2]

1. Jefferson 1787, 145–151.
2. Quoted in Bay 2000, 78.

THE TITRATION OF VIRTUE

In chemistry, *titration* refers to the process of determining the concentration of a substance in solution by adding another substance to it until it changes color. I adopt it here because it precisely describes the process whereby European admixture transformed the treatment and fortunes of many African American descendants. Despite rigid restrictions against intermarriage and sexual relations between light-skinned Euro-Americans and dark-skinned Africans, many children of mixed parentage and intermediate skin tone were born. The children of one darkly pigmented parent and one lightly pigmented parent have skin that looks to the eye to be somewhere in between. The precise shade of these children's skin had significant ramifications for their future.

The first-generation progeny of Africans and Europeans were referred to as mulattoes or half-castes. Even in the American colonies, where mulattoes were recognized as a separate census category, children born of an African or mulatto mother were automatically considered slaves. Once it was established in the American colonies that the child of an African slave took the status of its mother regardless of the child's skin tone, the two-tier system of black and white, slave and free, came into existence.[7] These colonial statutes presaged the notorious "one-drop rule," whereby a child born into slavery was considered "black" even if she could otherwise pass as "white."

As slavery became an entrenched part of America's economy in the nineteenth century, skin color became the standard by which slaves of African descent were judged suitable for various types of work. Notaries who recorded sales of slaves used the labels *Negro, griffe, mulatto,* and *quadroon,* while masters used colors of the spectrum— "purple," "deepest black," "dark brownish," "deep copper," and "yellow"—to describe skin color and transmit salient information about the physical and psychological suitability of slaves for diverse forms of labor. Darker skin hues were associated with vitality and strength. At slave markets, the skin of darkly pigmented slaves was oiled or enhanced with black grease prior to sale. In some places, a dark complexion was considered evidence of an innate talent for cutting cane. Slaves who became ill were said to have lost color, and according to one contemporary doctor, "Deviation from the black color, in the pure race [was] a mark of feebleness or ill health."[8] Light-skinned men, considered generally weaker and less hardy, were more likely to be assigned jobs as carpenters, ironmongers, or house servants.

Women were similarly graded by color. Darker women were thought to be stronger and healthier field workers and better "breeders," and lighter women were considered innately better suited to indoor pursuits (including sex). Always implicit in sales of women slaves was their potential value as sexual partners for the slave traders and buyers. Light-skinned women with straight hair commanded high prices and were much sought after. Opponents of slavery eagerly publicized reports about the forced sale of light-skinned slaves as concubines and vilified the men who attended "quadroon balls" to arrange liaisons with light-colored

FIGURE 26. Edouard Marquis, *Three Ladies of Color*, 1867. Some lightly pigmented women with African ancestry attended "quadroon balls" in New Orleans and other cities. If they were freed slaves, they could arrange liaisons themselves; if they were slaves, the arrangements were made by their owners or slave traders. Photo courtesy of the Collections of the Louisiana State Museum.

slave women (figure 26). Antislavery novels encouraged readers to identify with their nearly white heroines, who were portrayed as suffering the double crimes of enslavement and rape. It is ironic that, even among abolitionists, the brutality dealt out to the light-skinned—even in fiction—was deemed more heinous than that suffered by the dark-skinned.

Both before and after the U.S. Civil War, dark skin was increasingly associated with animal physicality and lighter skin with refinement and educability. These connotations of skin tone often reflected the self-interest of slave owners who were fathers of the "mixed-blood" children in their own homes. Many slave narratives describe how light-skinned children worked indoors "in the big house" or were assigned to less arduous outdoor duties. As a result of their parentage, many escaped the lash, even when their mothers did not.[9] Slaves as well as masters recognized that lighter-skinned slaves had higher status. The desirability of light over dark, as perceived by slavers and the enslaved alike, presaged the development of modern colorism, the systematic favoring of lightly over darkly pigmented people in employment, education, marriage, and other spheres of social life.

Despite the aspirations of the light-skinned for higher status, their classification as black within the two-tier racial system precluded their formal change of position. Light-skinned individuals judged to have "black blood" were forbidden from entering many establishments and were turned out if they did (figure 27). "The father of the slave may be the President of the Republic," wrote the former slaves William and Ellen Craft, "but if the mother should be a slave at the infant's birth, the poor child is ever legally doomed to the same cruel fate."[10] In addition, lighter-skinned individuals suffered a kind of backlash. Many slave owners disliked slaves who were "too white" because they were a risk for flight and because their "hidden blackness" was a threat to the integrity of the "white race."[11] In the American South, the presence of mulattoes was a constant reminder of sexual unions between masters and slaves and the social tensions that accompanied them.

Classification of people by skin color became an ineradicable part of American government as well as business and social life. In the first decades of the United States census, from 1790 to 1850, the only categories recorded were "white" and "black (Negro)," with black divided into categories of "free" and "slave."[12] As the population of individuals of mixed ancestry swelled in the years around the Civil War, a column titled "color" was added, and attempts were made to classify Africans and their descendants as "blacks" and "mulattoes." By 1890, the census had established categories for "blacks," "mulattoes," "quadroons," and "octoroons" in an attempt to categorize the descendants of African slaves.[13] Careful instructions were issued to "be particularly careful to distinguish between blacks, mulattoes, quadroons, and octo-

THESE CHILDREN

Were turned out of the St. Lawrence Hotel, Chestnut St.,
Philadelphia, on account of Color.

FIGURE 27. This photograph depicts children who were turned out of a Philadelphia hotel in 1863 on account of their skin color. Individuals judged to have some "black blood" were not permitted to use many establishments in the United States during Reconstruction and in the Jim Crow years of the late nineteenth and early twentieth centuries. Photo by James E. M'Clees, courtesy Library of Congress, Prints & Photographs Division [LC-DIG-ppmsca-11150].

roons. The word 'black' should be used to describe those persons who have three-fourths or more black blood; 'mulatto,' those persons who have from three-eighths to five-eighths black blood; 'quadroon,' those persons who have one-fourth black blood; and 'octoroon,' those persons who have one-eighth or any trace of black blood."[14] The Bureau of the Census decided to abandon these subdivisions in 1900 because the principle of hypodescent—which held that any "black blood" in a person's ancestry made them black—rendered the categories superfluous. Although the labels that have been used in classification and race ranking have varied in number and specificity over time, the underlying scales of imputed intelligence, attractiveness, morality, and cultural potential have varied hardly at all.[15]

COLOR ON TRIAL

Blackness and whiteness, with their respective associations of slavery and freedom, were literally on trial in the United States in the middle of the nineteenth century. Two cases tried in 1857 involved the adjudication of color and freedom. The famed case of *Dred Scott v. Sandford* came before the U.S. Supreme Court after having been heard in state and federal courts in Missouri. Dred Scott, a slave, originally filed a "suit for freedom" based on having lived in the free lands of Illinois and the Wisconsin Territory prior to moving to the Missouri Territory with his current owner, John F. A. Sandford. Scott's lawyer argued that his previous residences in free lands made him free. Sandford's lawyers argued that Scott had no right to sue in the first place because he was not a citizen of Missouri. The Supreme Court, replete with five slave-owning judges (including Chief Justice Roger B. Taney), ruled decisively against Scott (box 26).[16] Taney averred that Negroes "had for more than a century before been regarded as beings of an inferior order, and altogether unfit to associate with the white race either in social or political relations, and so far inferior that they had no rights which the white man was bound to respect."[17] With this pronouncement, Taney cemented into law the hearsay, biblical misinterpretations, and cognitive biases of centuries and set the stage for heated battles over slavery and the meaning of blackness in the United States. Two of the enduring tragedies of the *Dred Scott* decision were the establishment of physical differences in skin color as the insignia of race and the reinforcement of the association of race with social divisions and status. When people then acted on their beliefs about race, they created a society in which individuals of one group had greater access to the goods of society than did the members of the other.[18]

The second court case, *Morrison v. White,* from 1857, was much less widely publicized and had fewer ramifications than the *Dred Scott* case. It was significant, rather, for its deliberations over whether skin color or birth to a slave mother determined whether a person was a slave or free. The case concerned the sale of a young woman, Jane Morrison, in a slave market. She was purchased by a man named James White, but shortly after her sale she ran away. Morrison filed suit against White for her freedom, claiming that her real name was Alexina and that she had been born free and of white parents in Arkansas. In her court affidavit, Alexina stated that she was "of white blood and free and entitled to her freedom and that on view this is manifest" because she had

BOX 26   **The Infamous Words of Roger B. Taney**

In his ruling on *Dred Scott v. Sandford* (1857), Supreme Court Chief Justice Roger B. Taney used his position to defend slavery and white supremacy even as the tide of public opinion was turning against slavery in much of the United States. Three key excerpts from Taney's verdict illustrate his tainted logic:

> The question is simply this: can a negro whose ancestors were imported into this country, and sold as slaves, become a member of the political community formed and brought into existence by the Constitution of the United States, and as such become entitled to all the rights, and privileges, and immunities, guaranteed to the citizen? One of which rights is the privilege of suing in a court of the United States in the cases specified in the Constitution?

> A free negro of the African race, whose ancestors were brought to this country and sold as slaves, is not a "citizen" within the meaning of the Constitution of the United States.

> When the Constitution was adopted, they [negroes] were not regarded in any of the States as members of the community which constituted the State, and were not numbered among its "people or citizens." Consequently, the special rights and immunities guaranteed to citizens do not apply to them. And not being "citizens" within the meaning of the Constitution, they are not entitled to sue in that character in a court of the United States, and the Circuit Court has not jurisdiction in such a suit.[1]

1. *Dred Scott v. Sandford.*

blond hair and blue eyes and looked "white."[19] This status, she protested, made her free. If she had any trace of "black blood," it would be visible. One witness assured the court that "colored blood will stick out." The slave owner, White, on the other hand, claimed that she was a slave because she allegedly had been born of a slave mother.

The case was tried before three New Orleans juries, with the evidence put forward becoming more lurid and bizarre with each successive case. Between trials, Alexina was forced to "testify" by displaying herself in public so that people could determine if she showed any "traces of the African." She was stripped to the waist and publicly exhibited in a hotel, where she submitted to repeated examinations by prodding, leering men who were supposedly engaged in a scientific investigation into her heritage. In the end, the second jury could not agree on a verdict, and it was decided that the case would be retried in a different court. In the absence of any proof that Alexina was a slave, the jury in that trial declared unanimously for her freedom. Similar cases of women being stripped before juries in order to establish their whiteness or blackness occurred elsewhere.[20] In every case, the "fact-finding" exercises were thinly disguised attempts to display or impugn the sexuality of the women on trial. The supposed wild and animal-like sexuality of dark-colored women was simultaneously threatening and enticing, and the sexual tension and uncertainty created by mulatto women and their descendants was often expressed, if not resolved, in the courtroom.

The United States after the Civil War became fixated on skin color, especially concerns that blacks could "pass" as whites. People with darkly pigmented skin bore a visible badge of inferiority, but those with lighter skin tones passing for white were considered evil in disguise. The word *miscegenation,* coined in 1864, quickly entered the American vocabulary. The fear of blackness led to heightened concern over the flouting of laws prohibiting interracial sexual relations and marriage, the threat of racial "amalgamation," and worries that sexual unions between dark and light were creating "invisible blackness" that polluted the white race.[21] Before the Civil War, a person could be legally white but still be a slave in many states if born of a slave mother. After the Civil War, the same people were white and free. To many others, their freedom was an intolerable threat.

MINSTRELS

In the early history of the United States, blackness was associated with slavery, and slavery, in turn, with plantation life in the South. The details of slave life were mostly unknown to Northerners, but the music of African slaves held great interest for many. Minstrels started appearing in the northern United States in the 1820s. These men were not Africans or African Americans: rather, they were white entertainers imitating the culture of the black slave entertainer for the benefit of mostly Northern audiences (figure 28). Minstrels wore blackface and donned costumes and performed songs and dances that incorporated "primitive" African musical elements.[22] They were caricatures of caricatures: white men imitating contented black slaves. Blackface allowed

FIGURE 28. Frances Benjamin Johnson, *Man in Blackface as Minstrel,* ca. 1890–1910. This unnamed performer displayed the typical appearance of the American minstrel, with blackface, exaggerated white lips, and a clownlike costume. Courtesy Library of Congress, Prints & Photographs Division [LC-USZ62–47073].

minstrels to act like Africans without the opprobrium that straight imitation of African musical and dance forms would have brought. The obviously false and temporary nature of their blackness made the entertainment acceptable. At the same time, the widespread popularity of minstrelsy promoted slavery by propagating false notions of happy-go-lucky slaves contented with their lot on a benevolently run plantation. Minstrelsy was one of the most popular entertainment traditions ever to emerge in the United States, and it sustained large audiences for more than a century. So contorted had the perception of blackness become in the United States by the early twentieth century that a lightly pigmented man with a blackened face could perform African-inspired entertainment in places where darkly pigmented men themselves could not set foot.

12

Skin Colors
and Their Variable Meanings

Colors may be neutral, but our minds and culture give them meaning. Over time, color labels like *white, black,* and *brown* have become freighted with messages of social worth when applied to people. These meanings have varied according to place and time. Most of the concepts of race that people understand or identify with today are socially weighted skin-color labels. Races are described as socially constructed categories because they are composite categories of physical and cultural attributes, and because they have meaning only under highly specific conditions of time, space, and culture. As categories go, they are slippery and arbitrary; but they are no less real in people's minds for being so.

There is no universal preference for a specific skin color. Our preferences develop on the basis of our early experiences and what we learn about other people from our parents and teachers. Because people in prehistory and early history never moved far from home, they generally preferred their own color. Anything noticeably different was viewed with suspicion or fear. During and after the Age of Exploration, for instance, light-skinned Europeans were referred to as demons or ghosts in traditional African or Asian cultures. But two other important factors have come to influence cultural attitudes toward color in the past four hundred years, and both have created preferences for lighter skin. The first and older of these is the preference for paler skin based on its association with freedom from outdoor toil. This is a widespread and probably universal preference among agricultural people, one that arose independently in different societies. Paler skin was that with little or no evidence of tanning. The second preference is for light over dark—strictly speaking, white over black—that derives from Christian symbolism. The association of white with purity, virtue, and Christ, and of black with impurity, evil, and the devil, pervades the Christian liturgy and popular belief. Medieval and early Renaissance images of Christ often depict him with skin and garments of pure white.

The light-dark polarity was extended to the human sphere with the increase in commercial contact between Europe and sub-Saharan Africa and the establishment of the slave trade and hereditary slavery in the Americas. As the transatlantic slave trade became more lucrative, the moral polarity of skin colors was accentuated to the extent that light and dark were respectively associated with human and animal, creating one of the longest-lasting and most pernicious patterns of bias that the world has ever known. A darkly pigmented African who attained social acceptance could be pardoned for having black skin only because, according to a commonly used expression, "his soul was white."

In recent centuries, the two preferences for paleness have sometimes reinforced each other, as in the valorizing of the "English rose," a woman whose almost transparent skin and blushing cheeks connoted both freedom from outdoor labor and incomparable virtue. The single most powerful factor reinforcing the preference for lightness in the last 150 years has been the dissemination of images in the popular media. When positive social messages and elevated social status are associated with images of people with lighter skin (as in much advertising), the effects are swift and sure.[1] Humans are ever imitative and suggestible and will work to transform themselves into a form or color associated with greater social acceptability and higher social status. Once established, attitudes toward skin color tend to be durable because they are reactions to known stereotypes and are faithfully transmitted by multiple cultural mechanisms.

It is against this backdrop that we can look at how skin color has come to be viewed in different parts of the modern world. Many places could be discussed here, but I have chosen the examples of South Africa, Brazil, India, and Japan to illustrate common themes and salient differences. Each of these countries has a long and complex social history and history of attitudes toward skin color.

SOUTH AFRICA

Southern Africa is home to a great diversity of human populations, many of which arrived in waves of migration overland and by sea over the past 5,000 years. The region's original inhabitants are the San people, or Bushmen, foragers who have lived in the region for more than 30,000 years. The pastoralist Khoi people are closely related to the Bushmen genetically and arrived in southern Africa more than 4,000 years ago. The San and Khoi are often referred to as the Khoisan or Khoe-San. They have the moderately pigmented skin typical of people living under strong but seasonal sun. The Bantu-language-speaking group is a collective term for a large number of agricultural peoples, originally from equatorial latitudes, who have darkly pigmented skin like that of other Africans living under intense UVR year-round. The archaeological record indicates that starting about 4,000 years ago, the areas originally inhabited by the Khoe-San were occupied by the Bantu-language speakers with their agriculture and metal tools. This transition was later described by European scholars as the ascendance of "Iron Age" agricultural peoples with strong "tribal" organization over the degenerate, "Stone Age," "Bush" races. Genetic studies of both groups attest to considerable admixture having occurred.[2] No written accounts exist from either group of their interactions or their impressions of one another's appearance.

The first light-skinned Europeans to settle in southern Africa were representatives of the Dutch East India Company, which established the Cape Colony on the Cape of Good Hope in 1652. The Dutch East India Company was the world's first multinational company. Its colony in South Africa began as a garrison to support the shipping trade between Europe and Asia, but within a few years, former employees of Dutch and French descent were allowed to settle there and farm. The Europeans mostly conquered and absorbed the Khoe-San as they created farms and expanded their settlement. They also imported slaves from Madagascar, from elsewhere in Africa, and from Indonesia and South Asia.

From the outset, the Dutch East India Company provided ministers of the Dutch Reformed Church to support the colony, and the church exercised a virtual monopoly over the expression of Christianity in the new colony.[3] Among the fundamental beliefs of the church were that the Bible was the sole authority over faith and life, and that individuals' lives and fates were predestined by God. Most church members embraced the "internal holiness" doctrine, which counted the entire European community as redeemed because they were born of believers and the non-European community—except for converts—as unredeemed. Colonial society in South Africa was built on the foundation of white European superiority, and it was unthinkable to the early colonists and their descendants that it could be otherwise. Some church members referred to the indigenous Khoe-San people as the cursed sons of Ham, and they were sometimes portrayed as being halfway between ape and human.[4]

The British took over the Cape Colony in 1795 and abolished the external slave trade in 1807. The colony grew quickly, and by 1820 it was composed of three distinct groups: the British; the descendants of the Dutch-speaking inhabitants (Afrikaners); and the descendants of the former slaves, together with the Khoe-San. The last was a highly heterogeneous group officially known as the Cape Coloureds. The interactions between the British and Afrikaners were complex and strained, but they did not inhibit the movement of settlers, speculators, and prospectors of European ancestry into the hinterland. The British belonged to different Christian denominations than the Dutch and supported the elimination of slavery, but they did not champion integrationist ideals.[5] By 1870, most of South Africa was divided into four states dominated by whites. The Union of South Africa was formed from these four states after the British defeated the Afrikaners in the South African War of 1899–1902.

European domination over the darker races was justified because of the unshakeable belief that physical type was inextricably linked to morality, economy, aesthetics, and language. South African attitudes toward human diversity were shaped by the post-Enlightenment European notion that culture was an inherent expression of race, along with nineteenth-century beliefs that certain "stocks" had evolved biologically and culturally superior "fitness" and "adaptations."[6] The superiority of the white race was part of the natural order.

The doctrine of white superiority coincided conveniently with the growth of European-owned agriculture and the lucrative gold- and diamond-mining industries, and it helped to justify policies of population segregation and hierarchy. The introduction of migrant labor and the pass system, which regulated the movement of black Africans into white urban areas, ensured supplies of large numbers of exploitable workers and marked the first steps in establishment of a formal color bar. The Native Land Act of 1913 formally divided South Africa into "White" and "Black" areas, with the latter amounting to only 7 percent of the country's area. These "Black" reserves had limited agricultural potential and became "reservoirs of cheap, unskilled labor for white farmers and industrialists."[7] The resulting physical and economic isolation formed the cornerstone of apartheid.

During the early decades of twentieth century, increasing numbers of non-Europeans were educated at mission schools throughout South Africa and began to advocate for political reform. This movement—associated most strongly with the African National Congress—was temporarily vanquished with the election of the National Party in 1948 on a platform of apartheid. Over the next two decades the South African government enacted a series of laws designed to repress and segregate people of non-European descent.

The first step in enacting segregation was the institution of a rigid system of population classification whereby everyone was assigned to a race at birth. The Population Registration Act of 1950 codified the characteristics to be used to assign individuals to races, with sets of rights and privileges titrated by color. Four broad groups were defined: Europeans (meaning white persons); Natives, Africans, or Bantus (meaning black persons); Coloureds (denoting those of mixed race); and Asiatics (embracing the "various races of Asia").[8] Legal authorities in South Africa recognized that in daily life, appearance, particularly skin color, furnished the principal criterion for group membership. But when decisions had legal consequences, other criteria were brought to bear, so that assessments were based not only on appearance (skin color, facial features, hair texture, and skeletal structure) but also on descent (the so-called test of blood), general acceptance and repute, and mode of living (including a person's associates, habits, dress, place and conditions of residence, and customary language).

Over time, legal authorities in South Africa came to rely more on the criterion of "general acceptance and repute" than on any other. This led to the development of absurd legal interpretations: "A person who is in appearance obviously a white person is presumed, for the purposes of the Act, to be a white person until the contrary is proved; but a person although obviously a white person in appearance, who is generally accepted as a coloured person, will not be regarded as a white person."[9] Because the general-acceptance and most of the other criteria were arbitrary and subjective, many individuals appealed their classification. The Population Registration Act included a provision for a Race Classification Review Board, and this and associated appeals boards met regularly from 1954 through 1991. Appeals were of practical importance because racial classifications directly affected a person's rights and mobility. Appeals were also essential in the bizarre and untenable situations in which children assigned to one race could not legally reside with parents classified as another.

Few details are known of what was actually measured or discussed by board members in their appeal decisions. Assessments appear to have been made mostly on the basis of skin color, hair texture, and clothing. In what came to be one of the strangest and most humiliating rituals of modern times, individuals were physically scrutinized and questioned for potential reclassification. Africans were reclassified as Coloured, and Coloureds were reclassified as Indians. Few people, understandably, appeared voluntarily for potential racial downgrading. People, including many children, assigned to the White race at birth were occasionally reclassified as Coloured if they were suspected of being Mixed by teachers or fellow students.[10] These situations often resulted in great psychological trauma because of the humiliation and rebuke associated with the subsequent mandatory relocation.

The abolition of the Race Classification Review Boards in 1991 ended the era of official racial classification in South Africa, but it did not bring an end to differential treatment of people according to skin color. Traditions of speech, habitual associations of skin color and character, color-coded expectations of performance, and deeply entrenched patterns of physical segregation and residence developed over three hundred years have created durable inequalities that have proved resistant to change. A particular stigma is attached to Khoe-San ancestry. Despite the fact that genetic tests of the anti-apartheid activists and national leaders Nelson Mandela and Desmond Tutu have revealed that both have Khoe-San ancestors, other South African celebrities have declined to be tested. South Africans refer to the need to eliminate "apartheid of the mind" now that the formal institution of apartheid is gone.

BRAZIL

Brazil's history of colonial contact is broadly similar to that of the United States, but it differs in one crucial aspect. In the United States, beginning with the earliest European colonization, indigenous Native Americans were almost extirpated by disease, warfare, forcible slavery, and a program of resettlement that relegated them to reservations. In Brazil, the indigenous peoples also died in large numbers for similar reasons under British, Dutch, French, and Portuguese colonial rule, but a larger proportion of the indigenous population was assimilated by the dominant Portuguese. King Joseph I of Portugal at one point encouraged his subjects to "populate themselves" and "join the natives through marriage." [11]

They obeyed. By the middle of the sixteenth century, with the native population decimated, the Portuguese introduced African slaves into Brazil to meet the increasing demand for labor on sugarcane plantations. Upward of five million African slaves were brought to Brazil, where many suffered and died in brutal working conditions. Their fate was seen as payment for their "savagery and barbarous ways." [12] At the same time, faced with a dearth of Portuguese women, male colonizers sought out mates from indigenous and African slave populations and produced large numbers of children—often by rape—who varied greatly in physical appearance and skin color. Throughout Brazil's colonial history, interbreeding between Portuguese, Indians, and Africans was tolerated but not officially sanctioned by the government or the Catholic Church. The commercial benefits were substantial, however, because marriage ties resulted in enhanced trade networks with more communities. [13]

After the abolition of slavery in Brazil 1888, new scientific philosophies influenced official attitudes toward the country's extensively mixed population. Social Darwinists and eugenicists in Europe and the Americas in the late nineteenth and early twentieth centuries viewed darkly pigmented peoples, especially African blacks and their descendants, as inferior and mulatto offspring as degenerate. For Brazil's rulers and scientific authorities, the large mulatto population therefore posed an enormous problem. Segregation by color, as practiced in the United States and South Africa, could not be established in Brazil because there was no agreement as to classification. Many members of the ruling elite were mulattoes who were not inclined to institute systems of segregation or color-coded treatment that would disadvantage them or their offspring. Tolerance of diversity was a practical necessity. A tacit skin-color hierarchy emerged nonetheless. The darker the skin, and the greater the proportion of assumed African ancestry, the lower a person's social position.

Beginning in 1872, Brazil addressed the perceived problem of mulatto degeneracy through the scientific solution of "whitening." Government policy encouraged large-scale European immigration and promotion of "constructive miscegenation." [14] The virtues of miscegenation were promoted as the foundation for racial harmony, unity, and "racial democracy." The absence of a legally sanctioned divide between black and white or between black, colored, and white led to the development of a finely graduated rainbow of names for skin colors. Color has always been considered more important than "race," a term that is synonymous with origin, in Brazil. The two cannot be disconnected, however, because color is derived from the admixture of the country's major founding populations, indigenous (Indian), European, and African. When the populace was asked to self-identify by skin color in 1976, they used 134 different terms.[15]

Descriptive names notwithstanding, discrimination by skin color was revealed by census statistics and social activists beginning in the late 1970s. Racial democracy was revealed as being a "bias that white is best and black is worst and therefore the nearer one is to white the better."[16] Advocates for the rights of dark-skinned populations have noted the tendency of most Brazilians to place themselves in a lighter color category on the census. The black-skinned, they argued, are in the lowest position on the color hierarchy: they have been disenfranchised and are the victims of continuing discrimination. In contrast to the situations in the United States and South Africa, the absence of a formal legal framework of color-based discrimination in Brazil has left advocates for the dark-skinned without an established structure to fight.[17] Nevertheless, movements to improve the social status and economic prospects of Afro-Brazilians have gained energy and adherents in recent decades. Brazil, like the United States and South Africa, is now wrestling with the challenges of recognizing and reversing centuries of faithfully transmitted and collectively reinforced discrimination against the naturally dark-skinned.

Under such conditions, it is painfully ironic that recreational suntanning and cultivation of the deeply bronzed look is one of the most popular pastimes of Brazil's naturally light- and medium-toned people. Having the social flexibility to be "healthily dark," an appearance associated with leisure and privilege, is just as important in Brazil as it is in the United States and many European countries.

INDIA

Attitudes toward skin color in India reflect the complexities of the country's geography, its long history of population incursions, and its intricate social and religious history. The preference of agriculturalists for lighter skin, because of its association with freedom from outdoor toil, obtains in India as elsewhere, but it has been inscribed with more detailed and subtle shades of meaning. Attitudes toward skin color in India have developed over more than two thousand years and reflect considerations of class (*varna*) and caste (*jati*).[18] *Varna* described different spheres of human activity, from the sacred to the profane, and each was in turn associated with a different color (see chapter 8). Members of the *brāhmana* led religious lives: because they were forbidden to harm living creatures, they were discouraged from active agricultural pursuits. Thus rarely exposed to the sun, they became associated with the color white. Members of the martial *kṣatriya* class were, by contrast, exposed to the sun regularly during military training, and they came to be associated with a ruddy complexion and the color red. The mostly mercantile class of *vaiśya* had the special responsibility of keeping cattle. Spending time outdoors as herders, cultivators, and merchants, members were associated with the color yellow. The class of *śūdra* was subservient to the other three classes. Considered peripheral and dark by birth, members were associated with the color black. External influences over the past five hundred years have reinforced existing skin-color preferences in India. Christian associations of light skin with virtue and godliness, and of dark skin with evil and baseness, for example, were transported to India with British and Portuguese colonizers and strengthened long-standing associations based on *varna*.

The reality of skin color in India is complex. Social preferences for lightness exist within a country that spans thirty-five degrees of latitude and experiences varying but generally strong levels of sunshine. Skin pigmentation varies from generally dark in the south to moderate or light (but able to tan) in the northern states. It also tends to vary by class and caste, with members of higher social groups being generally lighter in skin tone than those of lower groups. These two gradients cut across each other, however, to the extent that people of the lowest groups in the north are often lighter than those of the highest groups living in the south. In practical terms, this means that members of a particular social group in a particular place exhibit considerable heterogeneity of skin color but express a preference for light skin. This is most strongly expressed in the predilection for light-skinned brides. Families go to considerable lengths to seek out light-skinned brides for their sons, even if it means "marrying down" into a lower caste. The ideal bride is light-skinned and virginal; a dark girl is a liability to her family because of the difficulty of arranging a marriage for her. In a son, the deficiency of dark skin can be mitigated if he acquires other socially desirable qualities, like a good job or a good education.

FIGURE 29. Models from the cover of the April 2010 issue of *Vogue India*, which heralded the emergence of a new era of color tolerance in India and a celebration of the country's "dusky" women. The same issue included two advertisements for skin-lightening agents. Photo courtesy of Prabuddha DasGupta.

The culturally reinforced preference for light-skinned women in most of India is one of the best examples of sexual selection operating in humans today.

Today, women from diverse backgrounds in India are better educated and enjoy greater social and physical mobility than in the past. Relatively dark-skinned women are gaining in popularity and social acceptability, at least judged by the barometer of popular magazines and movies. The cover of *Vogue India* for April 2010 heralded "the Dawn of Dusk," and the accompanying story celebrated the "stunning earthiness" and "duskiness" of Indian women (figure 29). It referred to the "evolutionary process" whereby dark-skinned Indian women were being gradually accepted and labeled as beautiful. The unfolding of this process, which has been widely discussed on blogs, talk shows, and other popular media, will be fascinating to observe.

JAPAN

The Japanese preference for lightness and whiteness in skin tone can be traced to ancient symbolic associations of color, concepts of purity and pollution rooted in folk religion, and traditional ways of making distinctions between insiders and outsiders. Skin color in Japan has been a metaphor for a complex of attractive and objectionable social traits. Since the eighth century, the Japanese have considered themselves imbued with an esteemed "whiteness," which refers not only to skin complexions but also to spiritual purity.

As in other agricultural societies, untanned skin was a symbol of the privileged class that was spared from outdoor labor. Pale skin was also equated with personal beauty. Dark-skinned people were deprecated because they were of the laboring class that worked out in the sun. Heavily applied cosmetics could temporarily conceal dark skin but could not protect against the scorn meted out to the dark-complexioned.[19] Prior to contact with Europeans, the only words used to describe skin color were white (*shiroi*) and black (*kuroi*). Residents of the southern Japanese island of Okinawa were traditionally held in low regard, for instance, because their naturally light brown skin and good tanning abilities made them "black." After European contact, Japanese artists tended to depict the skin of Europeans in flesh tones or gray but depicted Japanese people—particularly women—with white skin.

This convention was retained in Japanese paintings and cartoons during World War II that depicted war scenes across Asia and the Pacific. Chinese, Southeast Asian, and Polynesian combatants were invariably depicted with dark skin, while the Japanese were illustrated with white or near-white skin.[20] This tactic visually reinforced the Japanese concept of the pure, white self but belied the fact that the Japanese soldiers would have been just as darkened by sun exposure as the others. The concept of spiritual whiteness was more important than the reality of the skin tone.

As in India, very pale skin in Japan was considered to be an essential characteristic of feminine beauty and could compensate for other physical shortcomings. For centuries, Japanese women have taken great care to avoid sun exposure. Although some evidence of sun exposure on a woman's skin is now thought to be "healthy" and "athletic," near-white skin remains the feminine beauty ideal and a highly prized attribute of a potential wife. Whiteness in a man's skin is also considered beautiful but is less avidly sought in a mate because of its association with fragility and femininity. Japanese women favor men with light brown skin because they think of them as energetic, masculine, sincere, and self-assertive.[21] The strong favoring of white-skinned brides among the Japanese is very similar to that in India and presents another important example of sexual selection.

THE RECENT TREND TOWARD COLORISM

Attitudes toward skin color are similar, but not identical, in the United States and the four countries examined here. Bias based on skin color has developed most strongly in places where people originally physically distant from one another came into contact on an unequal social footing. In the United States and Brazil, darkly pigmented slaves were transported involuntarily to places dominated by lightly pigmented slave owners and slave traders. In South Africa, lightly pigmented people introduced themselves into a country inhabited by moderately and darkly pigmented people. In all three places to varying degrees, threat and force, sanctioned by biblically inspired notions of inherent supremacy, established light-skinned people in positions of power. Hierarchies of color were maintained by legal institutions and rhetorical traditions of superiority and inferiority. Over many generations, ideologies of color became rigid as they were collectively reinforced by stereotypes and multiple cultural traditions.

In India and Japan, skin-color based classifications and hierarchies of color favoring the light-skinned have developed from within. The hierarchies have been more casual, less rigid, and not legally mandated but no less potent as social forces influencing the fates of less-favored individuals and groups. Foreign (mostly Euro-American) preferences for light skin have reinforced those that already existed in these countries.

The increased pace of exchange of people, ideas, images, and advertising in the twenty-first century is creating a worldwide preference for lighter skin tones. As the systematic preference for the lighter-colored becomes universalized, the specific justifications for it are often no longer clearly remembered. We now live in a world in which colorism, the discriminatory treatment of individuals based on skin color, is a major social force and a challenge to human equality.

13

Aspiring to Lightness

Preferences for light skin have arisen independently in many cultures, and they have been reinforced when different "cultures of lightness" have come into contact. Because having lighter skin has often been associated with higher social status, success, and happiness, people over the ages have sought to become lighter by various means. In parts of the world today, the simple knowledge that lightness is associated with higher status elsewhere is sufficient to promote the desire for skin lightening and sales of lightening products. Skin lightening is not a fad: it is the ineluctable commercial extension of the now-worldwide phenomenon of colorism. Discussion of the history of skin lightening and the social contexts in which it developed brings together themes introduced elsewhere in this book, including humanity's preoccupation with the visual, status seeking, suggestibility, and susceptibility to social contagion.

SHADES OF PALE

Skin can be made to look lighter by applying whitening cosmetics, through the use of bleaching agents to decrease the production of pigment in the skin, or both. Whitening cosmetics and skin bleaches have been used for nearly two thousand years in the agricultural societies of Europe and Asia. The public display of white skin was of great social importance in eastern Asia and in western Europe from the sixteenth through the eighteenth century, and lightness acquired new meanings and enhanced value as European colonies in the Americas prospered through the labor of imported, dark-skinned slaves. In the twentieth century the production of skin-lightening compounds became sophisticated, commercialized, and highly profitable.

The early history of skin lightening is not well known because the earliest formulations belonged to concealed traditions of cooking, healing, and beautification that found their way into written records only when they became associated with a famous name. White lead (ceruse) was used by the ancient Greeks and Romans as a cosmetic, but it is from the Egyptian queen Cleopatra (69–30 BCE) that we know that a mercury compound was used for the same reason. Cleopatra is said to have taken pains to keep her skin light, and her practice of bathing in asses' milk for the same purpose is legendary but possibly apocryphal. Cleopatra's skin color is not known with certainty, but her genetically determined color was probably moderately pigmented and capable of tanning. Her renowned lightness has been imitated and celebrated in writing and art for centuries (figure 30), but it probably owed more to parasols and general sun avoidance than to active skin lightening. Far from the Nile, in Japan, the appearance of a pure white skin was simulated using makeup made from rice powder and white lead that was mixed with starch. These preparations were popular with both men and women of high rank from the eighth through the twelfth century but later became more closely associated with women.

Starting in the mid-sixteenth century, "books of secrets" described the proportions of mercury or lead compounds along with other ingredients needed to produce effective skin-lightening compounds. Formulas developed independently in continental Europe and China spread to Britain and Japan, where they became central to the beauty routines of upper-class men and women. The popularity of white makeup and lightening preparations increased despite the fact that sustained use was known to produce "withered faces like an ape," stinking breath, rotting teeth, and an "evil air surrounding the entire body."[1] Toxic lighteners and white face powders caused health problems in those who used them and in the children who came in contact with them. In Europe, the children of sixteenth-century women who used white makeup were said to lose their teeth before they could walk, and Japanese children born to samurai mothers who used white-lead face paint suffered what we now know to be lead toxicity and disturbances of bone growth.

FIGURE 30. Gerard de Lairesse, *Cleopatra's Banquet*, 1680. Cleopatra's allegedly light skin was part of her allure, and her name has been used to sell millions of dollars' worth of merchandise, from skin-lightening creams to bathtubs. Photo courtesy of Rijksmuseum Amsterdam [Object No. SK-A-2115].

Neither sickness nor denunciations of vanity curbed the use of white cosmetics and lighteners. For many, the pursuit of social approval or advancement through lightness was worth the risk. What was remarkable about the history of skin whitening before the nineteenth century was that it was the province of those who were already light-skinned.[2] They wanted to look lighter because whiteness was a powerful signifier, representing freedom from outdoor toil and spiritual purity. Skin lighteners and lightening cosmetics took on different roles when they were adopted by people with dark skin, especially by the descendants of former slaves in the New World and by others who experienced discrimination because of dark color. To some, these products were agents of social elevation and personal transformation. To others, they were instruments of subjugation that diminished the value of dark skin and reinforced the self-doubt associated with it. To all, cosmetics were political.

THE ORIGINS OF COLORISM

Colorism is a type of skin-color bias that involves systematic discrimination against the darker-skinned members of a particular group. It is primarily a product of the skin-color hierarchy that became entrenched and institutionalized with the transatlantic slave trade, and it has been collectively reinforced ever since. During the era of slavery in the United States, as discussed in chapter 11, people of African descent who were lighter-skinned enjoyed advantages: light skin, in the words of one historian, became their "most precious possession"[3] After the Civil War, lighter-skinned men of mixed ancestry continued in high-status positions. They enjoyed better educational opportunities, and many rose to positions of great social influence. Preferences for light-skinned students were common at many of the historic black colleges and universities established in the late nineteenth century because some school administrators considered it a waste of time to educate dark-skinned men and women for career paths that would be closed to them.

After Reconstruction, legally enforced segregation of "Negroes" and "whites" further heightened the awareness of skin tone among people with African ancestry. Negroes, as Chief Justice Taney observed when ruling in the *Dred Scott* case, were "far below" whites "in the scale of created beings."[4] In his novel *Pudd'nhead Wilson* (1894), Mark Twain used the fictional account of light-skinned boys switched as infants— one being $1/32$ Negro—to expose the hypocrisy of a system that apportioned basic rights according to presumed race. Negroes were relegated "by a fiction of law and custom" to lives without privilege. Twain's protagonist, fearing that his Negro ancestry would be exposed, "came to have a hunted sense and a hunted look, and then he fled away to the hilltops and solitudes. He said to himself that the curse of Ham was upon him."[5] Individuals able to pass as white enjoyed immense social advantages and were spared the segregation and shame associated with blackness. "Passing" became so common in the early twentieth century that some establishments in Washington, DC, employed African-American doormen "to spot and bounce intruders whose racial origins were undetectable by whites."[6]

The decades from the 1880s through the 1940s witnessed the rise of a mulatto elite in the United States. Preferences for lighter skin tones within the African-American community were pronounced, and darker skin tones were increasingly stigmatized. Skin color defined personal choice and prospects, and the names associated with skin colors created what was, effectively, a caste system: high yellow, high yella, crème-colored, ginger, saffron, octoroon, quadroon, bronze, mulatto, red-bone, light brown, black as tar, coal, blue-veined, café au lait, pinkie, blue-black. Girls and young women, especially, were encouraged not to play in the sun because darkened skin would reduce their chances of attracting a light-skinned husband and having light-skinned children. Individuals who could pass usually did so. Some light-skinned individuals, like the acclaimed *New York Times* book critic Anatole Broyard (1920–90), became famous as whites and never revealed their ancestry, even to their children. Others wrestled with internal conflicts over self-identification. The author Jean Toomer (1894–1967) identified himself at different times in his life as "white," "Negro," and, finally, "American": his renunciation of his African ancestry late in life represented a wish not to be judged within the narrow confines of "Negro literature."[7] In social contexts defined by color, becoming lighter improved prospects for education and employment, social mobility, and marriage. Selective breeding toward whiteness was advanced as a long-term solution, but in the short term, many resorted to harsh chemicals to bleach their skin to a more socially acceptable shade.

SKIN BLEACHING

The commercial development, production, and marketing of skin-bleaching products began in the United States in the post-Reconstruction era, as segregationist Jim Crow laws restricted the opportunities and prospects of African-Americans, especially in the South. At a time when American culture was suffused with caricatures of African Americans with dark skin, "vicious" and kinky hair, and apelike features, these new cosmetic preparations promised relief from discrimination along with social advancement. The Madam C. J. Walker Company encouraged buyers with its invocations to "add beauty to brains for success," while Palmer's Skin Success cream promised that its users would experience "a whole new world." The lofty rhetoric of this advertising competed with sharp criticism from social reformers, educators, ministers, and journalists in African American communities, who argued that skin bleaching only reinforced the association between color and character that had already caused so much suffering and disenfranchisement. The social activist E. Azalia Hackley (1867–1922) stated the problem clearly: "The time has come to fight, not only for rights, but for looks as well."[8]

Over time, marketing of skin bleaches became more nuanced, evok-

FIGURE 31. In the United States, advertisements for skin bleaches during the early twentieth century connected skin lightening with enhanced beauty and social betterment. Photo courtesy Chicago History Museum (Manuscript ICHi-64852).

ing images of mythic and exotic beauty to encourage consumers to pursue a universal ideal of beauty. The Kashmir Chemical Company, manufacturers of Nile Queen skin and hair products, invoked the sensual imagery associated with Cleopatra (figure 31). These refined advertising messages succeeded insofar as sales of skin lighteners increased during the 1920s and 1930s, and the iconography of lightness prevailed in the media. The blues singer Bessie Smith (1894–1937) was not alone, however, in literally singing the praises of blackness in her "Young Woman's Blues": "I'm as good as any woman in your town / I ain't no high yella, I'm a deep killer brown" (figure 32).[9]

Through the first half of the twentieth century, the "bleaching syndrome" had a strong hold on African-American culture.[10] In 1949,

FIGURE 32. Lyrics sung by the jazz great Bessie Smith flouted the social conventions of her time by promoting pride in dark skin. Photo by Carl Van Vechten, 1936, courtesy of the Library of Congress, Prints & Photographs Division [LC-DIG-ppmsca-09571].

the civil rights leader Walter White declared in *Look* magazine that "science [had] conquered the color line" through the discovery of a chemical that could "change the color of skin from black to white." "If completely perfected and widely used," White averred, "this chemical could hit the structure of society with the impact of an atomic bomb." Himself one-fourth African, White was convinced that use of the new chemical bleaching agent, monobenzyl ether of hydroquinone, would allow dark-skinned people to pass as whites, thereby eliminating "the color line, the shame of the twentieth century."[11] Hydroquinone—a related chemical with fewer side effects—did become popular, but it never achieved the universal adoption or the liberating effects for which White had hoped.

During the 1960s and 1970s the popularity of skin bleaching in the United States waned temporarily with the rise of the Black is Beautiful movement and with the 1973 ban on sales of mercury-containing skin bleaching creams because of their toxicity (box 27). The skinbleaching industry and ideology did not disappear, however; they just mutated, created a new language for themselves, and migrated into new markets. New bleaching agents were developed, and in the late 1960s, many African American–owned cosmetics companies that produced skin bleaches and hair straighteners were bought by multinational conglomerates such as L'Oreal and Revlon. Sales of skin-bleaching agents in the United States recovered, buoyed by sales messages emphasizing "brightening" and the development of a "glowing" complexion. Skin lightening also received boosts from the popularity of light-skinned African-American celebrities whose complexions—whether produced by chemical bleaching or sun avoidance—were widely admired. Markets for skin lighteners were also expanding in South Africa, the Caribbean, and Asia, fueled by the real and perceived social benefits of lighter skin and the marketing expertise of multinational cosmetics companies.

The popularity of skin-bleaching creams in South Africa during the apartheid era was predictable. The largest markets for skin lightening have developed in places where the social costs of darkness have been greatest. Mercury-based skin bleaches, introduced into South

---

BOX 27   **Coming Clean on Skin-Bleaching Agents**

Skin-lightening chemicals decrease the production of melanin in melanocytes (melanin-producing cells). Most of them work by suppressing tyrosinase, an enzyme governing melanin production. The oldest known skin bleaches are mercury-based creams and ointments, sometimes known as mercurials. Although banned by the Food and Drug Administration (FDA) of the United States in 1973 and by the countries of what is now the European Union (EU) in 1976, mercurials continued to be produced in the EU and exported to countries in Africa and the Caribbean until recently.

Mercurials were mostly superseded by hydroquinone-based preparations in the 1970s and 1980s. Hydroquinone lightens the skin by suppressing tyrosinase and by releasing chemicals that are toxic to melanosomes (melanin-containing bodies within skin cells). Banned by the EU and Japan in 2001, hydroquinone continues to be used in the United States in over-the-counter skin-lightening preparations (containing up to 2 percent hydroquinone) and prescription-only creams (containing up to 4 percent). It is often combined with corticosteroids, which also have lightening effects. A ban on sales of hydroquinone-containing creams was proposed by the FDA in the United States in 2006 but was opposed by many dermatologists.

The dangers of mercurials and hydroquinone have spurred the search for other compounds that can suppress melanin production without harmful side effects. Some of these are chemical relatives of hydroquinone, such as arbutin, which is derived from cranberries and other fruits. Others, such as kojic acid and azelaic acid, are derived from microorganisms, and many others, like aloesin, licorice extract, and hydroxystilbene compounds, are flavonoids derived from plant leaves, bark, and flowers. Many commercial preparations combine several lightening agents. All skin-lightening agents, even ones now considered safe, have side effects, which are summarized in the table below.

Agent	Mechanism of action	Harmful side effects
Mercurials	Suppression of tyrosinase	Dermatitis (skin inflammation), hyperpigmentation (excess pigmentation), permanent kidney damage, neurological symptoms (anxiety, depression, and psychosis)
Hydroquinone	Suppression of tyrosinase	Dermatitis, hyperpigmentation, redness, stretch marks, ochronosis (darkening and thickening of skin), squamous-cell carcinoma
Arbutin, kojic acid, azelaic acid, and flavonoids	Suppression of tyrosinase	Dermatitis, redness, increase in melanin production after prolonged use
Niacinimide	Inhibition of melanosome transfer into keratinocytes	Dermatitis, redness
α-hydroxy acids (glycolic, retinoic, salicylic, and linoleic acids)	Exfoliation and inhibition of tyrosinase	Dermatitis, redness, scaling, and drying
Vitamin C, Vitamin E	Reduction of melanin production through antioxidant activity	Dermatitis, redness

SOURCES: Gillbro and Olsson 2011; Ladizinski, Mistry, and Kundu 2011.

Skin lightening creams: a big new problem

LEARN AND TEACH 1982

1

FIGURE 33. The use of skin bleaches in South Africa was discouraged through educational posters like this, which were published in widely circulated periodicals. This example comes from *Learn and Teach* 2, no. 5 (1982): 1.

Africa from the United States in the 1930s, became enormously popular, especially among people classified as Coloured or Black.[12] Skin lighteners were praised for "smoothening" the skin of the face and for elevating the social status of both men and women. During apartheid, Black women used skin bleaches to obtain jobs often reserved for Coloured women. The unsightly skin blotches that often appeared following repeated use of skin lighteners were seen as positive evidence of being modern. Skin lighteners took away "the Blackness." Darkly pigmented skin had become a disease in need of a cure. After mercurials were banned in 1973, bleaches containing hydroquinone or monobenzyl ether of hydroquinone became more popular. Mercury-based preparations were still considered the most efficacious, however, and illegal imports of mercurial creams and soaps from Europe, Great Britain, and Ireland persisted until the making of these products was finally discontinued less than a decade ago.

Recent studies on the use of and opposition to skin lightening products in South Africa have highlighted "the dense interaction of racial hierarchies, capitalist commerce, and individual desires for betterment" that parallel the American situation.[13] Opposition to skin bleaching in South Africa gained strength when antiapartheid activists emphasized that lightening agents were harmful to health and individual self-image (figure 33). The Black is Beautiful campaigns of late-twentieth-century South Africa probably had more long-term success in reducing the popularity of skin lighteners than those in the United States because they combined social and medical information into comprehensive messages of personal empowerment and national pride. The market for skin lightening products in South Africa is still large, however, and cosmetics and skin-care companies have modified their advertising and ingredients to attract new users. These companies have also been resourceful in extending their markets throughout sub-Saharan Africa. Selling their products is easy when beauty, success, and happiness are linked to lightness. Demand for skin lighteners is high in African countries such as Nigeria, Ghana, Tanzania, and Kenya that have burgeoning economies and people eager to improve their status and prospects. Advertising has mostly targeted women of marriageable age, but it has also been credited with helping to shift male preferences toward women with light-colored skin.[14] Widely circulated images of light-skinned African American and Indian celebrities also contribute to aspirations to lightness on the part of both women and men. When women can't afford to buy lighteners containing "safe" skin bleaches, they buy illegally imported hydroquinone-based products or resort to under-the-counter, locally manufactured mercury-based preparations, often with disastrous effects.

COLORISM AS A GLOBAL PHENOMENON

Preferences for light skin and biases against dark skin are among the most serious social problems in the world today. These preferences are not innate.[15] The dominant culture sets and perpetuates the standards of physical attractiveness, and these standards are overwhelmingly Euro-American and biased toward light skin. Media-driven messages emphasizing the beauty and success associated with light skin amplify existing societal preferences, creating a vicious cycle of aspiration to an unattainable ideal that affects men as well as women. In India, the most popular brand of skin lightener has been marketed through the promise of making a positive first impression with lighter skin.

BOX 28 **The Costs of Colorism**

Skin tone affects ratings of attractiveness by others and self-empowerment, especially in women. The relationship is complex, and women who are judged to be unattractive are more likely to experience discrimination based on dark skin color than those judged attractive.[1] Skin tone also affects personal income and social position. According to a 2004 study among African Americans, 37 percent of people with dark skin tones were classified in the category of postindustrial poverty-stricken (or the underclass), while 25 percent were in a category considerably above poverty (or affluent).[2] The figures were almost reversed for light-skinned African Americans: 40 percent were classified as affluent, and 23 percent were classified as underclass.

Among all new legal immigrants to the United States—including those from Latin America, Mexico, and Asia—those with darker skin tones earn 17 percent less than those with lighter skin.[3] Despite the effects of colorism, most of these lighter-skinned people are likely to be considered "honorary whites." Some scholars contend that they will always, however, be considered an intermediate category in the emerging American "pigmentocracy," between "whites" and "collective blacks," and that they will never be regarded as legitimate representatives of the nation.[4]

1. This is one of the salient findings in a study of African Americans conducted by Maxine Thompson and Verna Keith (2004).

2. See Bowman, Muhammed, and Ifatunij 2004.

3. Based on the 2003 New Immigrant Survey, as cited by Hersch 2010.

4. Eduardo Bonilla-Silva and David Dietrich describe an emerging triracial, stratified system in the United States composed of "whites" (including "new whites," such as Russians and assimilated Latinos), "honorary whites" (including light-skinned Latinos and most multiracial individuals), and "collective blacks" (including African Americans and dark-skinned Latinos). See Bonilla-Silva and Dietrich 2009, 153–154.

In the past twenty years, many social science scholars have turned their attention to documenting colorism around the world.[16] From the communities of color in the United States and South Africa to the Caribbean, India, the Philippines, Korea, Latin America, and Mexico, skin tone is a major determinant of social stratification and its outcomes: education, occupation, income, and health status (box 28). Skin tone has more significant consequences for women than for men, because men are partial to lighter women. For very dark women, the word *dark* has consequently acquired the loaded meanings of lower-class, ugly, and unimportant. When described as dark, impressionable teens can become obsessed with skin color and consumed with a desire to be light, with predictable negative effects on their self-esteem and academic performance.[17] Chronic use of skin lighteners tends to lower self-esteem further, especially when the complications from persistent use result in the deterioration of facial skin and lead to ostracism.

The problems of colorism and skin lightening are conjoined: they have spread and been magnified by the rapid dissemination of electronic images and the advertising power of multinational companies. The potential of visual media to determine the preferences of suggestible and status-conscious people has never been greater.

14

Desiring Darkness

As we have seen, for much of recent history and around the world, pale skin has been prized, to such a degree that people have been willing to risk illness and disfigurement to obtain it. It is paradoxical, then, that tanned skin became fashionable and glamorous in Europe and the Americas in the mid-twentieth-century—to such a degree that people have been willing to risk painful burns and skin cancer to obtain it.

THE ORIGINS OF RECREATIONAL TANNING

After agriculture became widespread and complex societies developed, visible skin darkening was associated with sun exposure from outdoor labor. It is hard to know when this association became socially important, but paintings dating from about 500 BCE and earlier from Egypt, Greece, northern Italy, India, and China show people with broad-brimmed hats or parasols who are clearly using these items for sun protection. Written accounts from these societies attest that untanned, nearly white skin was strongly preferred in women and loved ones in general, and that this preference developed independently in many parts of the world.[1]

Untanned skin became associated with two different but not mutually exclusive characteristics. The first is social privilege. Pale skin signaled that an individual had the means to avoid outdoor toil and to be protected from strong sun when out of doors: it was a mark of upper-class status.[2] The second is sexual desirability. Pale and untanned skin was associated with beauty and youth. From its association with outdoor labor, sun-darkened skin was also associated with masculinity, but higher-ranking men protected their skin from the sun when possible.

People worked hard to be pale by staying out of the sun, developing ingenious devices and costumes to protect themselves from the sun, and applying cosmetics that simulated a pale and untanned look. Clothing and hats protected wearers from the sun for centuries and are still used in many parts of the world (figure 34). Parasols were added later in Egypt and—along with hats—served as fashion statements as well as sun shields. In some cultures, large parasols, and attendants who held them, were symbols of royalty. This cultural framework remained in place through the early twentieth century.

Tans became fashionable when the people who had them were of high status and widely visible to those who weren't. Prior to the development of print media such as newspapers and magazines, images of important people were circulated on coins and, later, stamps, as well as in sculptures and paintings. For the most part, the people depicted were royalty, military leaders, and religious figures: famous entertainers, authors, and athletes rarely merited celebrity status as they do today. For most of human history, fashion was modeled after a look that people had seen in person or in the disseminated likenesses of revered and exalted figures. The Roman emperor Nero's attempts to emulate the look and lifestyle of Alexander the Great—based on various depictions of Alexander—offer a good, if somewhat preposterous, example.

The trend toward socially acceptable tans began in the early twentieth century, when women—whose paleness had previously been highly prized—began spending more of their leisure time outdoors with exposed skin. It was reinforced by images of celebrities (in the modern sense of the word) with obvious, confidently displayed suntans widely disseminated by magazines and newspapers.[3] After Coco Chanel proclaimed in the late 1920s that tanning was fashionable and set a personal example, tanning was pursued as an activity, and a tan became a symbol of leisure, high status, and style. Images of visibly tanned women began appearing in *Vogue* magazine.

Tanning was also, to a degree, a sign of freedom. As women in Europe and the Americas achieved more legal rights and social freedoms in the 1920s, norms of dress relaxed considerably, and it became

FIGURE 34. Before the era of chemical sunscreens, modes of sun protection included concealing clothing, hats, and parasols. (Top) This nineteenth-century Indian painting depicts a lightly pigmented European woman being shielded from the hot sun by a darkly pigmented native man. © British Library Board. All rights reserved. (Bottom) Victorian-era beachwear protected both a woman's modesty and her skin. Photo courtesy Library of Congress, Prints & Photographs Division [LC-USZ62–116423].

socially acceptable to bare more skin to the sun and to the eyes of people outside the home. Sunbathing was indirectly promoted by fashion designers who created new outfits—including the bikini, invented in 1946—to maximize sun exposure while on the beach. When photographs of female celebrities in bikinis and other revealing attire hit the newspapers and fashion magazines in the 1960s, the effect was sensational (figure 35). The suntanning craze was also embraced by many men, who eagerly followed the examples of prominent male movie stars who would not be caught dead without a tan.

Fads catch on when many people can follow them easily without spending a lot of money, and they endure if there is continued social reinforcement of the behavior. In the 1960s and 1970s, getting a tan didn't require a trip to the French Riviera: it could be achieved in the backyard. It imparted a sense of well-being and glamour. Social reinforcement of tanning came in many forms, including Mattel's Malibu Barbie doll, which brought the glamour of a tanned Southern California girl into the hands of pallid tweens across America in the early 1970s. Fifty years on, the tanning craze has not yet run its course.

The popularity of sunbathing was also fueled by the discovery of vitamin D, the "sunshine vitamin," and recognition of the salutary effects of heliotherapy in reversing the course of rickets and tuberculosis. But it wasn't just this knowledge, or the association of tanning with glamour and the high life, that made recreational tanning into one of the most durable and widespread leisure pastimes ever. It was the feel-good factor: the feeling of well-being and relaxation that many people felt after being in the sun. It is still not clear exactly why tanning makes people feel good. There is some evidence that the habit of tanning is reinforced in some people because UVR produces natural opioids in the skin, specifically the potent neurotransmitter beta-endorphin. Endorphins produce the pleasant feeling sometimes known as runner's high: it is associated with prolonged aerobic exercise and implicated in exercise addiction. The deduction follows that suntanning may be addictive. In one study, frequent tanners were given a drug that blocked the action of opioids. Four out of eight experienced withdrawal symptoms before UVR exposure.[4] This finding suggests that UVR tanning has addictive effects in frequent tanners and that these effects are based on the production of opioids in the body. This conclusion was strengthened by the results of a recent survey showing that more than 30 percent of undergraduates frequenting indoor tanning facilities in a north-

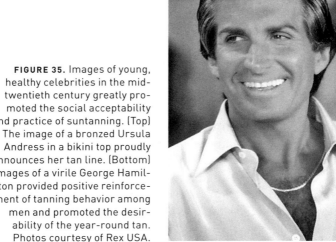

FIGURE 35. Images of young, healthy celebrities in the mid-twentieth century greatly promoted the social acceptability and practice of suntanning. (Top) The image of a bronzed Ursula Andress in a bikini top proudly announces her tan line. (Bottom) Images of a virile George Hamilton provided positive reinforcement of tanning behavior among men and promoted the desirability of the year-round tan. Photos courtesy of Rex USA.

eastern American city met standard criteria for addiction.[5] The urge for tanning was reinforced by a desire for appearance enhancement, feelings of relaxation, improved mood, and better socialization. Much remains to be learned about the brain's responses to UVR and the physiological mechanisms of tanning addiction, but the reality of the phenomenon is no longer denied.

Tanning, or at least having a tanned look, can also be reinforced by social interactions with family members, close friends, and romantic partners. Young women, especially, are much more likely to want to get a tan if their friends enjoy tanning and if friends, family, and significant others tell them that they look more attractive with a tan. Conversely, if family or close friends discourage tanning, they are much less likely to engage in it. In Asia, tanning never became popular in the mid-twentieth century because tanned or dark skin was still associated with low status and poor marriage prospects. Another reason for its lack of popularity may have to do with the physical reactions to UVR among people from East Asia (China, Korea, and Japan). A higher dose of UVR is required to induce melanin production in the first place, but once a tan is achieved, it lasts much longer.[6] Marriageable young women, in particular, were disparaged and scolded if they came home with a tan. Asians living in Europe and the Americas tend to have more permissive attitudes toward tanning with each successive generation, but deliberate tanning is still not as popular as it is among most people of European descent.

Deep tanning became very popular in Europe and the Americas from the mid-1960s through the mid-1980s, before the risks of skin cancer from UVR exposure were widely known. Baby oil or heavily scented tanning oil was sometimes applied to the skin for a basting effect (figure 36). As the dangers of UVR exposure started to become more widely known in the 1980s, tanning products started including ingredients that provided sun protection, but these were often spurned by serious tanners. For many years, it seemed impossible to be too tanned, although people who obviously worked to maintain their tans were considered vain. Images of spontaneous and "sun-kissed" tans were wildly popular and spurred the development of cosmetic bronzers that imitated the pattern of sunlight falling on the face. Synonymous with glamour, the good life, and good health, suntans were used to advertise everything from chewing gum to motorcycles.

FIGURE 36. Recreational tanning took off in the 1960s and 1970s, when it was common to see people "working on their tans" at the beach, at the pool, and in the backyard. Photo by Jack Dallinger, courtesy of Matthew Dallinger.

THE TANNING INDUSTRY

Although outdoor tanning had the advantage of being free, it wasn't possible for everyone who wanted a tan to lie outside in the middle of the day to catch rays. The first tanning salon in the United States opened in 1978, and by 1988 more than 18,000 tanning establishments were in business. By 2010, the number had grown to nearly 24,000, and the tanning industry was estimated to be worth $2.82 billion. Tanning parlors made it possible to get a tan at any time of the day or year and promised to deliver tans quickly and safely. The highest densities of tanning facilities in the United States developed in cities with low UV indexes and lots of lightly pigmented people.[7] On-demand tanning in posh salons acquired its own special cachet and has remained popular because of its association with busy celebrities—and the possibility of getting the "vacation look" without the vacation.

When the risks of skin cancer associated with UVR started to be publicized in the 1980s and 1990s, tanning remained popular. Informed of the dangers of skin cancer, many people displayed an unrealistic belief that they were not at risk.[8] Campaigns aimed especially at indoor tanners in the late 1980s emphasized the tremendously elevated risk (a 75 percent greater chance) of melanoma among frequent indoor tanners. These campaigns were effective, but only to a point. In surveys, the percentage of individuals who knew about the importance of limiting tanning to prevent melanoma increased greatly between 1988 and 1994, from 25 percent to 77 percent, but by 2007 the percentage had dropped to 67 percent. The titles of scientific papers published during the 1990s about the risks of tanning (especially in salons) betrayed the growing exasperation in medical circles over tanning behavior: "North Carolina Tanning Operators: Hazard on the Horizon?" (1992), "New Campaigns Needed to Remind the Public of the Dangers of Tanning Salons" (1994), and "There's No Such Thing as a Healthy Glow: Cutaneous Malignant Melanoma" (1997).[9]

Public health messages about the hazards of UVR tanning met with resistance or were ignored, in large part because tans were still considered attractive. The compliment "You look great with a tan" was sufficient to induce most people to continue tanning even if they knew it was harmful. Improvements in chemical sunscreens in the 1990s made it possible for people to feel safe while spending more time in the sun (box 29). Sunscreens with higher SPFs made it possible to get a "slow tan" and implied a reduced cancer risk.[10]

BOX 29   **Chemical Sunscreens and SPF**

Sunscreens are generally classified as organic or inorganic. The organic variety includes old formulations like PABA (para-aminobenzoic acid) and various cinnamates (related to the flavor components of cinnamon), along with newer compounds like Mexoryl SX (terephthalydene dicamphor sulphonic acid). These sunscreens work by absorbing UVR and then dissipating the energy via heat or light.[1] Inorganic sunscreens like titanium dioxide and zinc oxide reflect or scatter UVR by creating a physical barrier layer between sunlight and the skin.

Chemical sunscreens are rated according to their sun protection factor, or SPF. The SPF is a measure of how much UVR is required to produce sunburn in the presence of sunscreen relative to the amount required to produce sunburn on unprotected skin. As the SPF value increases, sunburn protection increases. The SPF is related not to the length of time of UVR exposure but to the amount, which is always highest at midday. Lightly pigmented people, who absorb more UVR than darkly pigmented people, require a higher-SPF sunscreen to protect themselves from UVR damage.

In the United States, the Food and Drug Administration has recently required that manufacturers of chemical sunscreens be able to prove protection against both UVA and UVB when claiming that an agent is "broad spectrum." It also stipulates that a sunscreen's water resistance be stated on the packaging. Sunscreens can be stated to offer protection for either forty or eighty minutes without reapplication.[2] The agency has also recommended that the maximum SPF claimed on product labels be "50+." For adequate sun protection, chemical sunscreens of at least SPF 15 should be applied according to manufacturers' directions and reapplied at least every two hours, or more frequently if the user is swimming or sweating.

1. For a comprehensive review of the mechanisms of action of chemical sunscreens, see Antoniou et al. 2008.

2. See United States Food and Drug Administration 2011.

TANOREXIA AND SUNLESS TANNING

Positive images of tanned people continued to grace video screens and magazines through the 1990s even as the risk of skin cancer from sun exposure became more widely known. Popular reaction to skin cancer risk from sun exposure was predictable. Many people used more sunscreen or sun protection and avoided intense sun exposure. Others did not change their behavior because a "natural tan" felt too good, "looked better," and brought compliments and approval. Between 1988 and 2007, indoor tanning among young adults in the United States increased from 1 percent to 27 percent.[11]

The persistence of tanning behavior in the face of known risks of skin aging and skin cancer is a major public health problem similar to smoking. "Like a drink or a cigarette," one study reported, "a sort of elation or relief offered by a tanning bed seems to eclipse thoughts of cancer patients, premature aging, or even physical disfigurement."[12] Those who seemed to be addicted to tanning were called "tanorexics" (box 30).

Many people who heeded warnings about the risks of UVR and reduced or eliminated UVR tanning still wanted a tanned look. During the 1990s and 2000s, they increasingly turned to sunless tanning agents to compensate for the lost glow. Sunless-tanning or self-tanning products are based on the action of dihydroxyacetone, or DHA, a com-

BOX 30   **Tanorexia**

The word *tanorexia* was coined in 2005 as a catchy descriptor for skin-tanning addiction. The connection to anorexia was intended to convey the seriousness of the compulsive disorder that led some to engage in UV tanning even when it led to burning, visibly accelerated skin aging, and a remarkably elevated risk of skin cancers, including melanoma. Tanorexia is considered a type of body image disorder, or body dysmorphic disorder, in which affected individuals engage in repeated checking of their appearance in the mirror, grooming, scrutinizing, and picking at their skin. Tanning addicts sometimes endure burns and subject themselves to UVR beyond the threshold necessary to get a tan. The high frequency of scorching sunburns experienced by frequent tanners leads, on average, to 700 emergency room visits per 10,000 tanning parlors every year.

Compulsive tanners are highly knowledgeable about the risks of UV tanning, but this knowledge doesn't decrease their desire to tan or discourage their pursuit of tanning opportunities. It's clearly not just the bronzing effect of UV tanning that is driving the compulsion of the tanorexic. As one tanner put it, "You might feel the same amount of self-image confidence from a spray-on tan, but it really won't affect your mood like UVB/UVA will."[1]

1. Tanning addiction has been expertly reviewed by Arienne Kourosh and colleagues (2010); quote at p. 284.

pound that reacts with proteins in the stratum corneum of the skin to impart a brown color similar to that produced by the tanning response. The same chemical reaction occurs when bread browns during baking in the oven. DHA is a safe coloring agent and has been approved for cosmetic use by the United States Food and Drug Administration and many other comparable authorities. The skin darkening produced by DHA confers minimal UVR protection. And because a DHA tan is a cosmetic dyeing of the surface of the skin, it lasts only a few days.[13] A natural tan is a complex mixture of yellow and red colors, but a DHA "tan" is yellower in most light-skinned people. The sallow color of DHA-tanned skin discouraged many people from using sunless tanning agents when they first appeared. This drawback has been remedied by the addition of antioxidants to DHA formulations. Even so, sunless tanning products used by people with naturally pale or lightly pigmented skin can produce an obviously artificial, deeply bronzed,

FIGURE 37. At a celebrity event, the naturally lightly pigmented actor Anne Hathaway stands next to the visibly artificially tanned clothing designer Valentino. Sunless tans provide the social benefits of a natural tan without the risk of UVR exposure, but deep artificial tans can look incongruous. Photo courtesy of Rex USA.

deck-stained look (figure 37). The social calculus that goes into determining the most desirable level of artificial tan is complex, and errors are widely ridiculed.

Sunless tanning agents, which can be applied as creams or liquids at home, or sprayed on at a tanning facility, have provided people with a safe alternative to UVR tanning. Those who use such products, however, are generally older, female, and more educated. Many teens and younger adults—those most susceptible to tanning addiction—have succumbed to the joint promotion of UVR tanning and sunless tanning at tanning parlors, often referred to as the "booth and bottle option." The indoor tanning industry endorses "controlled tanning," which is touted as being safer than "uncontrolled" beach tanning, and fights for the legal right to "protect the freedom of individuals to acquire a suntan, via natural or artificial light."[14] Thus sunless tanning can be misused in the continued promotion of a tanned look to young, suggestible people.

After it became unfashionable to talk about celebrity suntanning, the rhetoric shifted to extolling the "healthy glow." Although the phrase was later appropriated by the "Go with Your Own Glow" nontanning movement (see below), it described for many years the "sun-kissed" look of celebrities, achieved through a combination of sunscreen-mediated UVR exposure, spray-on tanning, and cosmetics. This look remains durably associated with glamour and sex appeal, partly as a result of heavy promotion among teens by the indoor tanning industry. Highly visible and widely imitated female celebrities such as Jennifer Lopez combine UVR and sunless tanning and sustain the association of a tanned appearance with prestige and popularity.

THE NONTANNING AND "GO WITH YOUR OWN GLOW" MOVEMENT

More female celebrities today are proudly pale, including some—like Victoria Beckham and Nicola Roberts—who have explicitly abandoned the bronzed look.[15] The "Go with Your Own Glow" campaign of the Skin Cancer Foundation champions the ideal of radiant, natural, untanned skin and has declared the tanned look passé. This movement has gained impetus among socially responsible female celebrities who recognize that their looks and behavior powerfully influence millions of young women who are in their most vulnerable years for sun exposure that could lead to cancer later in life. Suntanning and artificial tanning will wane in popularity only when there is no longer social reinforcement for the tanned look. Pallor and even unnatural paleness are currently in fashion because of the popularity of attractive vampires, but it is hard to know if this fascination will last. A survey of 2,000 British women between the ages of 18 and 44, conducted in 2011 for the launch of a new television channel, found that 69 percent felt that having a tan made them feel healthier, and more than half said that a tan gave them more confidence when socializing.[16] These results suggest that it will take a long time before the tanned look fades.

15

Living in Color

There is no topic more illustrative of human history than skin color. It unites us in evolution and divides us by walls of bias and stereotype. It invites us to learn about the life and times of our distant ancestors and taunts us with evidence of the psychological manipulation of modern peoples. Human beings are highly visually oriented and suggestible primates, ever willing to accede to the beliefs of people who have power over us and ever able to change our behavior.

Skin and skin pigmentation were intensely influenced by evolutionary processes for hundreds of thousands of years of human evolution because skin, and skin alone, was our interface with the environment. Variation in human skin pigmentation was produced by evolution, and the processes by which this variation came about are well understood. Different skin tones evolved as humans dispersed into places with different levels of UVR. Adaptive changes in skin color depended first on the occurrence of random mutations to produce the genetic variation necessary to change skin pigmentation and then on natural selection to make those mutations the norm. The melanin that imparts color to human skin is an excellent natural sunscreen that protects the body from the most destructive effects of UVR while allowing some of this radiation to penetrate and stimulate vitamin D production. The degree of melanin pigmentation in the skin is thus an exquisite evolutionary compromise.

For most of human history, people's skin pigmentation was well matched to their varying environments. Dark pigmentation protected people living in places with high UVR, and varying degrees of depigmentation allowed people to live healthily by enabling vitamin D production even in places with moderate or low levels of UVR. This equilibrium has been upset, especially in the past four hundred years, by long-distance travel and indoor lifestyles. Many people live in places distant from their ancestral homelands and often under UVR conditions dramatically different from those experienced by their ancestors for thousands of years. Mismatches between skin pigmentation and local UVR conditions have led to a host of health problems. People with little skin pigment suffer from the effects of too much UVR, and those with considerable melanin pigment suffer from the effects of too little. Now that a working understanding of both of these situations is at hand, serious health problems like skin cancer, folate and vitamin D deficiency, and the many diseases caused by vitamin D deficiency can be avoided. Knowledge of human evolution and of the movements and habits of people throughout history can lead to immediate improvements in human health.

There have never been any "pure" human populations or races. Archaeological and genetic evidence show us that during Neolithic times (roughly 10,000–3000 BCE), considerable intermingling of populations occurred. This was mostly a gradual ebbing and flowing of people according to changes in weather and climate and the introduction of agriculture and growth of populations. This mixing resulted in human populations on all continents being mutts and mongrels, some more so than others. Just as rapid and long-distance migrations affected our health, they also affected the ways people regarded and treated others. For thousands of years, the physical differences between "us" and "them" were generally minor. Even in ancient Egypt, where people of different skin tones and appearances came into regular contact, differences in appearance were not impediments to social and economic exchange, and meetings were mostly among social equals.

From the fifteenth century onward, abrupt encounters between different populations became frequent as seafarers, explorers, and traders in modern sailing boats came into contact with people on distant shores. These meetings often brought together people not only of different skin colors but also of different languages, cultures, and habits. Skin color nonetheless emerged as the most salient characteristic, around which stereotypes coalesced. More than anything else, it signified otherness.

Preliminary voyages and meetings matured into regular trading routes and associations. Some of these involved the mutual exchange of lucrative objects, but most involved highly asymmetrical relationships in which one side benefited inordinately at the expense of the other. At first, humans constituted a small fraction of trade objects, but by the mid-fifteenth century slaves had become commodities essential to the emergence and growth of modern commerce. The negativity of stereotypes associated with African slaves increased over time. Black and white polarities of color and morality were reinforced and biblical justifications invoked to render the dark-skinned less than human and defend their continued exploitation as slaves. The European intelligentsia contributed to these attitudes by supporting the development of schemes of human classification that ranked the peoples of the world by skin color, cultural potential, and social worth.

Races were born from this urge to categorize. Created by men considered to be intellectual leaders, races were defined as authoritative categories. Skin color was the essential characteristic that gave a race its social valence and established its place in an explicit hierarchy. Other traits considered definitive were physiognomy, temperament, and culture. From the outset, there was never anything objective or scientific about races. They were congeries of physical and cultural traits, defined by people who had a steadfast belief in their own superiority and most of whom had never seen those they were defining. Race definitions changed over time and from one place to another, so that a partial list of race names reads like a catalog of arbitrariness: Aborigine, African, alpine, Arab, Asian, Australoid, Bantu, black, Caribbean, Capoid, Caucasoid, coloured, Indian, Jew, Latino, Malay, Mediterranean, mestizo, Mongoloid, mulatto, Negro, Nordic, Oriental, Semitic, white. In the twentieth century, defining the Jewish race by religion rather than skin color set the stage for arbitrary discrimination and brutal subjugation.

The ordering of races according to skin color has been one of the most stable intellectual constructs of all time, even though the number, inclusivity, and acceptability of racial categories have varied greatly. Races are socially constructed and regularly reconstructed. Because they have become institutional facts, races have persisted along with the implicit hierarchies from which they arose. When people persist in acting on their beliefs about race, they maintain a society in which access to the goods of society—such as quality education, high-status jobs, good housing, and good medical care—is stratified by race. Race becomes a destination, not just a label. Perpetuation of the false idea that races represent real biological entities promotes the notion that racial inequities are acceptable and lessens the interest of people in interacting with those placed in racial out-groups.[1]

Skin color is a lasting statement of our evolutionary history. It is a biological trait—an adaptation to the environment—that has come to have many layers of social meaning. It has continued to be important in human affairs despite laws in many countries prohibiting formal color- or raced-based discrimination. The already robust associations of skin tone with human worth have been further reinforced by the world- wide marketing of skin-lightening agents by international cosmetics conglomerates and the widespread propagation of images depicting people with lighter skin tones as being happier and more successful than those with dark skin. The so-called postracial era in the United States and other developed nations is one in which the most darkly pig- mented people of varying ancestries still occupy the periphery of soci- ety. The negative effects of dark skin pigmentation on health and socio- economic status are magnified by physical marginalization, by lack of access to better food, education, and health care, and by stress result- ing from persistent discrimination.

We understand how skin color evolved, how it is perceived, how it came to be judged, how it came to be associated with other traits in race categories, and how judgments about it have come to be rigid, col- lectively reinforced, and spread through time and space. We also know from ancient and recent history that the suffering caused by color-based discrimination has cost millions of lives and, for many, is still acute. The diminishing of a human being on the basis of skin color lays bare the worst aspects of our visual orientation, suggestibility, imitativeness, and status consciousness.

Motivation is critical to the elimination of color-based discrimina- tion. The bodies of understanding we now have about skin color need to be matched by the will to change. This is a process in which no one is a spectator: we are all participants.

Notes

1. Sanjek 1994.

1. SKIN'S NATURAL PALETTE

1. The structure, properties, and evolutionary history of human skin are discussed in the first three chapters of my book *Skin: A Natural History* (Jablonski 2006).

2. Dilation of blood vessels in the skin as a response to exercise, orgasm, or emotional stimuli occurs in all people, but the redness may be masked by melanin in the skin. It was once thought that people with darkly pigmented skin did not blush with embarrassment or flush with anger, but this belief is false: the same physiological responses occur, even if they are not obvious. Blushing is discussed in Jablonski 2006, chapter 8, and at length in Gerlach et al. 2001 and Bogels and Lamer 2002.

3. Recent studies indicate that eumelanin can take a wide variety of forms because of the different ways in which the several building blocks of the color-bearing portion (or chromophore) of eumelanin combine with different proteins. Thus chemists are becoming more interested not only in the primary structure or elemental composition of the compound, but also in the secondary structure—the physical arrangement into helixes or sheets—that the different forms of the substance take during life. See Meredith and Sarna 2006.

4. Free radicals, or reactive oxygen species, are small molecules produced when UVR or other forms of high-energy radiation affect cells. UVR damage in the body results not only from the radiation itself but also from the free radicals it generates. The properties of UVR and its effects on biological systems are discussed in greater detail in Jablonski 2006, chapter 4. Many other

accessible and comprehensive references describe the effects of UVR on life in general and in humans: see Caldwell et al. 1998; Hitchcock 2001; Sinha and Hader 2002; Pfeifer, You, and Besaratinia 2005.

5. The antioxidant properties of the melanin in the retinal pigment epithelium (RPE) help to maintain the integrity of the retina during life and preserve the acuity of our vision. These properties appear to diminish with age (Wang, Dillon, and Gaillard 2006; Zareba et al. 2006).

6. Zecca et al. 2001.

7. Elucidation of the nature of the relationship between keratinocytes and melanocytes, and of the mechanisms of melanin production and delivery in mammalian cells, has required intensive, long-term research (Jimbow et al. 1976; Quevedo 1976; Schallreuter 2007; Goding 2007). Disruption of the control of keratinocytes over melanocytes is the fundamental cause of melanoma.

8. The regulation of tyrosinase activity in melanocytes in differently colored people is complex: see Sturm, Teasdale, and Fox 2001; Alaluf et al. 2002. Deliberate bleaching of skin, discussed in chapter 13, is achieved mostly by chemicals that disrupt the production or activity of tyrosinase.

9. Pheomelanin makes up only a small fraction of the melanin content in human skin, even in people with very fair skin, but its presence alters the reflection of visible light sufficiently to give certain skins a yellowish cast (Thody et al. 1991; Alaluf et al. 2002).

10. The genetic basis and different manifestations of albinism and vitiligo are discussed at length in Robins 1991 and Goding 2007.

11. People with albinism have long been targets of discrimination in Africa and other parts of the world, but the spate of recent killings in eastern Africa appears to be a recent phenomenon. Reports of these killings and the trials of accused murderers have been covered by various news media. See Kapama 2009; Siyame 2009. Some organizations, like the Tanzania Albinos Centre (www.tanzaniaalbino.org), provide social and medical support for people with albinism in Africa as well as physical protection and shelter from persecution.

12. Many measurements of skin pigmentation among the world's indigenous peoples, including some of the only measurements from extirpated or extinct native groups from Australia, were made using von Luschan skin-color tiles.

13. The measurement of skin pigmentation is succinctly reviewed by Pamela Byard in her classic paper on the genetics of skin color (Byard 1981). The outdated genetics in this paper detract relatively little from the value of the review.

14. This difference was measured precisely by Tadokoro and colleagues in skin samples from "black" and "white" American populations (Tadokoro et al. 2003). The same investigators also carefully measured the amount of DNA damage that occurred after UVR exposure in the same populations. The DNA of more darkly pigmented individuals suffered less damage than that of the lightly pigmented group.

15. This response characterizes people belonging to skin phototype I. Six human skin phototypes have been defined, ranging from type I, which never tans at all, to type VI, which is capable of prodigious melanin production. These are discussed in Jablonski 2006, chapter 5, and in dermatology textbooks: see Fitzpatrick and Ortonne 2003.

16. DNA can repair much of the damage caused to its structure by high-energy radiation, but insufficient repair can be followed by errors in DNA duplication that produce the mutations leading to cancer. For reviews of the relationship between UVR damage and skin cancer, see Cleaver and Crowley 2002; Matsumura and Ananthawamy 2004.

17. The redistribution of melanin within the epidermis as part of tanning has been documented in human subjects from eastern Asia, equatorial Africa, and northern Europe (Tadokoro et al. 2005).

18. See Ortonne 1990; Fisher et al. 2002.

19. Fink and Matts 2008.

2. ORIGINAL SKIN

1. Many excellent resources on the fossil and genetic evidence for human origins are available in printed and electronic form. Some of the most reliable electronic resources are the Becoming Human website of the Institute of Human Origins (www.becominghuman.org) and the American Museum of Natural History's Hall of Human Origins (www.amnh.org/exhibitions/permanent/humanorigins/). Good and up-to-date books include Carl Zimmer, *Smithsonian Intimate Guide to Human Origins* (2005) and Chris Stringer and Peter Andrews, *The Complete World of Human Evolution* (2005). The physical appearance of the last common ancestor of chimpanzees and humans and the reconstruction of the characteristics of the skin of the earliest members of the human lineage are discussed in Jablonski 2006, chapter 2. For more detailed accounts, see Jablonski and Chaplin 2000; Jablonski 2004.

2. Some of the more complete skeletons of early members of the genus *Homo* from West Turkana in Kenya and Dmanisi in Georgia indicate that by 1.5 million years ago, hominids had modern limb proportions: long thighs and short forearms. Studies of the limb proportions and joints show that these hominids were capable of long-distance travel, including sustained running. A wide range of studies on the relevant fossil evidence, the evolution of human walking and running, and the human diet include Walker and Leakey 1993; Leonard and Robertson 1994; Aiello and Wheeler 1995; Bramble and Lieberman 2004; and Lordkipanidze et al. 2007.

3. On the importance and evolution of eccrine sweating (that is, the process of producing watery sweat from eccrine sweat glands), see Jablonski 2006, chapter 3. All mammals sweat, but not all use sweating as their primary mode of cooling in hot environments or during exertion, as primates do. Chimpanzees, with sweat glands confined mostly to the armpits, overheat more quickly than primates like patas monkeys, which have sweat glands distributed over the surface of their bodies (Whitford 1976; Elizondo 1988). In some mammals, a mechanism known as selective brain cooling works together with sweating to help maintain body and brain temperatures within tolerable limits (Brinnel, Cabanac, and Hales 1987). The evolution of increased numbers of eccrine sweat glands in humans accompanied the trend toward hairlessness. Sweating requires routine rehydration (see Wheeler 1992).

4. The sequencing of the human and chimpanzee genomes confirmed infer-

ences that we differ from our close relatives in several genes related to brain structure and function. Comparative genomics has provided some interesting surprises, including some related to differences in the sense of smell and in the genes coding for the keratin proteins of the epidermis (Chimpanzee Sequencing and Analysis Consortium 2005). Differences in keratins between humans and chimpanzees are probably related to enhanced barrier functions of human skin, including improved resistance to abrasion, the functioning of human sweat glands, and the nature of human hair. Human sweat glands are lined by a large number of different types of keratin (including one unique to humans) that contribute to maintaining the integrity of the gland under mechanical stress (Langbein et al. 2005). Human skin contains more than fifty different types of keratin, and their properties are of great interest because of human interest in the natural and pathological appearance of skin and hair (Schweizer et al. 2007). The last major question remaining to be answered about the evolution of human skin is exactly how and when the number of eccrine sweat glands increased.

5. In their original paper, Alan Rogers and colleagues (2004) calculated an estimated time for the African *MC1R* selective sweep based on estimates of population size. The estimate of 1.2 million years was derived from a population estimate of 14,000. Even with a much larger population, the estimated time for fixation of the African *MC1R* would be 560,000 years. They consider the older estimate the more accurate.

6. The morbidity and mortality from all types of skin cancer in different human groups have been extensively studied. The most serious type of skin cancer, cutaneous melanoma, is also the rarest. Although the prevalence of this cancer is increasing in lightly pigmented populations, the average age of onset is fifty, long past the prime reproductive years (Bishop et al. 2007). The prevalence and effects of serious sunburns have been studied mostly in relation to skin cancer, and strong links between repeated painful sunburns before the age of twenty and cutaneous melanoma have been established (Kennedy et al. 2003). Serious sunburns alone are rarely linked to harmful immediate side effects other than pain. In only one study was the incidence of serious sunburn reported as part of overall statistics on burns. This was a one-year prospective study from an Irish hospital in which 16 of 336 cases (4.7 percent) of all burns were caused by serious sunburn. See Cronin et al. 1996.

7. See Chaplin and Jablonski 1998; Jablonski and Chaplin 2000; Jablonski 2004.

8. See Branda and Eaton 1978. Branda went on to write other papers on folate physiology but did not pursue the phenomenon of nutrient photolysis.

9. Studies conducted in Australia and the United Kingdom demonstrate a causal relationship between folate deficiencies and neural tube defects (NTDs) (Bower and Stanley 1989, 1992; MRC Vitamin Study Research Group 1991). These and other studies demonstrating the many important roles of folate were influential in the introduction in 1998 of folate fortification of the flour used to make most breads and breakfast cereals in the United States and Canada. Adequate folate intake is important for all women of reproductive age. Folate supplementation before and around the time of conception decreases NTDs by 50 to 70 percent (Copp, Fleming, and Greene 1998; Fleming and Copp 1998).

10. The probable importance of folate in spermatogenesis was first noted more than thirty years ago. Low folate levels are associated with damaged DNA in sperm and reduced male fertility (Boxmeer et al. 2009; Mathur et al. 1977).

11. The investigation of the effects of UVA on human plasma by Der-Petrossian and colleagues (2007) was the first to provide a controlled quantitative analysis of the chemical transformation of folate in human blood by UVR. Research to understand the effects of UVR on vitamin levels using model systems with the properties of skin has been led by Johan Moan and colleagues from the University of Oslo and other institutions in Norway. His group has produced a series of important technical papers on the kinetics of folate photolysis and the relevance of this problem to the evolution of skin pigmentation (Off et al 2005; Nielsen et al. 2006; Vorobey et al. 2006).

12. Investigations of the photosensitivity of folate under different conditions in vitro and in vivo have demonstrated that the relationship between skin pigmentation and folate metabolism is complicated. It involves direct photodegradation of folate (in its main form of 5-methyltetrahydrofolate, or 5-MTHF) as well as its photodegradation in the presence of flavins and porphyrins by reactive oxygen species. Considerable epidemiological work is needed to investigate the relationship between skin pigmentation, folate metabolism, and the prevalence of NTDs, but a protective effect of dark pigmentation against folate depletion is apparent (Off et al. 2005; Steindal et al. 2006, 2008; Tam et al. 2009; Lawrence 1983; Lamparelli et al. 1988; Leck 1984; Buccimazza et al. 1994).

13. The prevalence of NTDs in populations of different skin colors has been examined in South Africa and in the United States. The U.S. studies have investigated the effect of folic-acid fortification of foods on the frequency of NTDs in different groups. Rates of NTDs in these countries were not significantly affected by the introduction of folate fortification, but rates among the more lightly pigmented groups were (Buccimazza et al. 1994; Williams et al. 2005; Besser, Williams, and Cragan 2007).

14. Relatively few investigations of heat tolerance in humans have explored the effect of skin color on heat loads under various conditions. The most important was conducted by the biological anthropologist Paul Baker, on a sample of two hundred American enlisted soldiers (Baker 1958).

3. OUT OF THE TROPICS

1. The evolution of the human diet has been studied from many aspects. The transition from an exclusively or mostly vegetarian diet to one that included more meat occurred about 2 to 1.5 million years ago, as judged by anatomical, genetic, and chemical analyses. See Milton 1987, 1993; Leonard and Robertson 1994; Schoeninger et al. 2001; Finch and Stanford 2004.

2. J. Desmond Clark was an expert on the early evolution of the genus *Homo* and the rise of Paleolithic cultures. He conducted extensive archaeological studies in Africa and later in China. His insight into human behavior in the past was based on his compendious knowledge of stone tools and of all the

other challenges of the environment that humans coped with in the past. Our understanding of the early evolution of the genus *Homo* has increased in the past fifteen years with important fossil discoveries outside Africa. For a good review of the fossil evidence, dating, and natural history of early *Homo*, see Antón 2003. For a useful overview of the entire genus *Homo*, see Finlayson 2005. Evidence for the timing and nature of the first dispersal out of Africa has also grown considerably in recent decades. Good sources of information include Turner 1984, 1992, and Gabunia et al. 2001.

3. Fish have a limited ability to manufacture vitamin D in their skin and can do so only when exposed for a long time to short-wavelength UVR, a situation that would rarely occur in nature. Fish are one of the best dietary sources of vitamin D because they eat the organisms at the bottom of the food chain that manufacture vitamin D precursors. Fish that eat other fish are richer sources of vitamin D for the same reason. See Rao and Raghuramulu 1996; Lall and Lewis-McCrea 2007. Excellent reviews of the physiology of vitamin D and role of the vitamin in tetrapod evolution have been written by Michael Holick, known as the father of vitamin D research: see Holick 2003. I take exception only to his statements that vitamin D deficiency did not become a problem for humans until the industrial revolution: it has been an issue for humans for thousands of years.

4. In vitro and in vivo studies have shown that UVR penetration is related to the amount and distribution of melanin in the epidermis, with more super-ficial melanosomes closer to the surface being more effective in reducing pre–vitamin D production (Jablonski and Chaplin 2000; Clemens et al. 1982; Nielsen et al. 2006).

5. See Murray 1934; Loomis 1967. Loomis is generally credited with dis-covering the relationship between vitamin D and skin pigmentation, but the credit for the original insight goes to Murray.

6. Mawer's classic study showed that the main stores of vitamin D in the body were in fat and skeletal muscle; the viscera (including the liver), blood, and bone accounted for very small percentages (Mawer et al. 1972). Ash-ley Robins has persistently claimed that vitamin D stored in human tissues was sufficient to supply the body's needs during the months when cutane-ous production of the vitamin was impossible, and that no selective pressure for loss of skin pigmentation existed in hominids. His opinions are at odds with what is now known about the effects of dark skin pigmentation on vitamin D production and on the distribution of wavelengths of UVR suit-able to catalyze vitamin D production in the skin at higher latitudes during the year (Robins 2009). For the other side of the argument, see Chaplin and Jablonski 2009.

7. Research on skin and hair pigmentation genes in mammals is being con-ducted in many laboratories around the world, and the literature on genetic variation at pigmentation loci is now vast. The best current reviews of this literature are Sturm 2006 and 2009. For two other useful reviews, see Rees 2003; Barsh and Cotsarelis 2007. Variation in the *MC1R* (also known as the *agouti*) locus is widespread in mammals and underpins the variation that we observe in the hair colors of many mammals. For information on the relative

pheomelanin and eumelanin content of human skin and hair in different people, see Thody et al. 1991.

8. *MC1R* is the gene best known for its role in determining human skin, hair, and eye color, but numerous other genes have been related to subtleties of coloration and tanning ability in different human populations: see Sturm 2009.

9. The discovery of the *golden* gene in zebrafish was the result of elegant experimental design and tremendous amounts of work. The truly creative part of this work was the sequence of the investigation, which involved the inactivation of the golden zebrafish pigment gene, then the rescue of the gene by the mRNA of the human gene equivalent, as demonstrated by the production of golden pigment. The original paper (Lamason et al. 2005) is already a classic of experimental genetics.

10. The reconstruction of *Homo neanderthalensis* with relatively light (but tanned) skin and light hair appears as plate 8 in Jablonski 2006. The reconstruction was created by the expert paleo-reconstruction artist Mauricio Antón under my direction. A light-skinned condition for Neanderthals was discussed earlier by others (Michlovic, Hall, and Maggs 1977).

11. The sequencing of mitochondrial DNA (mtDNA) from a Neanderthal (Krings et al. 1997) was a momentous achievement that inaugurated the modern era of ancient DNA studies. The publication of the protein-coding sequence for the *MC1R* allele in a Neanderthal was another discovery that indicated that Neanderthals had evolved a functional variant form of a gene independently from modern humans (Lalueza-Fox et al. 2007).

12. The most recent comparisons of the Neanderthal and modern human genomes demonstrate that 3 to 4 percent of modern human DNA is identical to that of Neanderthals, suggesting that some interbreeding of the lineages occurred. The genes coding the MC1R protein are distinct, however, in the two lineages. This example illustrates how useful the sequencing of the Neanderthal genome has been in illustrating examples of probable positive selection in the genome. See Noonan 2010.

4. SKIN COLOR IN THE MODERN WORLD

1. Most of the hominid lineages that evolved in the past 5 million years are extinct. The fate of the descendants of the first dispersal from the African tropics is still much discussed and contested. Advocates of the Neanderthal introgression (interbreeding) model are still vocal, and new genetic evidence indicates that some interbreeding between modern humans and Neanderthals did occur, with the result that Neanderthal DNA represents a small fraction of the modern European genome. See Antón 2003; Finlayson 2005; Wall and Hammer 2006.

2. Discoveries in the Middle Awash area of Ethiopia have shed new light on the early history of modern humans. Remains of *Homo sapiens* dating to between 160,000 and 154,000 years ago have been found in association with a range of stone tools, including obsidian blades, and bones of butchered animals. Evidence of careful removal of flesh from some of the human bones suggests that ritual mortuary practices were undertaken. See Clark et al. 2003.

3. Paul Mellars (2006) provides an excellent review of the evidence for the

emergence of behavioral modernity in *Homo sapiens* in Africa and the likely timing and nature of the dispersal that occurred around 65,000 years ago.

4. Vigilant et al. 1991; Knight et al. 2003.

5. The genetic diversity within and between African populations has been ascribed to the length of continuous habitation and the influence of many historical migration events. Three excellent reviews of this subject are available: Relethford 2008; Tishkoff et al. 2009; MacEachern 2000.

6. Data on skin reflectance in sub-Saharan African populations recently collected by the anthropological geneticist Sarah Tishkoff (personal communication) indicates considerable variation within populations from the Horn of Africa. This probably comes from variation at genes other than the *MC1R* locus, which is virtually invariant among African populations. Research is now ongoing to determine the relative contributions to skin tone of genetic variation, environmental variation, and migration (gene flow).

7. The most comprehensive studies on Egyptian population history have been undertaken by the physician and anthropologist S.O.Y. Keita. Keita's evidence strengthens the case for the dynamic intermingling of African populations through time. See Keita 2005.

8. The history of contact between peoples of different colors in Greece, Rome, and ancient Egypt has been carefully documented in a readable and authoritative book by Frank Snowden (1983). The general descriptor *Mediterranean* is used to describe the skin of all peoples living around the Mediterranean. This region comprises many groups and countries and is characterized by seasonally variable levels of UVR. According to a recent paper, unexposed Mediterranean skin is "ten times lighter" than skin that is routinely exposed to the sun: see El-Mofty, Esmat, and Abdel-Halim 2007.

9. The reconstruction of Tutankhamun commissioned by the National Geographic Society is described on the Society's website in "King Tut's New Face: Behind the Forensic Reconstruction" (National Geographic Society 2005). This reconstruction effort was focused on the overall shape of the young king's head. The teams participating in the reconstruction specifically did not comment on skin color, but the magazine depicted the young king with a tawny skin tone as a reasonable approximation. This choice was contentious because some groups have contended that Tutankhamun had darkly pigmented skin and looked more "African."

10. The peopling of the Americas and of the Pacific has been studied extensively by archaeologists, historical linguists, and molecular geneticists. Colonization of the Americas occurred along the west coast and by hinterland routes, the coastal route offering particularly rich and dependable food resources. See Erlandson et al. 2011. By about 11,500 years ago, human populations extended through most of North and South America. An authoritative review of the molecular evidence for the earliest Americans by Goebel and colleagues (2008) is highly recommended, along with chapters from my edited volume, *The First Americans* (Jablonski 2002). There is less consensus concerning the peopling of the Pacific. Molecular markers suggest initial egress from Taiwan and subsequent movements from an expanded population base in Melanesia. See Hagelberg et al. 1999; Underhill et al. 2001.

11. See Makova and Norton 2005; Sturm 2009.

12. The prehistory of Melanesia has excited archaeologists and geneticists in recent years because the span of time involved is so long and the history of human interchange is so complex. Some of the most interesting research into patterns of human habitation in Melanesia has explored the genetics of the rats that accompanied humans when the latter dispersed to different islands in the region. The study by Norton and colleagues on the diversity of skin and hair pigmentation provides ample data and ideas about the factors that may have contributed to the great diversity of skin and hair colors in Melanesia. See Matisoo-Smith and Robins 2004; Norton et al. 2006.

13. Data on reflected UVR from various natural surfaces is plentiful in government publications from around the world. The World Health Organization's *Global Solar UV Index* can be downloaded from www.who.int/uv/publications/en/GlobalUVI.pdf. For a useful recent publication, see Chadysiene and Girgzdys 2008.

14. Many archaeologists have been interested in the colonization of far northern latitudes because of the physical challenges that such environments posed. Good reviews of the history of human habitation in far northern Europe and Siberia include Goebel 1999 and Bergman et al. 2004.

15. See Jablonski and Chaplin 2000.

16. Many of the people inhabiting the far north, including the Saami of Finland, the Chukchi of northeastern Asia, and the Inuit of northern Canada and Alaska, are divided by scholars, and the Saami themselves, into "maritime" and "reindeer" groups that pursue marine mammal and reindeer hunting, respectively. The reindeer are considered semidomesticated, and because of their importance, their foods have been studied in detail. Reindeer eat a variety of lichens, but the true reindeer lichen, *Cladina rangiferina,* contains high amounts of vitamin D_3. Some human populations in far northern Scandinavia and North America also eat well-cooked lichens and boil them to make beverages. See Bjorn and Wang 2000.

17. Goebel's review (1999) of research on the peopling of Siberia indicates that humans living in the northern boreal forests of Siberia today rely heavily on freshwater fish caught from forest streams and then dried for winter consumption. The earliest evidence of a barbed harpoon fashioned from antler comes from an archaeological site in Spain from around 13,000 years ago.

18. These data come from a recent review of UVR reflectance from natural surfaces (Chadysiene and Girgzdys 2008).

19. The frequency of nutritional rickets and other diseases caused by vitamin D deficiency is high among Inuit and Saami people who no longer eat traditional diets rich in fish, marine mammals, or other animal sources of vitamin D. These problems are a focus of great public health attention in Arctic countries.

20. The reaction of human skin to UVR is complex, and many variables must be considered in naturalistic or experimental studies. These include a person's genetically determined (constitutive) pigmentation, the amount of skin exposed, the duration of exposure, and the time of day and year. Experimental studies of human tanning have demonstrated that for most popula-

tions, the amount of extra melanin produced by the tanning reaction is small, and its effect on UV protection is modest. Lightly pigmented people make less melanin in response to UVR than those with more darkly pigmented skin. In lightly pigmented people, the thickened stratum corneum developed in response to UVR appears to be more important than melanin production in photoprotection. Two experimental studies that bear directly on this problem are Sheehan et al. 1998 and Tadokoro et al. 2005.

21. For details on distribution of land mass relative to UVR, see Chaplin and Jablonski 1998.

22. The abrupt climatic changes of the Late Pleistocene and early Holocene have been well documented using evidence from ice cores and marine sediment cores: see Taylor et al. 1993.

23. Hundreds of scholarly books and papers provide descriptions and interpretations of early *Homo sapiens* and the rise of complex civilizations. Readers seeking a single good, up-to-date source should consult the edited volume by Christopher Scarre (2005), which provides expert and engaging descriptions of the major events in prehistory.

24. See Abu-Amero et al. 2007.

5. SHADES OF SEX

1. Males are consistently darker than females in all indigenous populations in which skin pigmentation has been measured using standard protocols for reflectometry measurements of unexposed skin on the upper inner arm site. Before measurement protocols were standardized on this bodily site, some populations appeared not to follow this pattern: these exceptions are reviewed in Kalla 1974 and Byard 1981. A paper I coauthored on the evolution of skin pigmentation (Jablonski and Chaplin 2000) provides a reasonably complete appendix of skin-reflectance readings of males and females for many populations using standard protocols and the Evans Electroselenium Limited (EEL) reflectometer.

Many explanations for the origin of sexual differences in skin pigmentation have been put forward. Ours emphasizes the foundational role of natural selection, with additive effects of sexual selection operating more in some populations than in others. Peter Frost has emphasized the primacy of sexual selection and a secondary role of natural selection in establishing sexual differences. The debate continues: see Frost 1988, 1994; Aoki 2002; Madrigal and Kelly 2007.

2. Melasma, considered by many women to be undesirable and unattractive, has become a highly emotive topic. Many popular articles and blog postings are devoted to the subject, and some contain erroneous and even potentially harmful information. It is best to discuss concerns about melasma and other types of hyperpigmentation with a health-care professional. The best scientific discussion of the causes of melasma is included in a fact-packed academic paper on human skin pigmentation in response to stress by Costin and Hearing (2007). Melasma and treatments for it (with an emphasis on European women) are also discussed by Bolanca and colleagues (2008).

3. Breast pigmentation in women depends especially on levels of the gonadal hormones progesterone and estrogen and their effects on melanocyte-stimulating hormone (MSH). Irreversible darkening of the areolae occurs in women with lightly pigmented skin after three pregnancies. For details, see Pawson and Petrakis 1975.

4. Many workers have made contributions in this area of research. Peter Frost has written thoughtful papers on this topic for more than twenty years. His original paper (coauthored with Pierre van den Berghe) set out the hypothesis that lighter skin became preferred by men as a marker of female hormonal status and presumed enhanced fertility. In a series of single-author papers, Frost has advanced the idea that more lightly pigmented human females evolved as the result of changes in the operational sex ratio, that is, the ratio of men to women available as mates. During the last ice age, a reduction in the number of men due to early mortality likely resulted in intensified competition between females for males. This competition, Frost reasoned, would have been more intense at higher latitudes. Thus, sexual selection for lighter skin would also be more intense in these locations. Frost's hypothesis has been challenged most convincingly by Lorena Madrigal and William Kelly, who analyzed the skin-reflectance data of adult males and females from many populations and found no evidence of increasing color difference with increasing latitude that would support the sexual-selection hypothesis. Their analyses, in fact, found no evidence of sexual selection at all. See Van den Berghe and Frost 1986; Frost 1994; Guthrie 1970; Madrigal and Kelly 2007.

5. See Harris 2006.

6. Ethnographic accounts of foraging activities in modern traditional gathering and hunting societies stress the active contributions made by women to hunting activities, regardless of latitude. In some places, women hunt on their own or in groups with other women and children; in others, women accompany men on long-distance hunts and help ambush or dress large game animals. There is no modern example of a traditional gathering and hunting society in which women stay at home and wait to be provisioned solely with food provided by men. See Hawkes et al. 1997; Goodman et al. 1985; McDonald et al. 1990.

7. Some scholars maintain that natural selection to enhance the potential for vitamin D production has been unimportant in human evolution and, specifically, that it played no significant role in the evolution of depigmented skin in peoples living at high latitudes. In 2002, Kenichi Aoki proposed that at high latitudes, the selection pressure for maintaining dark pigmentation would have been relaxed and that the main force driving skin-pigmentation evolution in general—in both sexes—was a universal preference for lighter-than-average skin color in a sexual partner. In this reasoning, he followed Charles Darwin in his contention that differences in skin pigmentation between different peoples were due to sexual, not natural, selection. See Aoki 2002. A convincing rebuttal of his hypothesis is included in Madrigal and Kelly 2007.

8. The physiology of pregnancy and breastfeeding in women is complicated and interesting. Women transfer both stored nutrients and those gained from immediate consumption to their developing fetuses and neonates. Because

of changes during pregnancy in the levels of hormones that regulate calcium metabolism, even women who are deficient in vitamin D can produce infants with normal skeletons because the calcium reserves in their skeletons are depleted to supply the infant. The calcium and vitamin D needs of women during pregnancy and breastfeeding and after weaning are thoroughly summarized in a recent review by Christine Kovacs (2008).

9. The views of modern Japanese men on the preferred coloration of women are included as part of the comprehensive and fascinating review by Wagatsuma (1967) on attitudes of Japanese toward skin color.

6. SKIN COLOR AND HEALTH

1. The thinning of the ozone layer by manufactured chemicals such as chlorofluorocarbons has raised concern that increased levels of UVC and UVB reaching the Earth's surface may lead to a higher incidence of skin cancers. Mandated reduction in the emission of ozone-depleting substances has reduced but not eliminated this threat. The risk to humans is mitigated because the ozone layer is thinner over the virtually uninhabited poles than over other regions. Humans living in mid-latitudes of the Southern Hemisphere, in New Zealand, however, are still profoundly affected by ozone depletion.

2. Kiple and Kiple 1980, 216.

3. Observations on the near ubiquity of rickets in Washington, DC, in 1894 come from a paper by Thomas Mitchell (1930).

4. The role of Alfred Hess is emphasized here because of his prescient insight about dark skin pigmentation and its attenuating effect on sunlight being a predisposing factor to rickets. The long quotation from Hess comes from his classic paper on rickets (Hess 1922, 1183). See also Kiple and Kiple 1980; Rajakumar and Thomas 2005.

5. Several excellent reviews discuss the manifold and complex health problems associated with vitamin D deficiency: Norman 2008; Holick 2003, 2004; Kimball, Fuleihan, and Veith 2008. Researchers have also demonstrated that low vitamin D status is linked to impaired immune system activity, specifically Th1-mediated (T-helper-cell-type-1-mediated) autoimmunity and infectious immunity (Cantorna and Mahon 2005). Low levels of vitamin D are also correlated with a weakened immune response to the influenza virus and appear to predispose children to respiratory infections in general. See Holick and Chen 2008.

6. The illuminating review by Giovannucci and colleagues (2006) is especially recommended here. See also Holick 2004; Garland et al. 2006; Fleet 2008. A strong connection has emerged between vitamin D deficiency and prostate cancer in African American men, paralleling Alfred Hess's discovery of the association between skin pigmentation, sunlight attenuation, and rickets (see Grant 2008). The situation is complex, however, and a high-latitude location is not the only factor contributing to low vitamin D_3 levels in darkly pigmented people. High body mass index, low dietary vitamin D, and lower levels of outdoor physical activity are also contributing factors.

7. Archaeologists generally agree that the earliest cities arose in Mesopotamia around 3500 BCE and that cities sprang up quickly in many places soon

thereafter as agriculturally based populations became larger. The percentage of people living in cities has been tracked closely by the United Nations since 1950, and statistics by decade are available from the UN Population Division website (UNPD 2007). Studies of modern urban dwellers indicate that 80 to 90 percent of their time is spent indoors or in vehicles. The percentage varies according to place, season, and day of the week, but it is consistently high because most urbanites work or are educated indoors. See Andreev 1989; McCurdy and Graham 2003.

8. UVB is filtered out by all glass, but different kinds and colors of glass permit different amounts of UVA to pass through. The glass used in most houses and in the side windows of automobiles allows for some UVA transmission, and people sitting near these windows can experience high UVA exposure. The darkly tinted or reflective glass used in many office buildings greatly reduces UVA transmission, and the laminated glass used in car windshields is even more effective. UVA-filtering technology can now be incorporated into coatings for house glass and will be more widely used in the future. See Tuchinda et al. 2006.

9. The problem of vitamin D deficiency in the elderly is compounded because vitamin D production in the skin occurs more slowly in older people. See Davies et al. 1986; Solanki et al. 1995; Lauretani et al. 2010.

10. The excellent studies of Brian Diffey (2002, 2008) have contributed significantly to our knowledge of UVR and human exposure to UVR in different activities and lifestyles. His 2008 paper provides a superb description of the vacation effect on personal UVR exposure.

11. The group (a U.K. Food Standards Agency Workshop) concluded that exposure to UVB-rich sunlight for short periods in the summer would decrease the risk of vitamin D deficiency in the United Kingdom without significantly increasing rates of skin cancer and UVR-induced sun damage. See Ashwell et al. 2010.

12. See Matsuoka et al. 1992.

13. The ability of chemical sunscreens to reduce or eliminate pre–vitamin D_3 production in the skin has not been well studied. Few studies have been conducted under controlled conditions, and results have been equivocal because so many variables are involved, including a person's baseline skin pigmentation, the UVR conditions, and the way the sunscreen is applied. The literature on this topic is carefully reviewed by Springbett and colleagues (2010).

14. Among people with very lightly pigmented skin (including those with albinism), UVR exposure leads not to skin darkening through eumelanin production but to thickening of the stratum corneum. Thickening of the topmost layer of the skin provides a low level of protection against UVR but much less than that conferred by eumelanin tan, chemical sunscreens, or protective clothing. See Olivarius et al. 1997; Elias 2005.

15. The vacation effect has been well studied by scientists interested in quantifying the doses of UVR delivered to the skin under different conditions and schedules and by behavioral scientists working to determine why people intent on getting a tan will undertake painful and risky behavior to do so. See Diffey 2008; O'Riordan et al. 2008.

16. The risk of developing melanoma is increasing among young women, but the risk of dying from the disease is higher in men. Many excellent sources of information on melanoma are available, including websites maintained and routinely updated by the American Cancer Society (www.cancer.org/Cancer/SkinCancer-Melanoma/DetailedGuide/index) and the Skin Cancer Foundation (www.skincancer.org/Melanoma). A new scholarly review of the relationship between sunlight and melanoma has been published and is recommended (Garibyan and Fisher 2010), and a short summary of melanoma mortality rates in eleven countries from 1990 to 2006 is sobering (Marugame and Zhang 2010). Individuals with a history of nonmelanoma skin cancer have been shown to be at an increased risk for developing other cancers, but the reasons for this are not known (Wheless et al. 2010).

17. See Rouhani et al. 2010. Awareness of melanoma risk is lower in these communities than among lightly pigmented Floridians of European descent, and the disease tends to have a worse outcome because it is often diagnosed late.

18. The sunburn statistics for the United States come from American Cancer Society 2009.

19. The Fitzpatrick scale of tanning ability (see chapter 1) is based on the assumption that there is a reciprocal relationship between the tendencies to burn and to tan. People who always burn should never tan (type I) and people who always tan should never burn (types V and VI). The Fitzpatrick scale is used widely by dermatologists as a way of quickly evaluating a patient's risk of skin cancer.

20. The personal and health care costs of skin cancer in Australia are the highest in the world, as summarized by a recent government report (Australian Institute of Health and Welfare 2005). The success of the Slip! Slop! Slap! and SunSmart campaigns is reviewed in Montague, Borland, and Sinclair 2001. The policy guidelines for SunSmart schools are comprehensive and stress sun education of children along with sun protection: see Cancer Council of Western Australia 2011.

21. This is just one of several important conclusions reported in a recent comprehensive study of UVR and skin cancer prevention: see Saraiya et al. 2004.

7. THE DISCRIMINATING PRIMATE

1. A comprehensive review of the role played by imitation in the propagation of culture is provided by Nicolas Claidière and Dan Sperber (2010). The underlying neural mechanisms for imitation are the subject of intense debate. Mirror neurons have been proposed as the neural basis for human imitation (Caggiano et al. 2009; Iacoboni 2009). This view has been challenged recently by other neuroscientists (see Hickok 2009). A spirited blog on this and related subjects, *Talking Brains,* is moderated by Greg Hickok and David Poeppel: www.talkingbrains.org.

2. The behavioral and neurological basis for the development of "category activation"—the ability to place people or things into categories on a repeatable basis—and bias has been researched in detail since the 1950s, when social

scientists seeking to understand the biological and social bases of racial prejudice began to explore how stereotypes about groups were formed and how these lead to long-lasting biases. For an excellent background review of what categorical thinking is and how it develops, see Macrae and Bodenhausen 2000. Fiske 2002 offers a a plain-speaking but authoritative review on the subject as it refers specifically to racial classification. The landmark paper by Ross Hammond and Robert Axelrod (2006) on the likely evolutionary basis of in-group bias and ethnocentrism is also strongly recommended. The authors developed an abstract model in which competitors and cooperators had different colors. Individuals in the model that shared a specific color belonged to a specific in-group. They showed that colonies composed of those willing to cooperate with their own color grew faster than those in which individuals did not cooperate. This scenario for the development of in-group bias is consistent with behavior that could have evolved to promote social cohesion in small and vulnerable groups of early humans. Jennifer Eberhardt has been on the forefront of interpreting neuroscientific results in the context of the social psychology of race, and her review papers provide excellent syntheses of complex information on the subject, especially brain imaging: see, for example, Eberhardt 2005.

3. Such preferences have been studied extensively by sociologists and social psychologists, especially in the context of the development of racism (see Eberhardt and Fiske 1998).

4. Patterson and Bigler 2006.

5. Answering this question is one of the stated goals of the developers of the Implicit Association Test for Race (see Baron and Banaji 2006).

6. Jane Elliott's experiment was captured on film for the ABC News program "Eye of the Storm," aired in 1970. A book describing the experiment, *A Class Divided,* was first published by the filmmaker William Peters in 1971 and then as an expanded edition (Peters 1987; quote at p. 34). The experiment and original film gained enormous popularity after 1985, when they were shown as part of a Public Broadcasting System *Frontline* documentary of the same name. The documentary included footage of Elliott's reunion with members of her class, fourteen years after the experiment, and reflections by Elliott on the importance of the experiment then and now. The documentary can be watched in full online: www.pbs.org/wgbh/pages/frontline/shows/divided/etc/view.html.

7. The negative connotations of redheads in literature, and red-haired men in particular, are discussed in Cornwell 1998. The persecution of red-haired individuals because of their association with Satan is also explored by Mary Roach in a popular book on the social meanings of red hair (Roach 2006).

8. Lippmann 1929, 93. Lippmann's superb book on public opinion contains insightful chapters on stereotypes. Lippmann was the first person to use the word in its modern sense.

9. The highly contingent nature of the association between specific physical traits and inherent social rank is the cornerstone of Chris Smaje's excellent book on the social construction of race and caste (Smaje 2000). The acceptance of racial categories as fundamental truths is a pillar of the argument made by Don Operario and Susan Fiske (1998) on the nature of racism.

10. The philosopher John Searle stresses the difference between "institutional facts" and "brute facts." Brute facts are physical entities, like a mountain, that exist independent of human institutions such as language. Institutional facts include phenomena like money, marriage, and race that exist only because of human institutions such as language, and the shared belief in the significance of the words as symbols. See Searle 1995.

11. Lawrence Hirschfeld's study of the development of race awareness in young French schoolchildren demonstrated that the process was more complicated and multidimensional than previously thought and involved integration of visual information with conceptualizations (Hirschfeld 1993). The study also discusses the importance of verbal information in framing race perceptions in blind children. Naomi Quinn and Dorothy Holland (1997) discuss the importance of cultural transmission of attitudes about others and the cultural framing of cognition through what others say.

12. Daniel Levin has written thoughtful papers examining the nature of the cross-race recognition deficit. His review of the subject (Levin 2000) is worthwhile.

13. The subject of images as historical evidence of prevailing attitudes is explored in Peter Burke's superb short book *Eyewitnessing* (Burke 2001). Racial imagery and its influence on legal proceedings are discussed persuasively by Sheri Lynn Johnson (1992–93). Her excellent article surveys the effects on juries of pretrial publicity and imagery used during all stages of a trial, including witness testimony. She provides examples of the effects of blatant and subtle imagery and recommendations on how the prejudicial use of such imagery can be curbed.

14. This sentence paraphrases an excellent synopsis of race in David Zarefsky's lecture "Argumentation among Experts" (Zarefsky 2011).

15. Using functional magnetic resonance imaging (fMRI), Alumit Ishai and colleagues (2005) demonstrated that an extensive network of face-responsive regions exists in the human brain. Images of faces elicited responses from both sides of the brain, but the response in the right hemisphere was stronger. Images of famous and emotional faces resulted in stronger and more widespread activation of the brain. Lisa Barrett and colleagues' study of the effect of negative gossip on face perception demonstrates that negative gossip can generate negative emotions toward a neutral face and that it can affect whether the face is seen when it is competing with other stimuli (Anderson et al. 2011).

16. In 2000, Elizabeth Phelps and colleagues published a highly influential paper showing variation in brain reactions to "black" and "white" faces and how the strength of the amygdalar reaction varied according to degree of subconscious racial bias (Phelps et al. 2000). Andreas Olsson and colleagues showed that classical fear conditioning persisted for a longer period when people viewed photos of a "racial outgroup" (Olsson et al. 2005).

17. Fiske 2004.

18. After the victory of Barack Obama in the 2008 U.S. presidential election, a profound beneficial effect was detected in the examination performance of African Americans. It also resulted in a lowering of implicit bias and stereotyping. The term *Obama effect* was coined to describe the positive effects on

performance and implicit bias of a counterstereotypic African American exemplar (Marx, Ko, and Friedman 2009; Plant et al. 2009).

19. Fiske 2002, 124.

20. The original paper on stereotype threat was written by Claude Steele and Joshua Aronson (1995). Since then the subject has been exhaustively researched and published. Most literature on stereotype threat discusses the nature and consequences of negative stereotyping, including ways that negative stereotypes can be reduced through positive role models, as with the "Obama effect." See Columb and Plant 2010; Schmader, Johns, and Forbes 2008.

8. ENCOUNTERS WITH DIFFERENCE

1. The development of trade depended on innovations in transportation. Evidence exists in Europe and Africa for the widespread use by 9,000 to 8,000 years ago (7000–6000 BCE) of boats in gathering and distributing food and in facilitating trade on rivers, along lake shores, and even on the open sea. Boat technology made it possible for people to trade in a variety of perishable goods and precious materials as well as bulky and heavy objects that would have been difficult to transport on land.

Beginning about 5,500 years ago, the first horses were domesticated in the region now occupied by Kazakhstan and Ukraine. The introduction of domestic animals that could be ridden, milked, and used as draft animals permitted people to travel much farther and faster than they could on foot. The use of horses spread quickly throughout western and central Asia and eastern Europe, and just short of 4,000 years ago, there is evidence of the first two-wheeled chariots with carts that could carry people and some goods. The Silk Roads of Asia are the most famous examples of trade routes created by horse power, but horses and chariots were also widely used in ancient Egypt, beginning more than 3,500 years ago.

2. Western (initially European) attitudes toward skin color developed primarily as reactions to contacts with the deeply pigmented people of sub-Saharan Africa: see chapters 9 and 10.

3. The richness of Egyptian civilization owes much to the ecological stability and fertility of the Nile Valley, which were complemented by what we would now call sustainable agricultural practices that retained soil and enhanced fertility. Growth of and communication among human populations occurred without undue competition for food or water. Urban centers along the Nile supported higher population densities than elsewhere in the ancient Mediterranean because of the stability of the environment and agricultural resource base.

4. One of the best and most compact sources of information on Egypt and the lands of the Mediterranean is a timeline of the ancient world published by the British Museum: see Wiltshire 2004.

5. Definitions of peasants, serfs, and slaves are not always comparable across cultures and through time. Bruce Trigger provides a critical comparative discussion of the nature of serfdom and slavery in Egypt in *Ancient Egypt: A Social History* (Trigger 1983).

6. This discussion is synthesized from accounts of the history of Egyptian warfare and slavery by Paul Kern and Milton Meltzer, respectively, and of Egyptian and classical attitudes toward skin color awareness by Frank Snowden Jr. and David Goldenberg. See Kern 1999; Meltzer 1993; Snowden 1970, 1983; Goldenberg 2003.

7. An excellent review of Harappan civilization is provided by Kenneth Kennedy in his comprehensive *God-Apes and Fossil Men* (Kennedy 2000).

8. Evidence for a series of invasions of the Indian subcontinent by peoples typically called Aryans is supported by linguistic and archaeological evidence. In addition, genetic evidence has recently shown that the paternal lineages of Indian castes are primarily of Indo-European descent. The tribal peoples of India were not, however, affected by these influxes and were predominantly descended from the subcontinent's original inhabitants (Cordaux et al. 2004). A good introduction to early Indian history and Vedic literature is provided in the Introduction of Patrick Olivelle's translation of the Upanishads (Olivelle 1996).

9. In his historical overview of India, A.L. Basham briefly discusses the etymology of *varna*. He stresses that it is not synonymous with *caste* despite the fact that it is loosely translated thus (Basham 1985).

10. This quotation comes from *The Middle Length Discourses of the Buddha,* MN 79.10 (Nanamoli and Bodhi 1995). By the end of the Vedic period, classes of skin colors and of peoples had become codified by laws in the Laws or Codex of Manu, but the three highest classes were not distinguished by color. These classes were permitted to hear and learn the Vedas. Dietary formulas for producing children with fair, ruddy, or dark complexions exist in the literature of the time (see, e.g., *Brhadaranyaka Upaniṣad* 6.4.13–16). The serf class was prohibited from even hearing the Vedas.

11. The complex meaning of the term *varna*, as reflecting essential qualities of character and, later in history, being descriptive of complexion, is discussed by de Bary and colleagues in *Sources of Indian Tradition* (de Bary et al. 1958).

12. For a succinct summary of the history of the Mediterranean world, see Alcock and Cherry 2005.

13. For example, the Athenian general Nicias led his troops along the north coast of Sicily and captured the small town of Hyccara, which had few resources except its human population, which was captured and sold into slavery.

14. Westermann 1995, 23. Westermann's book is an exceptionally thorough study of Greek and Roman slavery. Another excellent and more broadly comparative source is Audrey Smedley's *Race in North America: Origin and Evolution of a Worldview* (1999).

15. Benjamin Isaac carefully reviews the environmental theory of Hippocrates and others in chapter 1 of *The Invention of Racism in Classical Antiquity* (2004).

16. See Goldenberg 2003.

17. Frank Snowden, in chapter 1 of *Blacks in Antiquity,* describes at length how skin color, especially dark color, was systematically observed and described by the Greeks and Romans (Snowden 1970).

18. There is considerable debate among historians and sociologists as to whether the kind of discrimination practiced in ancient Greece and Rome against noncitizens constituted racism (see Goldenberg 2003). To some, the presence of any hierarchy defines racism.

19. Ibid.

20. This point was made originally by Patricia Crone, who is quoted in Ronald Segal's fine book on Islamic slavery, *Islam's Black Slaves* (Segal 2001). In my discussion of Islamic attitudes toward skin color, I draw heavily on Segal's interpretations.

21. Ibid., 48–49.

9. SKIN COLOR IN THE AGE OF EXPLORATION

1. Samson 2005, 11–12. Samson's book is an excellent source of information on the changing perceptions of human diversity from the Middle Ages onward.

2. Irwin 1977, 127, 122.

3. Smaje 2000, 84–85. Lightly pigmented former slaves bore the mark of "transcendental slavery" in the minds of some: they could often assume other positions in society when freed. Darkly pigmented slaves, by contrast, bore the stain of slavery in their skin.

4. Northrop 2002, chapter 1. The cessation of the slave trade from eastern Europe at the end of the fifteenth century is not sufficiently recognized as a turning point in the history of slavery and colonialism.

5. For accounts of the lives of three former African slaves who became respected scholars in Europe during the Renaissance, see Fikes 1980.

6. Although the anecdote about the nobleman's veins may well be apocryphal, the phrase clearly derives from the time of the Inquisition in Spain and the importance of demonstrating pure and original Christianity.

7. The observations of Al-Idrisi on East Africa are summarized in Freeman-Grenville 1962.

8. Ibid., 19.

9. Ibid., 25.

10. Sue Niebrzydowski (2001) explores the development of the "fantastic other," especially in relation to views of women. Research by Malcolm Letts (1946) indicates that no real Sir John Mandeville had any part in writing or even translating the account.

11. Raymond Cole's account of sixteenth-century European travel books (1972) stresses the obsession of Europeans with the documentation of non-white skin tones.

12. The early history of Portuguese trade with Africa is summarized authoritatively in Crone 1937. The introduction is an excellent primer on the early development of the African slave trade, and its contents illustrate the fantastic nature of the reports that made their way back to Europe from explorers and travelers.

13. Cole 1972, 59.

14. Northrup 2002, 11.

15. Bernier 2000, 1.

16. A facsimile of the first edition of *Systema Naturae* by Linnaeus is available (Engel-Ledeboer and Engel 1964). Linnaeus and other early-eighteenth-century naturalists benefited greatly from the first systematic description of apes. Although other animals had been described as apes before, most were what we would now classify as monkeys. Various apes continued to be described and confounded for centuries afterward, but the discovery and description of a group of animals that closely resembled humans influenced the ways humans were classified and human variation was conceived (O'Flaherty and Shapiro 2002).

17. See Bernasconi 2001a. The entire eight-volume *Concepts of Race in the Eighteenth Century* is of great value to scholars interested in the development of race concepts in Western thought.

18. The eighteenth century witnessed many attempts by naturalists and natural philosophers to distinguish between "species," "races," and "varieties." Kant played an important role in this discussion by distinguishing a "variety" as an organism that would revert to a common stock in subsequent generations of breeding. A "race" would not.

19. A complete explication of Kant's views on human origins is provided in Bernasconi 2001b.

20. Kant 2000, 11–22.

21. Quoted in Bernasconi and Lott 2000, 26.

22. Blumenbach 2000, 37.

23. Mitchell and Collinson 1744, 140. Mitchell's use of the verb *tan* occurs on page 147. The full text is lengthy and makes for tedious reading, but Mitchell made significant and prescient observations about skin structure and function.

24. Smith 1965, 52.

25. Ibid., 65.

10. SKIN COLOR AND THE ESTABLISHMENT OF RACES

1. Robert Bernasconi has been a pioneer in exploring the origins and influence of Kant's views on race: his work is required reading for students interested in how the case for non-European inferiority was built in the late eighteenth century. See especially Bernasconi 2001b, 2002. The quotations from Kant come from Shell 2006, 56. Kant wrote many anthropological treatises that are available in translation: several are freely available online. A number of authoritative academic websites also provide thorough reviews and critiques of Kant's writings on human diversity and races. A particularly good one is Hachee 2011.

2. Kant developed his ideas about human diversity and races over more than twenty years. He relied on the accounts of travelers, explorers, naturalists, and traders for factual information on the people and environments outside Europe. His ideas also evolved as he read the work of other scholars and philosophers, notably Georg Forster. For an excellent source of information and interpretation on this topic, see Eigen and Larrimore 2006. See also Bernasconi 2006; Larrimore 2006.

3. This quotation comes from Kant's 1763 work *Observations on the Feeling of the Beautiful and the Sublime* (Kant 1960, 113).

4. Ladislas Bugner, quoted in Goldenberg 2003, 50. One of the best expositions of this subject is provided by Cohen 2003.

5. On the association of black with evil and negativity, see Goldenberg 2003, introduction and part 1.

6. Quoted in Cohen 2003, 85.

7. According to the Biblical account, the mark of Cain conferred God's protection and invoked a curse on anyone who harmed Cain in his exile; only later did the mark itself come to be associated with punishment and shame.

8. For a particularly helpful and thorough discussion of the influence of the curse of Ham on skin-color discrimination, the development of anti-African attitudes, and the promotion of African slavery, see Haynes 2002.

9. The etymology of the name *Ham* is discussed by Goldenberg (2003, 105). A brilliant discussion of the history of interpretation of the curse of Ham is provided by Braude 1997.

10. Samuel Purchas, *Hakluytus Posthumus, or Purchas His Pilgrimes* (1625–1626), book 6, quoted in Braude 1997, 137.

11. On the unique power of racial stereotypes, see Operario and Fiske 1998. On the concept of race as a stratifying practice reinforced by social interaction, see Ossorio and Duster 2005.

12. Robert Boyle was an alchemist and natural philosopher who is considered one of the founders of modern chemistry. A devout Christian, he committed much of his fortune to supporting missionary efforts. His quote refuting the interpretation of the curse of Ham as the cause of human blackness comes from his 1664 essay "Experiments and Considerations Touching Colours" (Boyle 2007, 261–62).

11. INSTITUTIONAL SLAVERY AND THE POLITICS OF PIGMENTATION

1. The obsession with labels for skin tones among the English is epitomized by the cultivation of the term *Negro*. This and related themes are developed in Sujata Iyengar's excellent book *Shades of Difference* (2005). The establishment of the "white" norm is the focus of Richard Dyer's book *White* (1997). Dyer observes that nonwhites receive race labels, whereas whites are "just people."

2. Few Americans realize that maintenance of the transatlantic slave trade and of chattel slavery were among the most important "freedoms" defended in the War of Independence. On the inextricable relationship between slavery, slaveholding, and the founding of the United States, see Oakes 1998.

3. The dehumanization of Africans began with an association with blackness and progressed through the invocation of a series of negative visual and auditory associations. This topic is thoroughly explored in Hoffer 2003.

4. Walvin 1986, 82. Walvin's commentary on the nature and effects of Edward Long's pernicious *History of Jamaica* is noteworthy.

5. The classic volume on the legal status of slaves in the American colonies is A. Leon Higginbotham Jr., *In the Matter of Color* (1978), which describes the laws and statutes of six colonies and their implications for the differential

treatment of servants and slaves by skin color. A good short summary is Wood 1995. The brutal mechanics of the slave trade and the nature of the rhetoric that turned people into commodities in American slave markets are masterfully summarized by Walter Johnson in *Soul by Soul* (1999). See also Audrey Smedley's *Race in North America* (1999) and Jane Samson's *Race and Empire* (2005).

6. Brown 1999, 340. This individual should not be confused with the abolitionist of the same name.

7. The relevant legal statutes are reviewed in Higginbotham 1978.

8. Quoted in Johnson 1999, 140.

9. Published slave narratives include individual histories such as that of the fugitive slave William W. Brown, who was the son of an African slave and an American slaveholder. While working as a house servant, Brown witnessed the whipping of his mother and other slaves (Brown 1970). The volume, edited and with an introduction by Henry Louis Gates Jr. (2002), provides an excellent introduction to this literature.

10. Craft and Craft 2001, 902. The position of mulattoes in the American South is discussed in Toplin 1979.

11. The slave narrative of Moses Roper (2001) describes how he barely escaped murder at the hand of his owner's wife at the time of his birth because he was "very white."

12. Publications by the U.S. Census Bureau and scholars of the census are important for understanding the history of government attempts at human classification and provide telling glimpses of American social history. Individual classifications were also devised by states, especially in the South, based on different measurements of the blood quantum of African ancestry. See Snipp 2003; Bennett 2000; Chestnutt 2000.

13. The concept of blood quantum is an attempt to quantify an individual's ancestry. In the American colonies and the United States, it has mostly been applied in attempts to ascertain an individual's degree of Native American ancestry, but it has also been applied, less rigorously and consistently, to African ancestry.

14. Nobles 2000, 1740.

15. Sanjek 1994, 1.

16. One of the best reviews of the meanings and implications of the *Dred Scott* decision is Bernasconi 1991–92.

17. *Dred Scott v. Sandford.*

18. On the stratifying effects of race on the access to the goods of society, and the biological consequences of differential access, see Ossorio and Duster 2005.

19. On *Morrison v. White,* see Johnson 2000.

20. During the infamous case of *Rhinelander v. Rhinelander* of late 1925, Alice Rhinelander (née Jones) was forced to expose her torso and legs to the jury to allow them to assess the skin color of her body. Her husband, Leonard Rhinelander, had sued her for an annulment of their marriage on the grounds that she had fraudulently claimed that she was white. For details of the case, along with an excellent commentary, see Wacks 2000.

21. Eva Saks (2000) has written a brilliant exposé on miscegenation law, discussing several cases that hinged on the explication of "hidden" ancestry.

22. For an excellent summary of the minstrel tradition in the United States, see Pieterse 1992, 132–36.

12. SKIN COLORS AND THEIR VARIABLE MEANINGS

1. The promotion of tanned skin in Europe and the Americas since the 1930s has yielded a similar effect. As discussed in chapter 14, tans achieved through leisure activities or suntanning became associated with leisure and higher social status in the later twentieth century, and images of tanned celebrities connected tanning with the promise of social elevation and approbation. White people can become tan and still enjoy the social benefits of lightness.

2. Saul Dubow describes the history of European scientific attitudes toward the "racial differentiation" of the Khoe-san and Bantu-language speakers in chapter 3 of *Scientific Racism in Modern South Africa* (Dubow 1995). For details, see the genetic studies conducted by Sarah Tishkoff and colleagues (2007).

3. On the history and attitudes of the Dutch Reformed Church in South Africa, see Gerstner 1997.

4. The practice of describing the Khoe-san as descendants of the sons of Ham, or representing humans that retained characteristics of monkeys and apes, can be traced to eighteenth-century Europe. Some of these attitudes developed in the wake of the public display of the Khoe-san woman Saarje Baartman in England and France in the late 1700s. After her death, her body was dissected by the French zoologist George Cuvier, and her body parts were variously displayed and stored. Her remains were finally repatriated to South Africa in 2003. See Tobias 2002.

5. A full exposition of the diversity of European Christian beliefs in colonial South Africa is presented in Elbourne and Ross 1997. Catherine Besteman provides an excellent and up-to-date synopsis of the history of population interactions and discriminatory practices in South Africa in *Transforming Cape Town* (Besteman 2008).

6. On the effects of post-Enlightenment European philosophy and social Darwinism on the development of white supremacist ideology in South Africa, see Dubow 1995.

7. Leonard Thompson, quoted in Besteman 2008, 5.

8. For a thorough legal interpretation of race classifications and definitions in South Africa from 1910 to 1960, see Suzman 1960.

9. Quoted in ibid., 354.

10. The personal turmoil caused by repeated racial classifications is epitomized by the story of Sandra Laing, who was successively classified as White, Coloured, and again as White. Laing's story is described by Judith Stone in *When She Was White* (2007).

11. Quoted in Telles 2004, 25. Edward Telles's excellent study should be consulted by readers seeking more detailed information about Brazil's long and complex social history.

12. Quoted in Vieira 1995, 228.

13. Attitudes toward miscegenation in European colonies varied. For a good summary, see Samson 2005.

14. See Telles 2004. The central differences between United States and Brazilian concepts of color and race are illustrated by the census categories that the two countries have employed in the past two hundred years: see Nobles 2000.

15. For the list of 134 skin-color names catalogued by Brazilian authorities in 1976, see Soong 1999.

16. A. Dzidzienyo, quoted in Guimaraes 1995, 217.

17. The irony of color-based discrimination in what was a nominally color-blind "racial democracy" is discussed in Vieira 1995.

18. *Varna* and *jati* are often and erroneously referred to together as "caste." The reality of the two systems of classification is much more subtle and reflects the interplay of Vedic and Hindu philosophy in Indian history. See Basahm 1985. André Beteille's account of race and descent in India (1968) provides an excellent summary of modern attitudes toward skin color.

19. On the meaning of skin color in Japan and the association of whiteness with purity, see Wagatsuma 1967; Dower 2004.

20. See Dower 2004.

21. See Wagatsuma 1967.

13. ASPIRING TO LIGHTNESS

1. Spanish humanist text, quoted in Swiderski 2008, 166. Swiderski observes that mercury-based compounds were central to skin-lightening and cosmetics formulations for more than four hundred years. Mercury's toxicity was recognized early, but for many, this was outweighed by its beneficial effects on the appearance of the skin and its effectiveness as a cure for syphilis. The harmful effects of white-lead cosmetics on the children of Edo-period samurai are described in Nakashima et al. 2011.

2. See Dyer 1997.

3. James 2003, 19.

4. Constance McClaughlin Green, quoted in Moore 1999, 58. On the history of colorism among African Americans, see James 2003. For a succinct overview of the historical background to American colorism, see Neal and Wilson 1989.

5. Twain 1997, 28, 66.

6. Gatewood 2000, 349.

7. The importance of light skin in African-American culture is the focus of Marita Golden's memoir *Don't Play in the Sun* (2004). The list of African-American skin color terms appears on page 7. The subject of passing—generally involving famous individuals—and of people being unaware of their ancestry has been the subject of many recent biographies, scholarly studies, and novels. See, for instance, Broyard 2007; Byrd and Gates 2011.

8. Quoted in Peiss 1998, 205. Peiss's monograph *Hope in a Jar* is one of the most insightful recent works on the politics of appearance.

9. Quoted in Walker 2007, 77.

10. The social historian Ronald Hall describes the bleaching syndrome in an excellent article discussing the obsession with lightness and skin bleaching among African Americans and comparing it to the preference for lightness among Indian Hindus (Hall 1995a).

11. White's article in *Look* (1949) is a product of its time in its construction of light-colored American society as an ideal and the post-Sputnik conviction that science could cure all of society's ills.

12. Evelyn Nakano Glenn (2008) includes South Africa in her excellent review of global skin-lightening practices. She describes the continued manufacture and export of mercurial bleaching products in countries of the European Union and Britain long after their sale had been banned in these countries. On the clinical and social aspects of the use of skin bleaches in South Africa, see also Bentley-Phillips and Bayles 1975.

13. Thomas 2009, 189.

14. This statement is based on my own informal survey of newspaper articles and editorials from Nairobi, Kenya, from 1987 through 2010. Skin bleaching is a recurrent and polarizing topic: letters to the editor from men who declare a preference for women with lighter skin became more common over this period.

15. Innate preferences for light skin, if they exist, may be related to the fact that adult females and babies in all populations have lighter skin than adult males (see chapters 5 and 12).

16. On colorism, see Glenn 2008; Keith and Herring 1991; Hall 1995b, 2001; Herring, Keith, and Horton 2004. On the effects of a preference for light skin on youth attitudes, see Rondilla and Spickard 2007.

17. See Glenn 2008; Thompson and Keith 2004.

14. DESIRING DARKNESS

1. The history of sun exposure in literature and art is briefly reviewed in Giacomoni 2001.

2. A similar observation was first made by the anthropologist Marvin Harris, whose research on attitudes toward tanning is summarized and quoted in Kerry Segrave's excellent book *Suntanning in 20th Century America* (2005). Segrave's book provides a thorough and provocative review of attitudes toward tanning and the development of recreational tanning as a pastime and industry.

3. On the decline of celebrity tanning, see Jablonski 2010. Thomas Rajakumar and Stephen Thomas have observed that the promotion of tanning followed the growth of heliotherapy for rickets and tuberculosis. On the changing perceptions of suntanning, see Randle 1997; Rajakumar and Thomas 2005.

4. Kaur et al. 2006. For a good recent review of the literature on tanning and physiological dependence, see Nolan and Feldman 2009. The behavioral reinforcement of tanning behavior has been studied extensively by Smita Banerjee and colleagues (2009). High-risk UVR tanning at tanning parlors appears to be particularly heavily influenced by peer pressure.

5. Mosher and Danoff-Burg 2010. See also Kaur et al. 2006; Bagdasarov et al. 2008; Banerjee et al. 2009; Nolan and Feldman 2009.

6. A good review of the effects of UVR on "Asian skin" is provided in Chung 2001.

7. The statistics on the tanning industry from 2010 come from Zwolack 2010. Katherine Hoerster and colleagues concluded that the association between a lower UV index and higher facility density "may be due to residents' desires to seek warmth, tanned skin, or both when natural sunlight is less available" (Hoerster et al. 2009, 3).

8. The "optimistic bias effect" comprises the dual perceptions that negative events are more likely to affect other people than oneself and that positive events are more likely to happen to oneself than to others. The effect, first described by Neil Weinstein in 1980, has been shown by Arthur Miller and colleagues (among others) to affect perception of risk of skin cancer from UVR exposure. See Weinstein 1980; Miller et al. 1990.

9. These titles are from Fleischer and Fleischer 1992; McPhail 1997; and Amonette 1994.

10. Use of chemical sunscreens with higher SPF values is associated with longer periods of UVR exposure among intentional tanners. Longer exposures to UVR, even with high-SPF sunscreen, are associated with more UVA penetration into the skin and elevated melanoma risk (Autier 2009).

11. Robinson et al. 2008.

12. See Kourosh, Keith, and Horton 2010; Nolan and Feldman 2009.

13. For more details about the chemistry and action of DHA, see Monfrecola and Prizio 2001.

14. On the fallacious claims of "controlled" and safe tanning being circulated to teenagers by the indoor tanning industry, see Balk and Geller 2008.

15. For more information about celebrity tanning and the "Go with Your Own Glow" campaign, see Jablonski 2010 and the Skin Cancer Foundation website, www.skincancer.org/glow-campaign.html.

16. Satherley 2011.

15. LIVING IN COLOR

1. See Williams and Eberhardt 2008. On the effects of race on differential access to the goods of society, see Ossorio and Duster 2005.

References

Abu-Amero, K., A. Gonzalez, J. Larruga, T. Bosley, and V. Cabrera. 2007. "Eurasian and African mitochondrial DNA influences in the Saudi Arabian population." *BMC Evolutionary Biology* 7 (1): 32–47.

Aiello, L.C., and P. Wheeler. 1995. "The expensive-tissue hypothesis." *Current Anthropology* 36 (2): 199–221.

Alaluf, S., D. Atkins, K. Barrett, M. Blount, N. Carter, and A. Heath. 2002. "Ethnic variation in melanin content and composition in photoexposed and photoprotected human skin." *Pigment Cell Research* 15 (2): 112–118.

Alcock, S.E., and J.F. Cherry. 2005. "The Mediterranean World." In *The Human Past: World Prehistory and the Development of Human Societies*, ed. C. Scarre, 472–517. London: Thames & Hudson.

Allen, L.C. 1915. "The negro health problem." *American Journal of Public Health* 5 (3): 194–203.

Amonette, R.A. 1994. "New campaigns needed to remind the public of the dangers of tanning salons." *Cosmetic Dermatology* 7: 25–28.

Anderson, E., E.H. Siegel, E. Bliss-Moreau, and L.F. Barrett. 2011. "The visual impact of gossip." *Science* 332 (6036): 1446–1448.

Andreev, Y.V. 1989. "Urbanization as a phenomenon of social history." *Oxford Journal of Archaeology* 8 (2): 167–177.

Antón, S.C. 2003. "Natural history of *Homo erectus*." *American Journal of Physical Anthropology* 122 (S37): 126–170.

Antoniou, C., M.G. Kosmadaki, A.J. Stratigos, and A.D. Katsambas. 2008. "Sunscreens: What's important to know." *Journal of the European Academy of Dermatology and Venereology* 22 (9): 1110–1119.

Aoki, K. 2002. "Sexual selection as a cause of human skin colour variation: Darwin's hypothesis revisited." *Annals of Human Biology* 29 (6): 589–608.

Armas, L.A.G., B.W. Hollis, and R.P. Heaney. 2004. "Vitamin D2 is much less effective than vitamin D3 in humans." *Journal of Clinical Endocrinology and Metabolism* 89 (11): 5387–5391.

Ashwell, M., E. M. Stone, H. Stolte, K. D. Cashman, H. Macdonald, S. Lanham-New, S. Hiom, A. Webb, and D. Fraser. 2010. "UK Food Standards Agency workshop report: An investigation of the relative contributions of diet and sunlight to vitamin D status." *British Journal of Nutrition* 104 (4): 603–611.

Australian Institute of Health and Welfare. 2005. *Health System Expenditures on Cancer and Other Neoplasms in Australia, 2000–01.* Canberra: Australian Institute of Health and Welfare.

Autier, P. 2009. "Sunscreen abuse for intentional sun exposure." *British Journal of Dermatology* 161 (S3): 40–45.

Bagdasarov, Z., S. Banerjee, K. Greene, and S. Campo. 2008. "Indoor tanning and problem behavior." *Journal of American College Health* 56 (5): 555–562.

Baker, P. T. 1958. "Racial differences in heat tolerance." *American Journal of Physical Anthropology* 16 (3): 287–305.

Balk, S. J., and A. C. Geller. 2008. "Teenagers and artificial tanning." *Pediatrics* 121 (5): 1040–1042.

Banerjee, S. C., K. Greene, Z. Bagdasarov, and S. Campo. 2009. "'My friends love to tan': Examining sensation seeking and the mediating role of association with friends who use tanning beds on tanning bed use intentions." *Health Education Research* 24 (6): 989–998.

Barnicot, N. A. 1958. "Reflectometry of the skin in Southern Nigerians and in some mulattoes." *Human Biology* 30 (2): 150–160.

Baron, A. S., and M. R. Banaji. 2006. "The development of implicit attitudes: Evidence of race evaluations from ages 6 and 10 and adulthood." *Psychological Science* 17 (1): 53–58.

Barsh, G., and G. Cotsarelis. 2007. "How hair gets its pigment." *Cell* 130 (5): 779–781.

Basham, A. L. 1985. *The Wonder That Was India: A Survey of the History and Culture of the Indian Sub-continent before the Coming of the Muslims.* London: Sidgwick & Jackson.

Bay, M. 2000. *The White Image in the Black Mind.* New York: Oxford University Press.

BBC News. 2008. "Living in fear: Tanzania's albinos." http://news.bbc.co.uk/2/hi/africa/7518049.stm. July 21.

———. 2009. "Albino trials begin in Tanzania." http://news.bbc.co.uk/2/hi/africa/8089351.stm. June 9.

Bennett, C. 2000. "Racial categories used in the decennial censuses, 1790 to the present." *Government Information Quarterly* 17 (2): 161–180.

Bentley-Phillips, B., and M. A. H. Bayles. 1975. "Cutaneous reactions to topical application of hydroquinone: Results of a 6-year investigation." *South African Medical Journal* 49 (34): 1391–1395.

Bergman, I., A. Olofsson, G. Hörnberg, O. Zackrissen, and E. Hellberg. 2004. "Deglaciation and colonization: Pioneer settlements in northern Fennoscandia." *Journal of World Prehistory* 18 (2): 155–177.

Bernasconi, R. 1991–92. "Constitution of the people: Frederick Douglass and the Dred Scott decision." *Cardozo Law Review* 13: 1281–1296.

———. 2001a. Introduction. In *Concepts of Race in the Eighteenth Century*, vol. 1, *Bernier, Linnaeus and Maupertuis*, ed. R. Bernasconi, 1: vii–xii. Bristol: Thoemmes Press.

———. 2001b. "Who invented the concept of race? Kant's role in the Enlightenment construction of race." In *Race*, ed. R. Bernasconi, 11–36. Malden, MA: Blackwell.

———. 2002. "Kant as an unfamiliar source of racism." In *Philosophers on Race: Critical Essays*, ed. J.K. Ward and T.L. Lott, 145–166. Oxford: Blackwell.

———. 2006. "Kant and Blumenbach's polyps: A neglected chapter in the history of the concept of race." In *The German Invention of Race*, ed. S. Eigen and M. Larrimore, 73–90. Albany: State University of New York Press.

Bernasconi, R., and T.L. Lott, eds. 2000. *The Idea of Race*. Indianapolis, IN: Hackett.

Bernier, F. 2000. "A new division of the Earth." In *The Idea of Race*, ed. R. Bernasconi and T.L. Lott, 1–4. Indianapolis, IN: Hackett.

Besser, L.M., L.J. Williams, and J.D. Cragan. 2007. "Interpreting changes in the epidemiology of anencephaly and spina bifida following folic acid fortification of the U.S. grain supply in the setting of long-term trends, Atlanta, Georgia, 1968–2003." *Birth Defects Research Part A: Clinical and Molecular Teratology* 79 (11): 730–736.

Besteman, C. 2008. *Transforming Cape Town*. Berkeley, CA: University of California Press.

Beteille, A. 1968. Race and descent as social categories in India. In *Color and Race*, ed. J.H. Franklin, 166–185. Boston, Beacon.

Bishop, J.N., V. Bataille, A. Gavin, M. Lens, J. Marsden, T. Mathews, and C. Wheelhouse. 2007. "The prevention, diagnosis, referral and management of melanoma of the skin: Concise guidelines." *Clinical Medicine, Journal of the Royal College of Physicians* 7 (3): 283–290.

Bjorn, L.O., and T. Wang. 2000. "Vitamin D in an ecological context." *International Journal of Circumpolar Health* 59 (1): 26–32.

Blayney, B., ed. 1769. *The Holy Bible, Containing the Old and New Testaments*. Oxford: T. Wright and W. Gill.

Blum, H.F. 1961. "Does the melanin pigment of human skin have adaptive value?" *Quarterly Review of Biology* 36 (1): 50–63.

Blumenbach, J.F. 2000. "On the natural variety of mankind." In *The Idea of Race*, ed. R. Bernasconi and T.L. Lott, 27–37. Indianapolis, IN: Hackett.

Bögels, S.M., and C.T.J. Lamers. 2002. "The causal role of self-awareness in blushing-anxious, socially-anxious and social phobics individuals." *Behaviour Research and Therapy* 40 (12): 1367–1384.

Bolanca, I., Z. Bolanca, K. Kuna, A. Vukovic, N. Tuckar, R. Herman, and G. Grubisic. 2008. "Chloasma: The mask of pregnancy." *Collegium Antropologicum* 32 (Suppl 2): 139–141.

Bonilla-Silva, E., and D.R. Dietrich. 2009. The Latin Americanization of U.S. race relations: A new pigmentocracy. In *Shades of Difference: Why Skin*

Color Matters, ed. E.N. Glenn, 40–60. Stanford, CA: Stanford University Press.

Bower, C., and F.J. Stanley. 1989. "Dietary folate as a risk factor for neural-tube defects: Evidence from a case-control study in Western Australia." *Medical Journal of Australia* 150: 613–619.

———. 1992. "The role of nutritional factors in the aetiology of neural tube defects." *Journal of Paediatrics and Child Health* 28: 12–16.

Bowman, P.J., R. Muhammed, and M. Ifatunij. 2004. "Skin tone, class and racial attitudes among African Americans." In *Skin Deep: How Race and Complexion Matter in the "Color-Blind" Era,* ed. C. Herring, V.M. Keith, and H.D. Horton, 128–158. Urbana, IL: Institute for Research on Race and Public Policy.

Boxmeer, J.C., M. Smit, E. Utomo, J.C. Romijn, M. Eijkemans, J. Lindemans, J. Laven, N.S. Macklon, E. Steegers, and R. Steegers-Theunissen. 2009. "Low folate in seminal plasma is associated with increased sperm DNA damage." *Fertility and Sterility* 92 (2): 548–556.

Boyle, R. 2007. "Experiments and considerations touching colours." In *Race in Early Modern England: A Documentary Companion,* ed. A. Loomba and J. Burton, 260–264. New York: Palgrave MacMillan.

Bramble, D.M., and D.E. Lieberman. 2004. "Endurance running and the evolution of *Homo.*" *Nature* 432 (7015): 345–352.

Branda, R.F., and J.W. Eaton. 1978. "Skin color and nutrient photolysis: An evolutionary hypothesis." *Science* 201 (4356): 625–626.

Braude, B. 1997. "The sons of Noah and the construction of ethnic and geographical identities in the medieval and early modern periods." *William and Mary Quarterly* 54 (1): 103–142.

Breunig, P., K. Neumann, and W. Van Neer. 1996. "New research on the Holocene settlement and environment of the Chad Basin in Nigeria." *African Archaeological Review* 13 (2): 111–145.

Brinnel, H., M. Cabanac, and J.R.S. Hales. 1987. "Critical upper levels of body temperature, tissue thermosensitivity, and selective brain cooling in hyperthermia." In *Heat Stress: Physical Exertion and Environment,* ed. J.R.S. Hales and D.A.B. Richards, 209–240. Amsterdam: Excerpta Medica.

Brown, J. 1999. "Slave life in Georgia: A narrative of the life, sufferings, and escape of John Brown, a fugitive slave, now in England." In *I Was Born a Slave: An Anthology of Classic Slave Narratives,* vol. 2, *1849–1866,* ed. Y. Taylor, 319–411. Chicago: Lawrence Hill Books.

Brown, W.W. 1970. *Narrative of William W. Brown, a Fugitive Slave.* New York: Johnson Reprint Corp.

Broyard, B. 2007. *One Drop.* New York: Little, Brown and Company.

Buccimazza, S.S., C.D. Molteno, T.T. Dunnem, and D.L. Viljoen. 1994. "Prevalence of neural tube defects in Cape Town, South Africa." *Teratology* 50 (3): 194–199.

Burke, P. 2001. *Eyewitnessing: The Uses of Images as Historical Evidence.* Ithaca, NY: Cornell University Press.

Byard, P.J. 1981. "Quantitative genetics of human skin color." *Yearbook of Physical Anthropology* 24 (S2): 123–137.

Byrd, R.P., and H.L. Gates, Jr. 2011. "Jean Toomer's conflicted racial identity." *Chronicle of Higher Education* 57 (23): B5–B8.

Caggiano, V., L. Fogassi, G. Rizzolatti, P. Their, and A. Casile. 2009. "Mirror neurons differentially encode the peripersonal and extrapersonal space of monkeys." *Science* 324 (5925): 403–406.

Caldwell, M.M., L.O. Bjorn, J.F. Bornman, S.D. Flint, G. Kulandaivelu, A.H. Teramura, and M. Tevini. 1998. "Effects of increased solar ultraviolet radiation on terrestrial ecosystems." *Journal of Photochemistry and Photobiology B* 46: 40–52.

Cancer Council of Western Australia. 2011. "SunSmart Schools." www.cancer wa.asn.au/prevention/sunsmart/sunsmartschools.

Cantorna, M.T., and B.D. Mahon. 2005. "D-hormone and the immune system." *Journal of Rheumatology* 76: 11–20.

Carden, S.M., R.E. Boissy, P.J. Schoettker, and W.V. Good. 1998. "Albinism: Modern molecular diagnosis." *British Journal of Ophthalmology* 82 (2): 189–195.

Chadysiene, R., and A. Girgzdys. 2008. "Ultraviolet radiation albedo of natural surfaces." *Journal of Environmental Engineering and Landscape Management* 16 (2): 83–88.

Chaplin, G. 2004. "Geographic distribution of environmental factors influencing human skin coloration." *American Journal of Physical Anthropology* 125 (3): 292–302.

Chaplin, G., and N.G. Jablonski. 1998. "Hemispheric difference in human skin color." *American Journal of Physical Anthropology* 107 (2): 221–224.
———. 2009. "Vitamin D and the evolution of human depigmentation." *American Journal of Physical Anthropology* 139 (4): 451–461.

Chestnutt, C.W. 2000. "What is a white man?" In *Interracialism: Black-White Intermarriage in American History, Literature, and Law*, ed. W. Sollors, 37–42. Oxford: Oxford University Press.

Chimpanzee Sequencing and Analysis Consortium. 2005. "Initial sequence of the chimpanzee genome and comparison with the human genome." *Nature* 437 (7055): 69–87.

Chung, J.H. 2001. "The effects of sunlight on the skin of Asians." In *Sun Protection in Man*, ed. P.U. Giacomoni, 3: 69–90. Amsterdam: Elsevier.

Claidière, N., and D. Sperber. 2010. "Imitation explains the propagation, not the stability of animal culture." *Proceedings of the Royal Society B: Biological Sciences* 277 (1681): 651–659.

Clark, J.D., Y. Beyene, G. WoldeGabriel, W.K. Hart, P.R. Renne, H. Gilbert, A. Defleur, G. Suwa, S. Katoh, K.R. Ludwig, et al. 2003. "Stratigraphic, chronological and behavioural contexts of Pleistocene *Homo sapiens* from Middle Awash, Ethiopia." *Nature* 423: 747–752.

Clarkson, T. 1804. *An Essay on the Slavery and Commerce of the Human Species, Particularly the African*. Philadelphia: Nathaniel Wiley.

Cleaver, J.E., and E. Crowley. 2002. "UV damage, DNA repair and skin carcinogenesis." *Frontiers in Bioscience* 7: 1024–1043.

Clemens, T.L., S.L. Henderson, J.S. Adams, and M.F. Holick. 1982. "Increased skin pigment reduces the capacity of skin to synthesise vitamin D3." *Lancet* 1 (8263): 74–76.

Cohen, W. B. 2003. *The French Encounter with Africans: White Response to Blacks, 1530–1880*. Bloomington: Indiana University Press.

Cole, R. G. 1972. "Sixteenth-century travel books as a source of European attitudes toward non-white and non-western culture." *Proceedings of the American Philosophical Society* 116 (1): 59–67.

Columb, C., and E. A. Plant. 2010. "Revisiting the Obama Effect: Exposure to Obama reduces implicit prejudice." *Journal of Experimental Social Psychology* 47 (2): 499–501.

Copp, A. J., A. Fleming, and N. Greene. 1998. "Embryonic mechanisms underlying the prevention of neural tube defects by vitamins." *Mental Retardation and Developmental Disability Research Reviews* 4: 264–268.

Cordaux, R., R. Aunger, G. Bentley, I. Nasidze, S. M. Sirajuddin, and M. Stoneking. 2004. "Independent origins of Indian caste and tribal paternal lineages." *Current Biology* 14 (3): 231–235.

Cornwell, N. 1998. "The rudiments of Daniil Kharms: In further pursuit of the red-haired man." *Modern Language Review* 93 (1): 133–145.

Costin, G.-E., and V. J. Hearing. 2007. "Human skin pigmentation: Melanocytes modulate skin color in response to stress." *FASEB Journal* 21 (4): 976–994.

Cowles, R. B. 1959. "Some ecological factors bearing on the origin and evolution of pigment in the human skin." *American Naturalist* 93 (872): 283–293.

Craft, W., and E. Craft. 2001. "Running a thousand miles for freedom." In *African American Slave Narratives: An Anthology*, ed. S. L. Bland Jr., 3: 891–946. Westport, CT: Greenwood Press.

Crone, G. R. 1937. *The Voyages of Cadamosto and Other Documents on Western Africa in the Second Half of the Fifteenth Century*. London: Hakluyt Society.

Cronin, K. J., P. E. M. Butler, M. McHugh, and G. Edwards. 1996. "A 1-year prospective study of burns in an Irish paediatric burns unit." *Burns* 22 (3): 221–224.

Dadachova, E., R. A. Bryan, R. C. Howell, A. D. Schweitzer, P. Aisen, J. D. Nosanchuk, and A. Casadevall. 2008. "The radioprotective properties of fungal melanin are a function of its chemical composition, stable radical presence and spatial arrangement." *Pigment Cell and Melanoma Research* 21 (2): 192–199.

Dadachova, E., R. A. Bryan, X. Huang, T. Moadel, A. D. Schweitzer, P. Aisen, J. D. Nosanchuk, and A. Casadevall. 2007. "Ionizing radiation changes the electronic properties of melanin and enhances the growth of melanized fungi." *PloS ONE* 2 (5): e457.

Davies, M., E. B. Mawer, J. T. Hann, and J. L. Taylor. 1986. "Seasonal changes in the biochemical indices of vitamin D deficiency in the elderly: A comparison of people in residential homes, long-stay wards and attending a day hospital." *Age and Ageing* 15 (2): 77–83.

de Bary, W. T., S. N. Hay, R. Weiler, and A. Yarrow. 1958. *Sources of Indian Tradition*. New York: Columbia University Press.

Der-Petrossian, M., M. Födinger, R. Knobler, H. Hönigsmann, and F. Trautinger. 2007. "Photodegradation of folic acid during extracorporeal photopheresis." *British Journal of Dermatology* 156 (1): 117–121.

Diffey, B. L. 2002. "Human exposure to solar ultraviolet radiation." *Journal of Cosmetic Dermatology* 1 (3): 124–130.

———. 2008. "A behavioral model for estimating population exposure to solar ultraviolet radiation." *Photochemistry and Photobiology* 84 (2): 371–375.

Dikotter, F. 1992. *The Discourse of Race in China.* London: C. Hurst.

Djukic, A. 2007. "Folate-responsive neurologic diseases." *Pediatric Neurology* 37 (6): 387–397.

Douthwaite, J. 1997. *"Homo ferus:* Between monster and model." *Eighteenth Century Life* 21 (2): 176–202.

Dower, J. 2004. "The pure self." In *Race, Ethnicity, and Migration in Modern Japan,* ed. M. Weiner, 1: 41–71. London: RoutledgeCurzon.

Dred Scott v. Sandford. 1857. 60 U.S. 393.

Dubow, S. 1995. *Scientific Racism in Modern South Africa.* Cambridge: Cambridge University Press.

Dyer, R. 1997. *White: Essays on Race and Culture.* London: Routledge.

Eberhardt, J. L. 2005. "Imaging race." *American Psychologist* 60 (2): 181–190.

Eberhardt, J. L., and S. T. Fiske. 1998. *Confronting Racism: The Problem and the Response.* Thousand Oaks, CA: Sage Publications.

Eigen, S., and M. Larrimore, eds. 2006. *The German Invention of Race.* Albany: State University of New York Press.

Elbourne, E., and R. Ross. 1997. "Combating spiritual and social bondage: Early missions in the Cape Colony." In *Christianity in South Africa: A Political, Social, and Cultural History,* ed. R. Elphick and R. Davenport, 31–50. Berkeley, CA: University of California Press.

Elias, P. M. 2005. "Stratum corneum defensive functions: An integrated view." *Journal of Investigative Dermatology* 125 (2): 183–200.

Elizondo, R. S. 1988. "Primate models to study eccrine sweating." *American Journal of Primatology* 14 (3): 265–276.

El-Mofty, M. A., S. M. Esmat, and M. Abdel-Halim. 2007. "Pigmentary disorders in the Mediterranean area." *Dermatologic Clinics* 25 (3): 401–417.

Engel-Ledeboer, M. S. J., and H. Engel. 1964. *Carolus Linnaeus Systema Naturae, 1735, Facsimile of the First Edition.* Nieuwkoop: B. de Graaf.

Erlandson, J. M., T. C. Rick, T. J. Braje, M. Casperson, B. Culleton, B. Fulfrost, T. Garcia, et al. 2011. "Paleoindian seafaring, maritime technologies, and coastal foraging on California's Channel Islands." *Science* 331 (6021): 1181–1185.

Fikes, R., Jr. 1980. "Black scholars in Europe during the Renaissance and the Enlightenment." *Negro History Bulletin* 43 (3): 58–60.

Finch, C., and C. Stanford. 2004. "Meat-adaptive genes and the evolution of slower aging in humans." *Quarterly Review of Biology* 79 (1): 3–50.

Fink, B., and P. J. Matts. 2008. "The effects of skin colour distribution and topography cues on the perception of female facial age and health." *Journal of the European Academy of Dermatology and Venereology* 22 (4): 493–498.

Finlayson, C. 2005. "Biogeography and evolution of the genus *Homo*." *Trends in Ecology & Evolution* 20 (8): 457–463.

Fisher, G.J., S. Kang, J. Varani, Z. Bata-Csorgo, Y. Wen, S. Datta, and J.J. Voorhees. 2002. "Mechanisms of photoaging and chronological skin aging." *Archives of Dermatological Research* 138 (11): 1462–1470.

Fiske, S.T. 2002. "What we know now about bias and intergroup conflict, the problem of the century." *Current Directions in Psychological Science* 11 (4): 123–128.

———. 2004. "Intent and ordinary bias: Unintended thought and social motivation create casual prejudice." *Social Justice Research* 17 (2): 117–127.

Fitzpatrick, T.B., and J.-P. Ortonne. 2003. "Normal skin color and general considerations of pigmentary disorders." In *Fitzpatrick's Dermatology in General Medicine*, ed. I.M. Freedberg, A.Z. Eisen, K. Wolff, et al., 819–825. New York: McGraw-Hill.

Fleet, J.C. 2008. "Molecular actions of vitamin D contributing to cancer prevention." *Molecular Aspects of Medicine* 29 (6): 388–396.

Fleischer, A.B., Jr., and A.B. Fleischer. 1992. "North Carolina tanning operators: Hazard on the horizon?" *Journal of the American Academy of Dermatology* 27 (no. 2, part 1): 199–203.

Fleming, A., and A.J. Copp. 1998. "Embryonic folate metabolism and mouse neural tube defects." *Science* 280: 2107–2109.

Freeman-Grenville, G.S.P. 1962. *The East African Coast: Select Documents from the First to the Earlier Nineteenth Century*. Oxford: Oxford University Press.

Frost, P. 1988. "Human skin color: A possible relationship between its sexual dimorphism and its social perception." *Perspectives in Biology and Medicine* 32 (1): 38–59.

———. 1994. "Geographic distribution of human skin colour: A selective compromise between natural selection and sexual selection?" *Human Evolution* 9 (2): 141–153.

Gabunia, L., S.C. Anton, D. Lordkipanidze, A. Vekua, A. Justus, and C.C. Swisher III. 2001. "Dmanisi and dispersal." *Evolutionary Anthropology* 10 (5): 158–170.

Garibyan, L., and D. Fisher. 2010. "How sunlight causes melanoma." *Current Oncology Reports* 12 (5): 319–326.

Garland, C.F., F.C. Garland, E.D. Gorham, M. Lipkin, H. Newmark, S.B. Mohr, and M.F. Holick. 2006. "The role of vitamin D in cancer prevention." *American Journal of Public Health* 96 (2): 252–261.

Gates, H.L., Jr., ed. 2002. *The Classic Slave Narratives*. New York: Signet Classics.

Gatewood, W.R. 2000. *Aristocrats of Color: The Black Elite, 1880–1920*. Little Rock: University of Arkansas Press.

Gerlach, A.L., F.H. Wilhelm, K. Gruber, and W.T. Roth. 2001. "Blushing and physiological arousability in social phobia." *Journal of Abnormal Psychology* 110 (2): 247–258.

Gerstner, J.N. 1997. A Christian monopoly: The Reformed Church and colonial society under Dutch rule. In *Christianity in South Africa: A Politi-*

cal, Social, and Cultural History, ed. R. Elphick and R. Davenport, 16–30. Berkeley, CA: University of California Press.

Giacomoni, P. U. 2001. "Women (and men) and the sun in the past." In *Sun Protection in Man,* ed. P. U. Giacomoni, 3: 1–10. Amsterdam: Elsevier.

Gillbro, J. M., and M. J. Olsson. 2011. "The melanogenesis and mechanisms of skin-lightening agents: Existing and new approaches." *International Journal of Cosmetic Science* 33 (3): 210–221.

Giovannucci, E., Y. Liu, E. B. Rimm, B. W. Hollis, C. S. Fuchs, M. J. Stampfer, and W. C. Willett. 2006. "Prospective study of predictors of vitamin D status and cancer incidence and mortality in men." *Journal of the National Cancer Institute (Bethesda)* 98 (7): 451–459.

Glenn, E. N. 2008. "Yearning for lightness: Transnational circuits in the marketing and consumption of skin lighteners." *Gender and Society* 22 (3): 281–302.

Goding, C. R. 2007. "Melanocytes: The new black." *The International Journal of Biochemistry and Cell Biology* 39 (2): 275–279.

Goebel, T. 1999. "Pleistocene human colonization of Siberia and peopling of the Americas: An ecological approach." *Evolutionary Anthropology* 8 (6): 208–227.

Goebel, T., M. R. Waters, and D. H. O'Rourke. 2008. "The Late Pleistocene dispersal of modern humans in the Americas." *Science* 319 (5869): 1497–1502.

Goff, P. A., J. L. Eberhardt, M. J. Williams, and M. C. Jackson. 2008. "Not yet human: Implicit knowledge, historical dehumanization, and contemporary consequences." *Journal of Personality and Social Psychology* 94 (2): 292–306.

Golden, M. 2004. *Don't Play in the Sun: One Woman's Journey through the Color Complex.* New York: Anchor Books.

Goldenberg, D. M. 2003. *The Curse of Ham: Race and Slavery in Early Judaism, Christianity, and Islam.* Princeton, NJ: Princeton University Press.

Goodman, M. J., P. B. Griffin, A. A. Estioko-Griffin, and J. S. Grove. 1985. "The compatibility of hunting and mothering among the Agta hunter-gatherers of the Philippines." *Sex Roles* 12 (11): 1199–1209.

Grant, W. B. 2008. "Solar ultraviolet irradiance and cancer incidence and mortality." *Advances in Experimental Medicine and Biology* 624: 16–30.

Gronskov, K., J. Ek, and K. Brondum-Nielsen. 2007. "Oculocutaneous albinism." *Orphanet Journal of Rare Diseases* 2 (1): 43–50.

Guernier, V., M. E. Hochberg, and J.-F. Guegan. 2004. "Ecology drives the worldwide distribution of human diseases." *PLoS Biology* 2 (6): e141.

Guimaraes, A. S. A. 1995. "Racism and anti-racism in Brazil." In *Racism and Anti-racism in World Perspective,* ed. B. P. Bowser, 208–226. Thousand Oaks, CA: Sage Publications.

Guthrie, R. D. 1970. "Evolution of human threat display organs." *Evolutionary Biology* 4: 257–302.

Hachee, M. R. 2011. "Kant, Race, and Reason." www.msu.edu/~hacheema/kant2.htm.

Hagelberg, E., M. Kayser, M. Nagy, L. Roewer, H. Zimdahl, M. Krawczak,

P. Lió, and W. Schiefenhövel. 1999. "Molecular genetic evidence for the human settlement of the Pacific: Analysis of mitochondrial DNA, Y chromosome and HLA markers." *Philosophical Transactions of the Royal Society B: Biological Sciences* 354 (1379): 141–152.

Hall, R. E. 1995a. "The bleaching syndrome: African Americans' response to cultural domination vis-a-vis skin color." *Journal of Black Studies* 26 (2): 172–184.

———. 1995b. "Dark skin and the cultural ideal of masculinity." *Journal of African American Studies* 1 (3): 37–62.

———. 2001. *Filipina Eurogamy: Skin Color as Vehicle of Psychological Colonization.* Quezon City, Philippines: Giraffe Books.

Hammond, R. A., and R. Axelrod. 2006. "The evolution of ethnocentrism." *Journal of Conflict Resolution* 50 (6): 926–936.

Harris, J. R. 2006. "Parental selection: A third selection process in the evolution of human hairlessness and skin color." *Medical Hypotheses* 66 (6): 1053–1059.

Hawkes, K., J. F. O'Connell, N. G. Blurton Jones, M. Gurven, K. Hill, R. Hames, T. Kano, et al. 1997. "Hadza women's time allocation, offspring provisioning, and the evolution of long postmenopausal life spans." *Current Anthropology* 38 (4): 551–577.

Haynes, S. R. 2002. *Noah's Curse: The Biblical Justification of American Slavery.* Oxford: Oxford University Press.

Herring, C., V. M. Keith, and H. D. Horton, eds. 2004. *Skin/Deep: How Race and Complexion Matter in the "Color-Blind" Era.* Urbana, IL: Institute for Research on Race and Public Policy.

Hersch, J. 2010. "Skin color, immigrant wages, and discrimination." In *Racism in the 21st Century: An Empirical Analysis of Skin Color,* ed. R. E. Hall, 77–90. New York: Springer

Hess, A. F. 1922. "Newer aspects of the rickets problem." *Journal of the American Medical Association* 78 (16): 1177–1183.

Hickok, G. 2009. "Eight problems for the mirror neuron theory of action understanding in monkeys and humans." *Journal of Cognitive Neuroscience* 21 (7): 1229–1243.

Higginbotham, A. L., Jr. 1978. *In the Matter of Color: Race and the American Legal Process, The Colonial Period.* New York: Oxford University Press.

Hirschfeld, L. A. 1993. "Discovering social difference: The role of appearance in the development of racial awareness." *Cognitive Psychology* 25 (3): 317–350.

Hitchcock, R. T. 2001. *Ultraviolet Radiation.* Fairfax, VA: American Industrial Hygiene Association.

Hoerster, K. D., R. L. Garrow, J. A. Mayer, E. J. Clapp, J. R. Weeks, S. I. Woodruff, J. F. Sallis, D. J. Slymen, M. R. Patel, and S. A. Sybert. 2009. "Density of indoor tanning facilities in 116 large U.S. cities." *American Journal of Preventive Medicine* 36 (3): 243–246.

Hoffer, P. C. 2003. *Sensory Worlds in Early America.* Baltimore, MD: Johns Hopkins University Press.

Holick, M. F. 2003. "Evolution and function of vitamin D." *Recent Results in Cancer Research* 164: 3–28.

————. 2004. "Vitamin D: Importance in the prevention of cancers, type 1 diabetes, heart disease and osteoporosis." *American Journal of Clinical Nutrition* 79 (3): 362–371.

Holick, M.F., and T.C. Chen. 2008. "Vitamin D deficiency: A worldwide problem with health consequences." *American Journal of Clinical Nutrition* 87 (4): 1080S–1086S.

Hollis, B.W. 2005. "Circulating 25-hydroxyvitamin D levels indicative of vitamin D sufficiency: Implications for establishing a new effective dietary intake recommendation for vitamin D." *Journal of Nutrition* 135 (2): 317–322.

Iacoboni, M. 2009. "Imitation, empathy, and mirror neurons." *Annual Review of Psychology* 60 (1): 653–670.

Ibrahim, A. 2008. "Literature of the converts in early modern Spain: Nationalism and religious dissimulation of minorities." *Comparative Literature Studies* 45 (2): 210–227.

Institute of Human Origins. n.d. *Becoming Human.* http://www.becoming human.org/. Accessed November 2011.

Institute of Medicine. 2010. *Dietary Reference Intakes For Calcium and Vitamin D.* www.iom.edu/Reports/2010/Dietary-Reference-Intakes-for-Calcium -and-Vitamin-D.aspx.

Irwin, G.W. 1977. *Africans Abroad.* New York: Columbia University Press.

Isaac, B. 2004. *The Invention of Racism in Classical Antiquity.* Princeton, NJ: Princeton University Press.

Ishai, A., C.F. Schmidt, and P. Boesinger. 2005. "Face perception is mediated by a distributed cortical network." *Brain Research Bulletin* 67 (1–2): 87–93.

Ito, T.A., and J.T. Cacioppo. 2007. "Attitudes as mental and neural states of readiness." In *Implicit Measures of Attitudes,* ed. B. Wittenbrink and N. Schwarz, 125–158. New York: Guilford Press.

Iyengar, S. 2005. *Shades of Difference: Mythologies of Skin Color in Early Modern England.* Philadelphia: University of Pennsylvania Press.

Jablonski, N.G., ed. 2002. *The First Americans: The Pleistocene Colonization of the New World.* San Francisco, CA: California Academy of Sciences.

————. 2004. "The evolution of human skin and skin color." *Annual Review of Anthropology* 33: 585–623.

————. 2006. *Skin: A Natural History.* Berkeley: University of California Press.

————. 2010. "From Bardot to Beckham: The decline of celebrity tanning." *Skin Cancer Foundation Journal* 28: 42–44.

Jablonski, N.G., and G. Chaplin. 2000. "The evolution of human skin coloration." *Journal of Human Evolution* 39 (1): 57–106.

James, W.A., Sr. 2003. *The Skin Color Syndrome among African-Americans.* New York: iUniverse.

Jefferson, T. 1787. *Notes on the State of Virginia.* London: Printed for J. Stockdale.

Jimbow, K., W.C. Quevedo, Jr., T.B. Fitzpatrick, and G. Szabo. 1976. "Some aspects of melanin biology: 1950–1975." *Journal of Investigative Dermatology* 67: 72–89.

Johnson, R. 2009. "European cloth and 'tropical' skin: Clothing material and

British ideas of health and hygiene in tropical climates." *Bulletin of the History of Medicine* 83 (3): 530–560.

Johnson, S. L. 1992–1993. "Racial imagery in criminal cases." *Tulane Law Review* 67: 1739–1806.

Johnson, W. 1999. *Soul by Soul: Life inside the Antebellum Slave Market.* Cambridge, MA: Harvard University Press.

———. 2000. "The slave trader, the white slave, and the politics of racial determination in the 1850s." *Journal of American History* 87 (1): 13–38.

Kalla, A. K. 1974. "Human skin pigmentation, its genetics and variation." *Human Genetics* 21 (4): 289–300.

Kant, I. 1960. *Observations on the Feeling of the Beautiful and the Sublime.* Berkeley, CA: University of California Press.

———. 2000. "Of the different human races." In *The Idea of Race,* ed. R. Bernasconi and T. L. Lott, 11–22. Indianapolis, IN: Hackett.

Kapama, F. 2009. "Magu trader 'was buyer of albino parts.'" *Daily News* (Dar es Salaam), June 11.

Kaur, M., A. Liguori, W. Lang, S. R. Rapp, A. B. Fleischer Jr., and S. R. Feldman. 2006. "Induction of withdrawal-like symptoms in a small randomized, controlled trial of opioid blockade in frequent tanners." *Journal of the American Academy of Dermatology* 54 (4): 709–711.

Keita, S. O. Y. 2005. "History in the interpretation of the pattern of p49a,f TaqI RFLP Y-chromosome variation in Egypt: A consideration of multiple lines of evidence." *American Journal of Human Biology* 17 (5): 559–567.

Keith, V. M., and C. Herring. 1991. "Skin tone and stratification in the black community." *American Journal of Sociology* 97 (3): 760–778.

Kennedy, C., C. D. Bajdik, R. Willemze, F. R. de Gruijl, and J. N. Bouwes Bavinck. 2003. "The influence of painful sunburns and lifetime sun exposure on the risk of actinic keratoses, seborrheic warts, melanocytic nevi, atypical nevi, and skin cancer." *Journal of Investigative Dermatology* 120 (6): 1087–1093.

Kennedy, D. 1990. "The perils of the midday sun: Climate anxieties in the colonial tropics." In *Imperialism and the Natural World,* ed. J. M. MacKenzie, 118–140. Manchester, U.K.: Manchester University Press.

Kennedy, K. A. R. 2000. *God-Apes and Fossil Men: Paleoanthropology of South Asia.* Ann Arbor: University of Michigan Press.

Kern, P. B. 1999. *Ancient Siege Warfare.* Bloomington: Indiana University Press.

Kimball, S., G. H. Fuleihan, and R. Vieth. 2008. "Vitamin D: A growing perspective." *Critical Reviews in Clinical Laboratory Sciences* 45 (4): 339–414.

Kiple, K., and V. Kiple. 1980. "The African connection: Slavery, disease and racism." *Phylon* 41 (3): 211–222.

Knight, A., P. A. Underhill, H. M. Mortenson, L. A. Zhivtovsky, A. A. Lin, B. M. Henn, D. Louis, M. Ruhlen, and J. L. Mountain. 2003. "African Y chromosome and mtDNA divergence provides insight into the history of click languages." *Current Biology* 13 (6): 464–473.

Kourosh, A. S., C. R. Harrington, and B. Adinoff. 2010. "Tanning as a behavioral addiction." *The American Journal of Drug and Alcohol Abuse* 36 (5): 284–290.

Kovacs, C.S. 2008. "Vitamin D in pregnancy and lactation: Maternal, fetal, and neonatal outcomes from human and animal studies." *American Journal of Clinical Nutrition* 88 (2): 520S–528S.

Krings, M., A. Stone, R.W. Schmitz, H. Krainitzki, M. Stoneking, and S. Pääbo. 1997. "Neandertal DNA sequences and the origin of modern humans." *Cell* 90: 19–30.

Kurzban, R., J. Tooby, and L. Cosmides. 2001. "Can race be erased? Coalitional computation and social categorization." *Proceedings of the National Academy of Sciences of the United States of America* 98 (26): 15387–15392.

Ladizinski, B., N. Mistry, and R.V. Kundu. 2011. "Widespread use of toxic skin lightening compounds: Medical and psychosocial aspects." *Dermatologic Clinics* 29 (1): 111–123.

Lall, S.P., and L.M. Lewis-McCrea. 2007. "Role of nutrients in skeletal metabolism and pathology in fish: An overview." *Aquaculture* 267 (1–4): 3–19.

Lalueza-Fox, C., H. Rompler, D. Caramelli, C. Staubert, G. Catalano, D. Hughes, N. Rohland, et al. 2007. "A melanocortin 1 receptor allele suggests varying pigmentation among Neanderthals." *Science* 318 (5855): 1453–1455.

Lamason, R.L., M.-A.P.K. Mohideen, J.R. Mest, A.C. Wong, H.L. Norton, M.C. Aros, M.J. Jurynec, et al. 2005. "SLC24A5, a putative cation exchanger, affects pigmentation in zebrafish and humans." *Science* 310 (5755): 1782–1786.

Lamparelli, R.D., T.H. Bothwell, A.P. MacPhail, J. van der Westuyzen, R.D. Baynes, and B.J. MacFarlane. 1988. "Nutritional anaemia in pregnant coloured women in Johannesburg." *South African Medical Journal* 73 (8): 477–481.

Langbein, L., M.A. Rogers, S. Praetzel, B. Cribier, B. Peltre, N. Gassler, and J. Schweizer. 2005. "Characterization of a novel human type II epithelial keratin K1b, specifically expressed in eccrine sweat glands." *Journal of Investigative Dermatology* 125 (3): 428–444.

Larrimore, M. 2006. "Race, freedom and the fall in Steffens and Kant." In *The German Invention of Race*, ed. S. Eigen and M. Larrimore, 91–122. Albany: State University of New York Press.

Lauretani, F., M. Maggio, G. Valenti, E. Dall'aglio, and G.P. Ceda. 2010. "Vitamin D in older population: New roles for this 'classic actor?'" *Aging Male* 13 (4): 215–232.

Lawrence, V.A. 1983. "Demographic analysis of serum folate and folate-binding capacity in hospitalized patients." *Acta Haematologica* 69 (5): 289–293.

Leck, I.A.N. 1984. "The geographical distribution of neural tube defects and oral clefts." *British Medical Bulletin* 40 (4): 390–395.

Leonard, W.R., and M.L. Robertson. 1994. "Evolutionary perspectives on human nutrition: The influence of brain and body size on diet and metabolism." *American Journal of Human Biology* 6: 77–88.

Letts, M. 1946. "Sir John Mandeville." *Notes and Queries* 191 (10): 202–204.

Levin, D.T. 2000. "Race as a visual feature: Using visual search and perceptual discrimination tasks to understand face categories and the cross-race recognition deficit." *Journal of Experimental Psychology: General* 129 (4): 559–574.

Lippmann, W. 1929. *Public Opinion*. New York: Macmillan.

Loomis, W. F. 1967. "Skin-pigment regulation of vitamin-D biosynthesis in man." *Science* 157 (3788): 501–506.

Lordkipanidze, D., T. Jashashvili, A. Vekua, M. S. Ponce de Leon, C. Zollikofer, G. P. Rightmire, H. Pontzer, et al. 2007. "Postcranial evidence from early Homo from Dmanisi, Georgia." *Nature* 449 (7160): 305–310.

Lucock, M., Z. Yates, T. Glanville, R. Leeming, N. Simpson, and I. Daskalakis. 2003. "A critical role for B-vitamin nutrition in human development and evolutionary biology." *Nutrition Research* 23 (11): 1463–1475.

MacEachern, S. 2000. "Genes, tribes, and African history." *Current Anthropology* 41 (3): 357–384.

Mackintosh, J. A. 2001. "The antimicrobial properties of melanocytes, melanosomes and melanin and the evolution of black skin." *Journal of Theoretical Biology* 211 (2): 101–113.

Maclaren, C., ed. 1823. "Negro." *Encyclopædia Britannica*. Edinburgh: Archibald Constable.

Macrae, C. N., and G. V. Bodenhausen. 2000. "Social cognition: Thinking categorically about others." *Annual Review of Psychology* 51: 93–120.

Madrigal, L., and W. Kelly. 2007. "Human skin-color sexual dimorphism: A test of the sexual selection hypothesis." *American Journal of Physical Anthropology* 132 (3): 470–482.

Makova, K., and H. L. Norton. 2005. "Worldwide polymorphism at the MC1R locus and normal pigmentation variation in humans." *Peptides* 26 (10): 1901–1908.

Mandeville, J., G. da Pian del Carpine, W. van Ruysbroeck, and O. de Pordenone. 1964. *The Travels of Sir John Mandeville: With Three Narratives of It: The Voyage of Johannes de Plano Carpini; The Journal of Friar William de Rubruquis; The Journal of Friar Odoric*. New York: Dover.

Marugame, T., and M.-J. Zhang. 2010. "Comparison of time trends in melanoma of skin cancer mortality (1990–2006) between countries based on the WHO Mortality Database." *Japanese Journal of Clinical Oncology* 40 (7): 710.

Marx, D. M., S. J. Ko, and R. A. Friedman. 2009. "The "Obama Effect": How a salient role model reduces race-based performance differences." *Journal of Experimental Social Psychology* 45 (4): 953–956.

Mathur, U., S. L. Datta, and B. B. Mathur. 1977. "The effect of aminopterin-induced folic acid deficiency on spermatogenesis." *Fertility and Sterility* 28 (12): 1356–1360.

Matisoo-Smith, E., and J. H. Robins. 2004. "Origins and dispersals of Pacific peoples: Evidence from mtDNA phylogenies of the Pacific rat." *Proceedings of the National Academy of Sciences* 101 (24): 9167–9172.

Matsumura, Y., and H. N. Ananthawamy. 2004. "Toxic effects of ultraviolet radiation on the skin." *Toxicology and Applied Pharmacology* 195 (3): 298–308.

Matsuoka, L. Y., J. Wortsman, M. J. Dannenberg, B. W. Hollis, Z. Lu, and M. F. Holick. 1992. "Clothing prevents ultraviolet-B radiation-dependent photosynthesis of vitamin D₃." *Journal of Clinical Endocrinology and Metabolism* 75 (4): 1099–1103.

Mawer, E.B., J. Backhouse, C.A. Holman, G.A. Lumb, and S.W. Stanbury. 1972. "The distribution and storage of vitamin D and its metabolites in human tissues." *Clinical Science* 43: 413–431.

McCullough, M.L., R.M. Bostick, and T.L. Mayo. 2009. "Vitamin D gene pathway polymorphisms and risk of colorectal, breast, and prostate cancer." *Annual Review of Nutrition* 29 (1): 111–132.

McCurdy, T., and S.E. Graham. 2003. "Using human activity data in exposure models: Analysis of discriminating factors." *Journal of Exposure Analysis and Environmental Epidemiology* 13 (4): 294–317.

McDonald, J.C., T.W. Gyorkos, B. Alberton, J.D. MacLean, G. Richer, and D. Juranek. 1990. "An outbreak of toxoplasmosis in pregnant women in Northern Quebec." *Journal of Infectious Diseases* 161 (4): 769–774.

McPhail, G. 1997. "There's no such thing as a healthy glow: Cutaneous malignant melanoma; The case against suntanning." *European Journal of Cancer Care* 6 (2): 147–153.

Mellars, P. 2006. "Why did modern human populations disperse from Africa ca. 60,000 years ago? A new model." *Proceedings of the National Academy of Sciences* 103 (25): 9381–9386.

Meltzer, M. 1993. *Slavery: A World History.* New York: De Capo Press.

Meredith, P., and T. Sarna. 2006. "The physical and chemical properties of eumelanin." *Pigment Cell Research* 19 (6): 572–594.

Michlovic, M.G., M. Hall, and T. Maggs. 1977. "On early human skin pigmentation." *Current Anthropology* 18 (3): 549–550.

Miller, A.G., W.A. Ashton, J.W. McHoskey, and J. Gimbel. 1990. "What price attractiveness? Stereotype and risk factors in suntanning behavior." *Journal of Applied Social Psychology* 20 (15): 1272–1300.

Milton, K. 1987. "Primate diets and gut morphology: Implications for hominid evolution." In *Food and Evolution,* ed. M. Harris and E.B. Ross, 93–115. Philadelphia: Temple University Press.

———. 1993. "Diet and primate evolution." *Scientific American* 269 (2): 86–93.

Mitchell, F.T. 1930. "Incidence of rickets in the South." *Southern Medical Journal* 23 (3): 228–235.

Mitchell, J., and P. Collinson. 1744. "An essay upon the causes of the different colours of people in different climates." *Philosophical Transactions (1683–1775)* 43: 102–150.

Monfrecola, G., and E. Prizio. 2001. "Self tanning." In *Sun Protection in Man,* ed. P.U. Giacomoni, 3: 487–493. Amsterdam: Elsevier.

Montague, M., R. Borland, and C. Sinclair. 2001. "Slip! Slop! Slap! and Sun-Smart, 1980–2000: Skin cancer control and 20 years of population-based campaigning." *Health Education and Behavior* 28 (3): 290–305.

Moore, J.M. 1999. *Leading the Race: The Transformation of the Black Elite in the Nation's Capital, 1880–1920.* Charlottesville, VA: University Press of Virginia.

Mosher, C.E., and S. Danoff-Burg. 2010. "Addiction to indoor tanning: Relation to anxiety, depression, and substance use." *Archives of Dermatology* 146 (4): 412–417.

MRC Vitamin Study Research Group. 1991. "Prevention of neural tube defects: Results of the Medical Research Council Vitamin Study." *Lancet* 338 (8760): 131–134.

Murray, F. G. 1934. "Pigmentation, sunlight, and nutritional disease." *American Anthropologist* 36 (3): 438–445.

Nakashima, T., K. Matsuno, M. Matsushita, and T. Matsushita. 2011. "Severe lead contamination among children of samurai families in Edo period Japan." *Journal of Archaeological Science* 38 (1): 23–28.

Nanamoli, B., and B. Bodhi. 1995. *The Middle Length Discourses of the Buddha: A New Translation of the Majjhima Nikaya.* Boston: Wisdom Publications.

National Geographic Society. 2005. "King Tut's New Face: Behind the Forensic Reconstruction." http://news.nationalgeographic.com/news/2005/05/0511 _050511_kingtutface.html.

National Institutes of Health. 2009. *Dietary Supplement Fact Sheet: Folate.* Office of Dietary Supplements. http://ods.od.nih.gov/factsheets/folate.

Neal, A.M., and M.L. Wilson. 1989. "The role of skin color and features in the black community: Implications for black women and therapy." *Clinical Psychology Review* 9 (3): 323–333.

Niebrzydowski, S. 2001. "The sultana and her sisters: Black women in the British Isles before 1530." *Women's History Review* 10 (2): 187–210.

Nielsen, K.P., L. Zhao, J.J. Stamnes, K. Stamnes, and J. Moan. 2006. "The importance of the depth distribution of melanin in skin for DNA protection and other photobiological processes." *Journal of Photochemistry and Photobiology B: Biology* 82 (3): 194–198.

Nobles, M. 2000. "History counts: A comparative analysis of racial/color categorization in US and Brazilian censuses." *American Journal of Public Health* 90 (11): 1738–1745.

Nolan, B.V., and S.R. Feldman. 2009. "Ultraviolet tanning addiction." *Dermatologic Clinics* 27 (2): 109–112.

Noonan, J.P. 2010. "Neanderthal genomics and the evolution of modern humans." *Genome Research* 20 (5): 547–553.

Norman, A.W. 2008. "From vitamin D to hormone D: Fundamentals of the vitamin D endocrine system essential for good health." *American Journal of Clinical Nutrition* 88 (2): 491S–499S.

Northrup, D. 2002. *Africa's Discovery of Europe, 1450–1850.* New York: Oxford University Press.

Norton, H.L., J.S. Friedlaender, D.A. Merriwether, G. Koki, C.S. Mgone, and M.D. Shriver. 2006. "Skin and hair pigmentation variation in island Melanesia." *American Journal of Physical Anthropology* 130 (2): 254–268.

Oakes, J. 1998. *The Ruling Race: A History of American Slaveholders.* New York: W.W. Norton.

Off, M.K., A.E. Steindal, A.C. Porojnicu, A. Juzeniene, A. Vorobey, A. Johnsson, and J. Moan. 2005. "Ultraviolet photodegradation of folic acid." *Journal of Photochemistry and Photobiology B: Biology* 80 (1): 47–55.

O'Flaherty, B., and J.S. Shapiro. 2002. *Apes, Essences, and Races: What Natural Scientists Believed about Human Variation, 1700–1900.* Columbia University Department of Economics Discussion Paper #0102-24. New York: Columbia University.

Olivarius, F.F., H.C. Wulf, P. Therkildsen, T. Poulson, J. Crosby, and M. Norval. 1997. "Urocanic acid isomers: Relation to body site, pigmentation, stratum corneum thickness and photosensitivity." *Archives of Dermatological Research* 289 (9): 501–505.

Olivelle, P. 1996. *Upaniṣads (translated from the original Sanskrit) by Patrick Olivelle.* New York: Oxford University Press.

Olsson, A., J.P. Ebert, M.R. Banaji, and E.A. Phelps. 2005. "The role of social groups in the persistence of learned fear." *Science* 309 (5735): 785–787.

Operario, D., and S.T. Fiske. 1998. "Racism equals power plus prejudice: A social psychological equation for racial oppression." In *Racism: The Problem and the Response,* ed. J.L. Eberhardt and S.T. Fiske, 33–53. Thousand Oaks, CA: Sage Publications.

O'Riordan, D.L., A.D. Steffen, K.B. Lunde, and P. Gies. 2008. "A day at the beach while on tropical vacation: Sun protection practices in a high-risk setting for UV radiation exposure." *Archives of Dermatology* 144 (11): 1449–1455.

Ortonne, J.-P. 1990. "Pigmentary changes of the ageing skin." *British Journal of Dermatology* 122 (S35): 21–28.

Ossorio, P., and T. Duster. 2005. "Race and genetics: Controversies in biomedical, behavioral, and forensic sciences." *American Psychologist* 60 (1): 115–128.

Patterson, M.M., and R.S. Bigler. 2006. "Preschool children's attention to environmental messages about groups: Social categorization and the origins of intergroup bias." *Child Development* 77 (4): 847–860.

Pawson, I.G., and N.L. Petrakis. 1975. "Comparisons of breast pigmentation among women of different racial groups." *Human Biology* 47 (4): 441–450.

Peiss, K. 1998. *Hope in a Jar: The Making of America's Beauty Culture.* New York: Metropolitan Books.

Peters, W. 1987. *A Class Divided: Then and Now.* New Haven, CT: Yale University Press.

Pfeifer, G.P., Y.H. You, and A. Besaratinia. 2005. "Mutations induced by ultraviolet light." *Mutation Research* 571 (1–2): 19–31.

Phelps, E.A., K.J. O'Connor, W.A. Cunningham, E.S. Funayama, J.C. Gatenby, J.C. Gore, and M.R. Banaji. 2000. "Performance on indirect measures of race evaluation predicts amygdala activation." *Journal of Cognitive Neuroscience* 12 (5): 729–738.

Pieterse, J.N. 1992. *White on Black: Images of Africa and Blacks in Western Popular Culture.* New Haven, CT: Yale University Press.

Plant, E.A., P.G. Devine, W.T.L. Cox, C. Columb, S.L. Miller, J. Goplen, and B.M. Peruche. 2009. "The Obama effect: Decreasing implicit prejudice and stereotyping." *Journal of Experimental Social Psychology* 45 (4): 961–964.

Quevedo, W.C. 1973. "Genetic control of melanin metabolism within the melanin unit of mammalian epidermis." *Journal of Investigative Dermatology* 60 (6): 407–417.

Quillen, E. 2010. "Identifying genes related to Indigenous American–specific changes in skin pigmentation." PhD diss., Pennsylvania State University.

Quinn, N., and D. Holland. 1997. "Culture and cognition." In *Cultural Models in Language and Thought,* ed. D. Holland and N. Quinn, 3–42. Cambridge: Cambridge University Press.

Rajakumar, K., and S.B. Thomas. 2005. "Reemerging nutritional rickets: A historical perspective." *Archives of Pediatrics and Adolescent Medicine* 159 (4): 335–341.

Randle, H.W. 1997. "Suntanning: Differences in perceptions throughout history." *Mayo Clinic Proceedings* 72 (5): 461–466.

Rao, D.S., and N. Raghuramulu. 1996. "Food chain as origin of vitamin D in fish." *Comparative Biochemistry and Physiology Part A: Physiology* 114 (1): 15–19.

Rees, J.L. 2003. "Genetics of Hair and Skin Color." *Annual Review of Genetics* 37: 67–90.

Relethford, J.H. 2000. "Human skin color diversity is highest in sub-Saharan African populations." *Human Biology* 72 (5): 771–780.

———. 2008. "Genetic evidence and the modern human origins debate." *Heredity* 100 (6): 555–563.

Roach, M. 2006. *The Roots of Desire: The Myth, Meaning, and Sexual Power of Red Hair.* New York: Bloomsbury USA.

Robins, A.H. 1991. *Biological Perspectives on Human Pigmentation.* Cambridge: Cambridge University Press.

———. 2009. "The evolution of light skin color: Role of vitamin D disputed." *American Journal of Physical Anthropology* 139 (4): 447–450.

Robinson, J.K., J. Kim, S. Rosenbaum, and S. Ortiz. 2008. "Indoor tanning knowledge, attitudes, and behavior among young adults from 1988–2007." *Archives of Dermatological Research* 144 (4): 484–488.

Rogers, A.R., D. Iltis, and S. Wooding. 2004. "Genetic variation at the MC1R locus and the time since loss of human body hair." *Current Anthropology* 45 (1): 105–124.

Rondilla, J.L., and P. Spickard. 2007. *Is Lighter Better? Skin-Tone Discrimination among Asian Americans.* Lanham, MD: Rowman and Littlefield.

Roper, M. 2001. "A narrative of the adventures and escape of Moses Roper, from American slavery." In *African American Slave Narratives: An Anthology,* ed. S.L. Bland Jr., 1: 47–88. Westport, CT: Greenwood.

Rouhani, P., P.S. Pinheiro, R. Sherman, K. Arheart, L.E. Fleming, J. MacKinnon, and R.S. Kirsner. 2010. "Increasing rates of melanoma among nonwhites in Florida compared with the United States." *Archives of Dermatology* 146 (7): 741–746.

Saad, E.N. 1983. *Social History of Timbuktu: The Role of Muslim Scholars and Notables, 1400–1900.* Cambridge: Cambridge University Press.

Saks, E. 2000. "Representing miscegenation law." In *Interracialism: Black-White Intermarriage in American History, Literature, and Law,* ed. W. Sollors, 61–81. Oxford: Oxford University Press.

Sambon, L. W. 1898. "Acclimatization of Europeans in tropical lands." *Geographical Journal* 12 (6): 589–599.

Samson, J. 2005. *Race and Empire*. Harlow, U.K.: Pearson Education Limited.

Sanjek, R. 1994. "The enduring inequalities of race." In *Race*, ed. S. Gregory and R. Sanjek, 1–17. New Brunswick, NJ: Rutgers University Press.

Saraiya, M., K. Glanz, P. Nichols, C. White, D. Das, S. J. Smith, B. Tannor, et al. 2004. "Interventions to prevent skin cancer by reducing exposure to ultraviolet radiation: A systematic review." *American Journal of Preventive Medicine* 27 (5): 422–466.

Satherley, J. 2011. "From 'Cole Cappuccino' to 'Katona Karrot': Pippa Middleton's 'Royal Mocha' leads the celebrity tan tone scale as the most desirable shade in Britain." *Mail Online*. August 2. www.dailymail.co.uk/femail/article-2021360/Pippa-Middletons-Royal-Mocha-tan-desirable-shade-Britain.html.

Scarre, C., ed. 2005. *The Human Past: World Prehistory and the Development of Human Societies*. London: Thames & Hudson.

Schallreuter, K. U. 2007. "Advances in melanocyte basic science research." *Dermatologic Clinics* 25 (3): 283–291.

Schmader, T., M. Johns, and C. Forbes. 2008. "An integrated process model of stereotype threat effects on performance." *Psychological Review* 115 (2): 336–356.

Schoeninger, M. J., H. T. Bunn, S. Murray, T. Pickering, and J. Moore. 2001. "Meat-eating by the fourth African ape." In *Meat-Eating and Human Evolution*, ed. C. B. Stanford and H. T. Bunn, 179–195. Oxford: Oxford University Press.

Schweizer, J., L. Langbein, M. A. Rogers, and H. Winter. 2007. "Hair follicle-specific keratins and their diseases." *Experimental Cell Research* 313 (10): 2010–2020.

Searle, J. R. 1995. *The Construction of Social Reality*. New York: Free Press.

Segal, R. 2001. *Islam's Black Slaves: The Other Black Diaspora*. New York: Farrar, Straus, and Giroux.

Segrave, K. 2005. *Suntanning in 20th Century America*. Jefferson, NC: McFarland.

Sheehan, J. M., C. S. Potten, and A. R. Young. 1998. "Tanning in human skin types II and III offers modest photoprotection against erythema." *Photochemistry and Photobiology* 68 (4): 588–592.

Shell, S. M. 2006. "Kant's concept of a human race." In *The German Invention of Race*, ed. S. Eigen and M. Larrimore, 55–72. Albany: State University of New York Press.

Sinha, R. P., and D.-P. Hader. 2002. "UV-induced DNA damage and repair: A review." *Photochemical and Photobiological Science* 1 (4): 225–236.

Siyame, P. 2009. "Albino's skinned body found in swamp." *Daily News* (Dar es Salaam), February 12.

Smaje, C. 2000. *Natural Hierarchies: The Historical Sociology of Race and Caste*. Malden, MA: Blackwell.

Smedley, A. 1999. *Race in North America: Origin and Evolution of a Worldview*. Boulder, CO: Westview.

Smedley, A., and B. D. Smedley. 2005. "Race as biology is fiction, racism as a social problem is real: Anthropological and historical perspectives on the social construction of race." *American Psychologist* 60 (1): 16–26.

Smellie, W., ed. 1771. "Negroes." In *Encyclopædia Britannica*. Edinburgh: A. Bell and C. Macfarquar.

Smith, S.S., 1965. *An Essay on the Causes of the Variety of Complexion and Figure in the Human Species*. Cambridge, MA: Belknap Press of Harvard University Press.

Snipp, C.M. 2003. "Racial measurement in the American census: Past practices and implications for the future." *Annual Review of Sociology* 29: 563–588.

Snowden, F.M., Jr. 1970. *Blacks in Antiquity: Ethiopians in the Greco-Roman Experience*. Cambridge, MA: Belknap Press of Harvard University Press.

———. 1983. *Before Color Prejudice: The Ancient View of Blacks*. Cambridge, MA: Harvard University Press.

Solanki, T., R.H. Hyatt, J.R. Kemm, E.A. Hughes, and R.A. Cowan. 1995. "Are elderly Asians in Britain at a high risk of vitamin D deficiency and osteomalacia?" *Age and Ageing* 24 (2): 103–107.

Soong, R. 1999. "Racial Classifications in Latin America." Zona Latina: The Latin America Media Site. www.zonalatina.com/Zldata55.htm.

Spamer, E.E. 1999. "Know thyself: Responsible science and the lectotype of *Homo sapiens Linnaeus, 1758*." *Proceedings of the Academy of Natural Sciences of Philadelphia* 149: 109–114.

Springbett, P., S. Buglass, and A.R. Young. 2010. "Photoprotection and vitamin D status." *Journal of Photochemistry and Photobiology B: Biology* 101 (2): 160–168.

Steele, C.M., and J. Aronson. 1995. "Stereotype threat and the intellectual test performance of African Americans." *Journal of Personality and Social Psychology* 69 (5): 797–811.

Steindal, A.H., A. Juzeniene, A. Johnsson, and J. Moan. 2006. "Photodegradation of 5-methyltetrahydrofolate: Biophysical aspects." *Photochemistry and Photobiology* 82 (6): 1651–1655.

Steindal, A.H., T.T.T. Tam, X.Y. Lu, A. Juzeniene, and J. Moan. 2008. "5-Methyltetrahydrofolate is photosensitive in the presence of riboflavin." *Photochemical and Photobiological Sciences* 7 (7): 814–818.

Stone, J. 2007. *When She Was White: The True Story of a Family Divided by Race*. New York: Miramax Books.

Stringer, C., and P. Andrews. 2005. *The Complete World of Human Evolution*. New York: Thames & Hudson.

Sturm, R.A. 2006. "A golden age of human pigmentation genetics." *Trends in Genetics* 22 (9): 464–468.

———. 2009. "Molecular genetics of human pigmentation diversity." *Human Molecular Genetics* 18 (R1): R9–R17.

Sturm, R.A., R.D. Teasdale, and N.F. Fox. 2001. "Human pigmentation genes: Identification, structure and consequences of polymorphic variation." *Gene* 277 (1–2): 49–62.

Suzman, A. 1960. "Race classification and definition in the legislation of the union of South Africa 1910–1960." *Acta Juridica* 339–367.

Swiderski, R.M. 2008. *Quicksilver: A History of the Use, Lore, and Effects of Mercury*. Jefferson, NC: McFarland.

Tadokoro, T., N. Kobayashi, B.Z. Zmudzka, S. Ito, K. Wakamatsu, Y. Yamaguchi, K.S. Korossy, S.A. Miller, J.Z. Beer, and V.J. Hearing. 2003. "UV-induced DNA damage and melanin content in human skin differing in racial/ethnic origin." *FASEB Journal* 17: 1177–1179.

Tadokoro, T., Y. Yamaguchi, J. Batzer, S.G. Coelho, B.Z. Zmudzka, S.A. Miller, R. Wolber, J.Z. Beer, and V.J. Hearing. 2005. "Mechanisms of skin tanning in different racial/ethnic groups in response to ultraviolet radiation." *Journal of Investigative Dermatology* 124: 1326–1332.

Tam, T.T.T., A. Juzeniene, A.H. Steindal, V. Iani, and J. Moan. 2009. "Photodegradation of 5-methyltetrahydrofolate in the presence of uroporphyrin." *Journal of Photochemistry and Photobiology B: Biology* 94 (3): 201–204.

Taylor, K.C., G.W. Lamorey, G.A. Doyle, R.B. Alley, P.M. Grootes, P.A. Mayewskill, J.W.C. White, and L.K. Barlow. 1993. "The 'flickering switch' of late Pleistocene climate change." *Nature* 361: 432–436.

Telles, E.E. 2004. *Race in Another America: The Significance of Skin Color in Brazil*. Princeton, NJ: Princeton University Press.

Thebert, Y. 1980. "Reflections on the Use of the Foreigner Concept: Evolution and Function of the Image of the Barbarian in Athens in the Classical Era." *Diogenes* 28 (112): 91–110.

Thieden, E., M.S. Agren, and H.C. Wulf. 2001. "Solar UVR exposures of indoor workers in a working and a holiday period assessed by personal dosimeters and sun exposure diaries." *Photodermatology, Photoimmunology and Photomedicine* 17 (6): 249–255.

Thody, A.J., E.M. Higgins, K. Wakamatsu, S. Ito, S.A. Burchill, and J.M. Marks. 1991. "Pheomelanin as well as eumelanin is present in human epidermis." *Journal of Investigative Dermatology* 97 (2): 340–344.

Thomas, L.M. 2009. "Skin lighteners in South Africa: Transnational entanglements and technologies of the self." In *Shades of Difference: Why Skin Color Matters,* ed. E.N. Glenn, 188–210. Stanford, CA: Stanford University Press.

Thompson, M.S., and V.M. Keith. 2004. "Copper brown and blue black: Colorism and self evaluation." In *Skin Deep: How Race and Complexion Matter in the "Color-Blind" Era,* ed. C. Herring, V.M. Keith, and H.D. Horton, 45–64. Urbana, IL: Institute for Research on Race and Public Policy.

Thong, H.-Y., S.H. Jee, C.C. Sun, and R.H. Boissy. 2003. "The patterns of melanosome distribution in keratinocytes of human skin as a determining factor of skin colour." *British Journal of Dermatology* 149 (3): 498–505.

Tishkoff, S.A., M.K. Gonder, B.M. Henn, H. Mortenson, A. Knight, C. Gignoux, N. Fernandopulle, et al. 2007. "History of click-speaking populations of Africa inferred from mtDNA and Y chromosome genetic variation." *Molecular Biology and Evolution* 24 (10): 2180–2195.

Tishkoff, S.A., F.A. Reed, F.R. Friedlaender, C. Ehret, A. Ranciaro, A. Froment, J.B. Hirbo, et al. 2009. "The genetic structure and history of Africans and African Americans." *Science* 324 (5930): 1035–1044.

Tobias, P.V. 2002. "Saartje Baartman: Her life, her remains, and the negotiations for their repatriation from France to South Africa." *South African Journal of Science* 98 (3–4): 107.

Toplin, R.B. 1979. "Between black and white: Attitudes toward southern mulattoes, 1830–1861." *Journal of Southern History* 45 (2): 185–200.

Trigger, B.G. 1983. *Ancient Egypt: A Social History*. Cambridge: Cambridge University Press.

Tuchinda, C., S. Srivannaboon, and H.W. Lim. 2006. "Photoprotection by window glass, automobile glass, and sunglasses." *Journal of the American Academy of Dermatology* 54 (5): 845–854.

Turner, A. 1984. "Hominids and fellow travellers: Human migration into high latitudes as part of a large mammal community." In *Hominid Evolution and Community Ecology,* ed. R. Foley, 193–215. London: Academic Press.

———. 1992. "Large carnivores and earliest European hominids: changing determinants of resource availability during the Lower and Middle Pleistocene." *Journal of Human Evolution* 22: 109–126.

Twain, Mark. 1997. *Pudd'nhead Wilson*. New York: Simon & Schuster.

Underhill, P.A., G. Passarino, A.A. Lin, S. Marzuki, P.J. Oefner, L. Cavalli-Sforza, and G.K. Chambers. 2001. "Maori origins, Y-chromosome haplotypes and implications for human history in the Pacific." *Human Mutation* 17 (4): 271–280.

United States Food and Drug Administration. 2011. "FDA sheds light on sunscreens." Consumer Updates. www.fda.gov/forconsumers/consumerupdates/ucm258416.htm.

UNPD (United Nations, Department of Economic and Social Affairs, Population Division). 2007. *World Urbanization Prospects: The 2007 Revision Population Database*. http://esa.un.org/unup/index.asp?panel = 1.

Urbach, F. 2001. "The negative effects of solar radiation: A clinical overview." In *Sun Protection in Man,* ed. P.U. Giacomoni, 3: 39–67. Amsterdam: Elsevier.

Van den Berghe, P.L., and P. Frost. 1986. "Skin color preference, sexual dimorphism and sexual selection: A case of gene culture evolution?" *Ethnic and Racial Studies* 9: 87–113.

Vieira, R.M. 1995. "Black resistance in Brazil: A matter of necessity." In *Racism and Anti-racism in World Perspective,* ed. B.P. Bowser, 227–240. Thousand Oaks, CA: Sage Publications.

Vigilant, L., M. Stoneking, H. Harpending, K. Hawkes, and A.C. Wilson. 1991. "African populations and the evolution of human mitochondrial DNA." *Science* 253 (5027): 1503–1507.

Vorobey, P., A.E. Steindal, M.K. Off, A. Vorobey, and J. Moan. 2006. "Influence of human serum albumin on photodegradation of folic acid in solution." *Photochemistry and Photobiology* 82 (3): 817–822.

Wacks, J.L. 2000. "Reading race, rhetoric, and the female body in the Rhinelander case." In *Interracialism: Black-White Intermarriage in American History, Literature, and Law,* ed. W. Sollors, 162–178. Oxford: Oxford University Press.

Wagatsuma, H. 1967. "The social perception of skin color in Japan." *Daedalus* 96 (2): 407–433.

Walker, A., and R.E. Leakey, eds. 1993. *Nariokotome* Homo erectus *Skeleton.* Cambridge, MA: Harvard University Press.

Walker, S. 2007. *Style and Status: Selling Beauty to African American Women, 1920–1975.* Lexington: University of Kentucky Press.

Wall, J.D., and M.F. Hammer. 2006. "Archaic admixture in the human genome." *Current Opinions in Genetic Development* 16 (6): 606–610.

Walvin, J. 1986. *England, Slaves, and Freedom, 1776–1838.* Jackson: University Press of Mississippi.

Wang, Z., J. Dillon, and E.R. Gaillard. 2006. "Antioxidant properties of melanin in retinal pigment epithelial cells." *Photochemistry and Photobiology* 82 (2): 474–479.

Wassermann, H.P. 1965. "Human pigmentation and environmental adaptation." *Archives of Environmental Health* 11: 691–694.

———. 1974. *Ethnic Pigmentation.* New York: American Elsevier.

Watkins, T. 2005. "From foragers to complex societies in Southwest Asia." In *The Human Past: World Prehistory and the Development of Human Societies,* ed. C. Scarre. London: Thames & Hudson: 200–233.

Weinstein, N.D. 1980. "Unrealistic optimism about future life events." *Journal of Personality and Social Psychology* 39 (5): 806–820.

West, P.M., and C. Packer. 2002. "Sexual selection, temperature, and the lion's mane." *Science* 297: 1339–1343.

Westermann, W.L. 1955. *The Slave Systems of Greek and Roman Antiquity.* Philadelphia, PA: American Philosophical Society.

Wheeler, P.E. 1992. "The influence of the loss of functional body hair on the water budgets of early hominids." *Journal of Human Evolution* 23 (5): 379–388.

Wheless, L., J. Black, and A.J. Alberg. 2010. "Nonmelanoma skin cancer and the risk of second primary cancers: A systematic review." *Cancer Epidemiology Biomarkers and Prevention* 19 (7): 1686–1695.

White, W. 1949. "Has science conquered the color line?" *Look,* August, 94–95.

Whitford, W.G. 1976. "Sweating responses in the chimpanzee (*Pan troglodytes*)." *Comparative Biochemistry and Physiology Part A: Physiology* 53 (4): 333–336.

WHO (World Health Organization). 2002. *Global Solar UV Index: A Practical Guide.* WHO/SDE/OEH/02.2. www.who.int/uv/publications/en/Global UVI.pdf.

Williams, L.J., S.A. Rasmussen, A. Flores, R.S. Kirby, and L.D. Edmonds. 2005. "Decline in the prevalence of spina bifida and anencephaly by race/ethnicity: 1995–2002." *Pediatrics* 116 (3): 580–586.

Williams, M.J., and J.L. Eberhardt. 2008. "Biological conceptions of race and the motivation to cross racial boundaries." *Journal of Personality and Social Psychology* 94 (6): 1033–1047.

Wiltshire, K. 2004. *The British Museum Timeline of the Ancient World.* New York: Palgrave Macmillan.

Wood, P.H. 1995. "'If toads could speak': How the myth of race took hold and flourished in the minds of Europe's Renaissance colonizers." In *Racism and*

Anti-racism in World Perspective, ed. B. P. Bowser, 27–45. Thousand Oaks, CA: Sage Publications.

Zareba, M., G. Szewczyk, T. Sarna, L. Hong, J. D. Simon, M. M. Henry, and J. M. Burke. 2006. "Effects of photodegradation on the physical and antioxidant properties of melanosomes isolated from retinal pigment epithelium." *Photochemistry and Photobiology* 82 (4): 1024–1029.

Zarefsky, D. 2001. "Arguments among Experts." *Argumentation: The Study of Effective Reasoning.* DVD. The Teaching Company LLC.

Zecca, L., D. Tampellini, M. Gerlach, P. Riederer, R. G. Fariello, and D. Sulzer. 2001. "Substantia nigra neuromelanin: Structure, synthesis, and molecular behaviour." *Journal of Clinical Pathology: Molecular Pathology* 54 (6): 414–418.

Zimmer, Carl. 2005. *Smithsonian Intimate Guide to Human Origins.* Washington, DC: Smithsonian Books.

Zwolak, R. 2009. *IBISWorld Industry Report 81219c: Tanning Salons in the US.* Santa Monica, CA: IBISWorld Inc.

Index

Page references given with *fig.* indicate illustrations or material contained in their captions. Color plates are indicated with *pl.*

TEXT
10/13 Sabon (Open Type)

DISPLAY
Din

COMPOSITOR
BookMatters, Berkeley

INDEXER
Kevin Millham

PRINTER AND BINDER
Sheridan Books, Inc.